The Essential Writings of
Abraham Isaac Kook

Edited, Translated and Introduced by
Ben Zion Bokser

"In these pages dwells a paradoxical giant of both Lurianic Kabbalism and Talmudic scholarship, of meditative piety and active legislation. The writings emit an instructive, sacred and healing balm for these troubled times. The reader emerges with glints of Rav Kook's own light; and sees the total Jewish experience divorced from the petty politics of the day...

"As profoundly a master of the rational, Maimonidean way as of the mystical, Hassidic approach...

"The myopic views of the extreme right and left fall away before the grand vision... embodied in these writings. Here is a timely and a timeless masterpiece for the *erev shabbos* of human history."

– Isaac Mozenson in *Speaking of Books*

To the Memory of

Rabbi Ben Zion Bokser
July 4, 1907 — January 30, 1984

who lived his life in the spirit of Rabbi Kook

The Essential Writings of
Abraham Isaac Kook

Edited, Translated and Introduced by
Ben Zion Bokser

Ben Yehuda Press

Published by Ben Yehuda Press
430 Kensington Road
Teaneck, NJ 07666
http://www.BenYehudaPress.com

For permission to reprint, including distribution of the material in this book as part of a synagogue or school newsletter, please contact:
Permissions, Ben Yehuda Press, 430 Kensington Road, Teaneck, NJ 07666
Email: permissions@BenYehudaPress.com

Ben Yehuda Press books may be purchased for educational, business or sales promotional use. For information, please contact:
Special Markets, Ben Yehuda Press, 430 Kensington Road, Teaneck, NJ 07666
Email: markets@BenYehudaPress.com

ISBN 978-1-953-82998-6

Printing History:
Amity House edition published 1988

FIRST BEN YEHUDA PRESS EDITION 2006

06 07 08 09   /   10 9 8 7 6 5 4 3 2 1

Bonus Features & Special Offers

At the Ben Yehuda Press web site, you'll find a brief film clip of Rav Kook, as well as the opportunity to sign up for special pre-publication sales of forthcoming books.

Visit http://www.BenYehudaPress.com/kook for details.

Contents

Preface

Rabbi Kook was one of the most remarkable figures in the spiritual history of mankind. He was a rabbi of the old school, who grew up in a small town ghetto in Eastern Europe. He had no secular education. His world was dominated by traditional Jewish piety and learning. He had no contact with the secular world, or with non-Jews, even on a personal basis. And yet there emerged in him a vision of life that transcended all parochialism, and that embraced within its scope all people, all ideas, everything that expressed the stirring of life, whether physical or spiritual. And he responded to the most subtle ideas of philosophers, theologians, and scientists.

Much of his vast erudition, in areas outside the classic literature of Judaism, must have come to him from his own private reading. But he was more than a scholar in the sense of one who had mastered vast tomes of writing by other people. His ideas which proclaim his originality represent an inflow of thought which proceeded spontaneously, as he would call it, by the grace of God who ever illumines the world and releases His light to those ready to receive it. Rabbi Kook received it. It was the essence of his life, and he regarded himself as a channel through which this light was to reach other people.

Rabbi Kook was a master of the vast domain of Jewish law. As a rabbi, at first in Eastern Europe, and then in Jaffa, Palestine, and finally in Jerusalem, where he served as chief rabbi for Palestine Jewry, it was his duty to interpret the law in the specific cases that needed juridical guidance. His legal interpretations were essentially traditional. It was only when issues arose where the traditional interpretation of the law seemed to him as posing an undue hardship that he reinterpreted the law for the sake of equity. There is ample precedent in Jewish law to modify classic procedures in emergency situations where some gross harm to religion or life might result (cf. Ber. 54a). But these reinterpretations of the law made him a target of criticism by the advocates of an uncompromising traditionalism.

However, Rabbi Kook's major contribution was as a rabbinic scholar. Beneath the formalism of his legal responsibilities there was at work a creative spirit that stirred him to meditate on the meaning of human life, and to see man as but an incident in the mysterious drama of cosmic life. He wrote essays, meditations, and poems, and he maintained a vast correspondence with people who turned to him with questions — sometimes to challenge him for his views, sometimes to seek guidance in resolving doubts and perplexities they faced in their lives. Some of his letters were inspired by his own initiative in communicating his advice to someone or, in other cases, his protest because some inequity had been committed.

The present volume is an attempt to present the core elements in Rabbi Kook's thought, in the light of the unique contribution these can make to modern man in his bewilderment and his quest for guidance if he is to emerge from the confusion that surrounds him. It is divided into four sections. The first is a recall of the controversies in which he became embroiled as a result of his views. This is followed by a collection of some of his statements on major themes which offer us a general perspective or profile of his thought. The third is a collection of letters, and the fourth is a collection of meditations. The last section consists of diverse sayings on different aspects of religion and life, culled from his various writings and giving us succinct statements of his views.

A number of friends and colleagues assisted me, and I express my gratitude to them. My wife, as usual, offered me many critical suggestions, and her encouragement in all my literary labors has been a sustaining force through the years. My daughter, Miriam, and her husband Dov, have shown a continued interest in mysticism and have influenced me in my studies of the mystical dimensions of Rabbi Kook's thought. My son's scholarship has often helped me resolve problems, which has assisted me in the labor of producing this book. I am thankful to Rabbi Salomon Faber, to whom I often turned with specific problems in interpreting various texts and he was most helpful. Rabbi David Novick read much of the material and offered many suggestions which helped in better understanding the original and shaping it in an acceptable literary idiom. Prof. Israel Knox also read the manuscript and I am grateful to him for his many suggestions which improved the style of the work. Mrs. Shirley Tendler, my secretary, put the work in readable form, through many revisions, and otherwise gave me invaluable help during preparation of the manuscript. I finally offer thanks to my editor, Richard Payne, for his helpful suggestions and steady guidance in bringing this work into shape.

My thanks go forth to Him, who inspires our quest for truth, who has sustained me in my labors, and made it possible for me to reach this day.

My Yearning Heart

My heart is filled with yearning
For the higher vistas of the spirit.
Give me the Light of God,
The pleasure and the delight
Of the living God,
The privilege of standing in the palace
Of the King of the universe.
I always aspire for the God of my father,
My whole heart is devoted to His love,
My awe of Him exalts me.
I hope for deliverance and light,
For the dawn of knowledge and illumination.
I will find delight
In the goodness of the Lord,
In contemplating the vastness of His hiding place,
In His supernal might.

Sihot Harayah, Moreshet
(Tel Aviv 1979), p. 353

I.

Controversies

Rabbi Abraham Isaac Hakohen Kook was one of the great figures in the history of Jewish thought. But during his lifetime he was a highly controversial figure, who drew upon himself sharp criticism and even abuse. In some religious circles he was looked upon as a heretic, a deviant from the norms of classic Judaism, one who had strayed from the foundations of his faith and who influenced others to stray as well.

Rabbi Kook was born in 1865 in Grieve, Latvia, and was raised in the classic tradition of Eastern European Jewish scholarship and piety. At an early age he evinced an interest in the Jewish return to the Holy Land, and in 1904 he was invited to serve as rabbi in Jaffa and the colonies in its environs, after having served as rabbi in the Eastern European communities of Zoimen (1888-1895) and Boisk (1895-1904). During the First World War he was stranded while attending a conference of the Agudat Yisrael in Switzerland, and he was invited to serve as rabbi in London, England (1917-1918). He was then invited to become the chief rabbi in Jerusalem and, after a two-year delay, finally assumed this august office. In his general writings and in his legal decisions Rabbi Kook showed himself a master of classic rabbinic learning, but he also revealed a sensitivity to the problems of the contemporary world, and a tendency toward originality in his general philosophy of Judaism. It was these latter attributes of his work which drew upon him the sharp darts of critics who saw him as a deviant from the norms of classic Judaism.

Some misgivings about his orthodoxy are discernible, even among those who serve as the ostensible champions of his spiritual legacy. A great part of his writings have been withheld from circulation, no doubt out of fear that they might be misunderstood and prove disturbing to too many people. An additional volume of his letters and another volume of his mystical meditations, the Orot Ha-kodesh, are ready for publication but the custodians of his literary legacy have not given their final approval to publish them. One volume, Arpele Tohar, was suppressed while in the process of publication, and only some unbound copies came into the hands of a few students of his works. A volume of essays about Rabbi Kook's philosophy was published by the Mosad Harav Kook in 1966, and it has on the second page, as a kind of preface in large type, a responsum of his which forbids mixed dancing, as though to say: Look, he was really a pietist in the classic sense, and the charges of heresy are groundless.

Rabbi Kook's own writings, especially his voluminous correspondence, reflect the difficulties that many people, even friends and admirers, had with some of his positions. In one of his most seminal essays, "The Road to Renewal", Rabbi Kook had posited that there were two paths to religious truth: the study of classic texts, and an ongoing spiritual illumination which is experienced by sensitive spirits — a mystical experience, as we generally call it — through whom God continues to reveal ever newer dimensions of truth. But the latter, Rabbi Kook warned us, to be efficacious must be subjected to moral and rational refinement in the person through whom it is channeled, or the message will be distorted and become a source of stumbling. In the light of this, he surveyed the various stages of Jewish history, and found that one of the continuing problems which has faced the Jewish people has been a tendency to focus on texts and the outer performance of the commandments, while neglecting the mystical tradition and the many documents it has yielded in piety and morals on the level of inwardness. As a reaction to this, he explained, there have emerged various dissident movements in Judaism, such as Christianity, the messianism of Shabetai Zevi and Jacob Frank. These movements did not go through the process of moral and rational refinement, and they released fantasies and visions that were detrimental to the people; but, in Rabbi Kook's own words, "amidst all the evil they caused, there was not lost the tiny element of good that was hidden in them. They exemplified a psychic renewal as opposed to the sole dependence on the one foundation, the study of texts, and indoctrination in the disciplined, practical performance of the commandments." In the course of this discussion on Christianity he also made the statement: "Its founder was endowed with a remarkably charismatic personality who exerted great spiritual influence." He qualified this by adding: "But he had not escaped the defect of idolatry which is an intensification of spiritual influence without the prior training in the existing moral and cultural disciplines; and he and his followers were so committed to the cultivation of the spiritual life that they lost their spiritual characteristics and they became alienated, in deed and spirit, from the sources whence they had sprung."[1] The qualification which Rabbi Kook attached to his positive characterization was ignored, but his positive characterization of the founder of Christianity was seized on and it aroused consternation in many circles. It seemed as though he was sympathetic to the founder of Christianity and that he saw in him a bearer of positive spiritual influences.

Rabbi Dov Milstein, who admired Rabbi Kook and often turned to him for counsel on personal matters, wrote him of his troubled feelings about his expressions concerning the founder of Christianity. Rabbi Kook defended himself in an extended explanation, in the course of which he stated:

> Greater and better people than I suffered the critical comments from people because of matters such as this, when their noble spirit forced them, in order to mend the condition of their generation, to enunciate new ideas and to disclose what had been hidden, with which the popular mind was unfamiliar. Because of this many rose to complain against them, until the justice of their position was well established, and the holy cause was vindicated. If the time were opportune it would be appropriate to discuss this hidden subject at greater length, but at this time the brief comment I have made will suffice. Whoever judges me favorably, may he be judged favorably before the heavenly tribunal.[2]

Another colleague, Rabbi Benjamin Menashe Levin, had apparently raised the same issue with him, and Rabbi Kook, in the course of his reply, stated: At a time like this, it is necessary to clarify the general characteristics of religion, according to its diverse expressions, and not to be intimidated by the customary disdain and unmitigated hatred of everything unfamiliar which is deeply rooted in heart and soul.[3]

Rabbi Kook was often criticized because of his apparent disparagement of the Talmud and the legal codes as the main focus of Torah study, calling for an emphasis on the study of mystical and moralistic writings, and even a certain measure of worldly knowledge. We know of these criticisms only from Rabbi Kook's reply to them. One critical communication came to him from a Rabbi Yeshaya Orenstein, to which Rabbi Kook replied in a touching letter dated 12 Kislev 5667 (1907):

> Your important communication reached me. Truthfully I was uncertain whether to reply to you or not, because I was concerned that your honor might be disturbed by my letter, and why should I grieve an elder scholar like you, may you be blessed with life. I decided, however, to reply to you briefly. Perhaps God will grant it that you will heed my words, and then you would not longer be so troubled about the pamphlets. This would be my reward, to save a precious person like you from pain and worry.
>
> Your honor should know that my primary goal in these pamphlets and in all my writing is to stir the hearts of scholars, old and young alike, to concern themselves with the dimension of the Torah . . . To this one needs to study with great diligence, like the very diligence required to master the tractates of the Talmud and the legal codes.
>
> It is indeed true that because of the bent of human nature, not everyone is qualified to pursue this type of study. Therefore, whoever is not equipped for this . . . should surely pursue the dialectical study of the Talmud and the codes. But whoever is equipped to engage in the deeper study of theosophical wisdom and Cabbala must arrange for himself short units of this type of study as compared with the more elaborate studies in Talmudic dialectics . . .
>
> And in our time when, because of our many sins, a great number of our young people are lured by the attractions of the literary style of the rebels among our people, it is important to show the world that scholars who engage in the holy pursuit of studying the true dimension of the Torah are not lacking in the graces of a good literary style. This was the objective which inspired the saintly Rabbi Moses Hayim Luzatto to write his books on literary style. I, in my humble way, aspire to follow in his footsteps to the extent of my ability.
>
> And in order to fully understand the Torah, it is also necessary to possess worldly knowledge in many areas, especially in order to be able to respond to the arguments of heretics, which is most urgent in our time . . .
>
> If there are some people who err in interpreting what I say and distort my position — this is no reason for suppressing the good from those who prepared to profit from it. One is reminded of what Maimonides said in one of his letters in a similar situation, quoting the verse: "The ways of the Lord are upright, the righteous walk in them but sinners stumble over them" (Hosea 14:10). By

regularly studying the satisfying inner dimension of our holy Torah a light of joy and higher love will shine on the person pursuing it, with spiritual delights which are intimations of the world to come, and he will have no need whatever to invoke the lower fear, the fear of retribution, except in a very small measure . . . This is the substance of what I intended to convey, to which your honor reacted. How good and how agreeable it would be if we each judged one another charitably. Thereby the honor of God would be exalted and magnified, as well as the honor of the holy land, and the honor of the scholars in Eretz Yisrael.

As for me, I am, thank God, far from taking great pleasure when people praise me, nor am I unduly disturbed when they insult me. I thank God, praised be He, that my constant pursuit of the study of morals and the inner dimension of our holy Torah has had this effect on me. I, therefore, see no need to apologize before your honor, only to calm your honor's heart, that you should not suffer anguish, for all my desire is to bring happiness to people and, to the extent of my ability, to fulfill the expectation expressed in the verse: "Those who revere You will see me and rejoice" (Psalm 119:74). I have therefore said: May these words of mine bring peace to the heart of your honor. And may the Holy One, praised be He, bless you with a good old age, you and all that are yours, and may we be privileged to see the rejoicing that will come to Zion and the rebuilding of Jerusalem, when the glory of the divine kingship will be manifest for us, raising us to acclaim and praise among all the nations of the earth, and the whole earth will be filled with the knowledge of the Lord, as befits your noble spirit, and as is aspired by your youthful friend, the trodden on doorstep, who hopes for light and deliverance.

The lowly Abraham Isaac Kook

P.S. I am surprised that your honor criticizes me because of what someone wrote in *Havazelet*. Do I know him, and what can I or anyone else who releases his writings in public do if some people will react to them with nonsensical remarks?

I have subsequently examined what that person had written in *Havazelet* and it became clear to me that they do not contain those objectionable remarks which your honor attributed to them, God forbid. It is in order that he, too, be judged charitably, and that we love peace and truth.[4]

Another issue on which Rabbi Kook was criticized was his support of Zionism. The Zionist activists, specifically the pioneers who came to settle in Palestine, preparing the ground for the later emergence of the state of Israel, were nonreligious in most cases, some of them even tinged with socialism. The entire idea of a human initiative in the rebuilding of the Holy Land, without waiting for the divine initiative by sending the long hoped-for messiah, seemed heretical to many of the Jewish pietists. To them, the secularism of the Zionist pioneers was particularly offensive. Rabbi Kook often decried the parochial culture of the Zionist builders in the cities and villages as a tragic shedding of the religious dimension of Jewish history and tradition. Nevertheless, he supported their efforts and maintained a friendly relationship with them. It was his conviction that through this there was the possibility of influencing them to return to the moorings of their faith, while hostility would only result in greater alienation. Apart from this, he valued their pioneering efforts as a good in itself. In one of his letters he expressed himself thus: "One cannot altogether dismiss the success of the Zionists. Though this is pervaded by many deficiencies, there must also be here a spirit of the divine, to build souls for the Holy Land. Through all does the Holy One, praised be He, accomplish His mission. Who can discern the mysterious workings of God, to fathom why there should be among those who serve this cause people who are so thoroughly tainted with heresy?"[5]

The religious Jewish community in Palestine that predated the Zionist efforts was vehemently opposed to the Zionist movement as a whole, and especially to the Zionist pioneers who brought with them a lifestyle totally divergent from the traditional and antagonistic to it. Rabbi Kook's support for their efforts was therefore another cause for scandal. One correspondent, Rabbi Joseph David of Safed (Ridvaz), reproached him that "he had become a Zionist in his old age, and was ready to sacrifice his soul for the settlement of Jews in Eretz Yisrael." To this he replied:

> My beloved one, if all 'Zionists' loved Eretz Yisrael and sought the development of the Holy Land with the holy goal and purpose which directs me . . . it would be a source of great pride for every great person in Israel, for every scholar and *zaddik* to be a 'Zionist', and even your honor would not need to be ashamed of such 'Zionism'. Whoever bends the scale of justice toward charity, and speaks in defense of Jews even when they do not fulfill God's will, is praiseworthy. Certainly one can find in every Jew, even in the lowest one, many precious jewels of good deeds and of good qualities of character, beyond enumeration. Eretz Yisrael will surely help to bring them out and to hallow them. If these attributes cannot

be seen in them, they will become revealed in their children and their children's children.[6]

Another issue which proved troublesome for Rabbi Kook, shortly after he became rabbi in Jaffa, was his action suspending the restriction in agricultural labor during the sabbatical year. It would have ruined all agricultural efforts if the land were to remain fallow once every seven years, as Biblically ordained. He acted therefore on the basis of a previously promulgated ordinance (which had the support of important legal authorities, including Rabbi Isaac Elkanan of Kovno) to go through the form of selling the land to a non-Jew, and to have non-Jews do the basic work on the land during the sabbatical year. At the same time he urged that Jews avoid nonessential labor on the land, while he pledged full support to those who wished to keep the Biblical law in its prescribed rigor. He regarded his ordinance as an emergency measure to cope with an emergency situation. Soon many rabbis of the old *yishuv* (the pre-Zionist community) denounced him for his bold step in contributing to a violation of a Biblically ordained law. Rabbi Joseph David of Safed (Ridvaz) especially challenged Rabbi Kook's ordinance and advocated that the law be kept according to and in all its Biblical requirements. The rabbinic circles in Jerusalem, who were remote from the problems of the new Zionist settlers, were particularly active in denouncing Rabbi Kook's ordinance.

The anguish which this controversy caused Rabbi Kook is clearly indicated in the defensive letter which he wrote to Rabbi Joseph David:

> I am replying briefly to your honor's statement. You blamed me for the fact that the colonists employed Jews to sow the land in the sabbatical year. The fact is that I announced a prohibition against a Jew sowing or performing any other labor forbidden in the sabbatical year, even if after the formal "sale" of the land to a non-Jew... As to your second criticism, I would like you to know that in the past as in the present, I loathe the evil in the wicked, but the good that is in them I have always esteemed highly, and loved, for this is an aspect of the divine. When I see even among our lowest ones some good quality, any feeling for equity and truth, even if only a courteous conversation or an act of good manners, I draw him closer, always hoping that as a result he will turn toward the good, in some measure, and if my encouragement should stimulate in his heart the tiniest degree of penitence, whether inspired by fear or love, all the effort in the world will have been justified...
>
> And as to your argument that they claim me to be one of them,

God forbid, please consider that our father Abraham was promised that 'all the nations of the world will be blessed through you'. And even the nations of the world take pride in the prophets and the early *zaddikim*. Does this, God forbid, stain their honor? Thank God, my intention is not to win their good graces, or the good graces of any other person. Thank God, the primary motivation of my thought is only to serve God, praised be He and praised be His name.

And when you ask how any food can be agreeable to me, when I see the treatise [ridiculing those who forbid work in the sabbatical year] written by those rebels, it surprises me to have you think that any food is agreeable to me. You should know that it is not so. There is no limit to the pain they have caused me. It has made me sick, this mockery of our holy Torah at the hands of these heretics. But I thought that by protesting I would not redress the condition, I would only add fuel to the fire. The protest would surely have provoked them to add to their rebelliousness, and I, therefore, felt constrained to keep silent, for the honor of the Torah. It surprises me that your honor whose heart is filled with respect and love for the Torah did not judge me charitably. One is obligated to do so even for an ordinary layman in Israel.

I am especially surprised that you wondered why I do not repudiate publicly my voiding the law of the sabbatical year in the holy land. How can you attribute to me something that never occurred to me to do. In what way did I void the law of the sabbatical year? Are you saying that I voided the law because I ruled that the condition of the *yishuv* during the last sabbatical year made it necessary to follow the ruling issued previously by many important scholars? They may not measure up to your honor's scholarship, but they are authoritative interpreters of the law. It was not up to me to suspend the prohibitions of the sabbatical year; on the contrary, my effort was to see to it that the land be 'sold', so as to avoid a greater stumbling, by not having any permissible option for working the land at all. Above all, am I astonished at the advice your honor suggested to me, to leave for the diaspora and there to accept a rabbinic position...

Your honor is fortunate that he is privileged to be free of the burden of public service and he can withdraw and pursue the truth in its full perfection, but I am deprived, being burdened all day with the responsibilities of serving those people of God. My only delight is that I remind myself that my feet are stationed on the holy soil, on the land God has called His portion and His inheritance and characterized with various expressions of endearment. If someone gave me all the land in the world, it would not compare with one moment of breathing the holy air of Eretz Yisrael. I trust in Him to help me, for the honor of His name, that no stumbling results from my work, and that I never pronounce anything against His will.

I conclude with a blessing, and with a renewal of the covenant of love, as in the past.[7]

All the polemics we have referred to thus far were relatively mild. They were expressed largely in correspondence by rabbis with whom he had a somewhat friendly relationship. The period when this polemic took place was while Rabbi Kook still served as rabbi in Jaffa, before his elevation to the chief rabbinate.

The polemic exploded with greater bitterness after 1919 when he was invited to serve as chief rabbi. Rivka Shatz has written a well-documented study of this phase of the controversy, which appeared in the Hebrew journal *Molad*.[8] An organization of religious extremists, "The Holy Association" (*Agudat Ha*-Kodesh), began an active propaganda campaign to nullify this invitation. They sought to establish a rabbinic authority under the sponsorship of the super-Orthodox community in Jerusalem that would ban his legal decisions and his writings, and invalidate marriages and divorces issued under his authority.

The extremists cited three arguments in their attack on Rabbi Kook: First, they cited statements from his writings which revealed him to be an adversary of Orthodoxy. Rabbi Kook, we recall, had often decried the neglect of the spiritual dimension of Judaism in the established religious community, its tendency to focus on the outer aspect of *halakha*, on the study of classic texts, and the indifference to the mystical and moralistic elements. He also advocated a responsiveness to modern cultural developments. It was his judgment that the alienation of many of the younger generation from Jewish tradition was the result of the inner decadence in Jewish life as exemplified by the conventional expressions of Judaism.

Second, they quoted from the controversial essay, "The Road to Renewal", a statement deriding the rabbinate in this decadent state of Jewish piety. When the spiritual becomes a weak auxiliary to the practical, he had written,

> the rabbinate will then be judged according to the administrative role it plays and its educational function will be assessed according to the monetary value of the animals and the fowl, the pots and spoons and all other such petty items it has declared *kosher*, for it

is only by such criteria that the practical sense of the multitude understands a service of usefulness. In the end such values are bound to decline and to sink ever lower, unless a mighty spiritual force should arise to support them according to their original inspiration that lifts all spiritual needs to their full stature.[9]

A third statement which was quoted against him appeared in a letter to Rabbi Judah Leib Seltzer which the latter made public by citing it in his own volume, *Masa Yehuda* (Jerusalem 1914). In this letter Rabbi Kook again decried the neglect of the inner dimension of Judaism and the over-emphasis on the purely legal aspects. The passage cited is a sharp rebuke to the Orthodox mentality:

As long as Orthodoxy maintains stubbornly: No, we will only study Gemara and the Codes, but not Aggadah, not morals, not Cabbala, not research, not worldly knowledge, not Hasidism, it impoverishes itself, and all the strategies it adopts in self-defense, without embracing the true life-giving therapy, the inner light of the Torah, will prove of no efficacy. In the face of all this, I will continue my battle against all who have risen against me from all sides.[10]

There were two other arguments cited against him on a practical rather than an ideological plane. It was argued that the invitation to Rabbi Kook to serve as rabbi in Jerusalem had not been agreed on by the people generally, nor by their authoritative religious representatives. The final argument was that he was an impractical person given to flights of imagination which would keep him from discharging effectively his administrative responsibilities. Thus the approximately five hundred dollars a month that would be paid him as salary would be a waste of funds that could be better spent as charity for the poor. The pamphlet adds: "We do not excommunicate him, but this rebel is excommunicated on the basis of the teachings of the sages. It is forbidden to stand before him, to study Torah from him, and it is a *mitzvah* to show *disdain* for him, and whoever supports him is as one who plants a tree for idol worship (an *ashera*) close to the altar of God."[11]

An effort was subsequently made to induce Rabbi Kook not to accept the invitation to serve as chief rabbi in Jerusalem on the ground that the invitation had not been issued with the proper authorization by the competent representatives of the religious community. One letter addressed to him in the spirit of prudent counsel bore the signatures of the venerable rabbis in the super-Orthodox Jerusalem community, Rabbis Joachim

Diskin and Hayim Sonenfeld. Considering the mounting opposition to his choice as chief rabbi, he was advised that it would be prudent on his part to decline the invitation. Indeed, Rabbi Kook remained for two years in Jerusalem without assuming that role. In the end, he became the chief rabbi of Jerusalem and of the Palestine Jewish community as well and though the zealots identified with the extremists continued their attacks, the general community rallied to him and he became the recognized chief rabbi of Palestine Jewry. However, the ultra-Orthodox community in Jerusalem established a *Beth Din*, or a rabbinic authority of its own, which ignored the authority of Rabbi Kook.

An especially scurrilous attack on Rabbi Kook was launched by members of the same group, in a pamphlet that began to make its appearance in 1922. Rabbi Kook was called a *Shabbetai Zevi*, the nefarious false messiah. A letter by a son of the Hasidic Rebbe of Belz was quoted, branding Rabbi Kook a *rasha gamur*, in these words: "It is known that the rabbi there in Jerusalem whose name is Kook, may his name be blotted out, is a *rasha gamur* [a completely wicked man], who has already defiled many of our young people with his smooth talk and contaminated books."

A vitriolic attack against everything which Rabbi Kook advocated was issued by Yeshaya Asher Zelig Margoliot in 1927, in a small volume entitled *Ashre Haish*. The title is an allusion to the first verse in the opening Psalm: "Happy is the man who has not walked in the counsel of the wicked, not stood in the way of sinners, nor sat in the seat of the scornful." The thrust of the book is a denunciation of the notion that by friendly relations with the secularists one will win them back to Judaism. He contends that every relation with them is sinful; that one is to shun them with total disdain as the bearers of an infectious disease, of heresy. He denounces the effort to rebuild a Jewish presence in the Holy Land, that there is merit in individuals coming to live in the Holy Land, but as an overall effort of the people as was promoted under Zionist auspices, it was foolish, sinful and was bound to fail. He also denounces the effort to popularize the use of the Hebrew language as a general medium of communication as a desecration of the language that should be used for holy purposes solely. He warns against allowing one's home to be contaminated by permitting into it books of the new literature. He also warns against allowing vocational training to be included in the Jewish schools, demanding that the hours should only be devoted to the study of Torah.

After citing all the sins of the times, he accuses Rabbi Kook of being the sponsor of all these evils, charging that he had rationalized them through a false interpretation of the Torah. He does not mention Rabbi Kook by name but by a derisive reference as chief rabbi:

> Their 'chief rabbi' [*harav rosham*], the *Haman* from the perspective of the Torah [*Hehaman min Hatorah*] finds justifications and supportive precedents for all their sins and faults and evils and transgressions by invoking the tendency to permissiveness and he misinterprets the Torah . . . and in the Temple of the Lord he places the idol of their national renewal.[12]

In a footnote he clarifies the source whence this "evil" person has drawn his perilous ideas:

> Those who fear God and pure of heart and soul state that this person who is wise to do evil, who entices others to heresy and deflects them from the right course drew his inspiration (his 'waters') from various heretical books, the wisdom of ancient times from the mountains of darkness and death.[13]

Rabbi Kook also had his defenders. During the controversy inspired by his ruling concerning the sabbatical year, a letter signed by seven rabbis was published in the religious periodicals *Hador* and *Haherut* which defended his competence and authority and castigated his adversaries as rebels against a recognized and renowned Torah authority. In part, this letter read as follows:

> We are forced to issue an open protest. This is not a time to be silent, we dare not inhibit ourselves. An affront to the Torah, and an insult to a great scholar and a *zaddik* has taken place in our very midst. . . The Lord has seen our sinful state, and He has stirred a spirit of jealousy in the hearts of a small number of people, some of them students of the Torah who are of our own fellowship, and in the name of the Torah, they perpetrate acts that should not be done, which are offensive to the dignity of a rabbi and scholar in Israel, as well as the dignity of all our people.
> He is not a newcomer to us, the revered and righteous Rabbi Kook who serves with distinction as chief rabbi in Jaffa and the colonies in its environs. Apart from his genius as a scholar, he has been graced by God with remarkable talents, with a heart overflowing with knowledge of and reverence for God. Who dare stand in the presence of this giant and dispute his actions which are inspired from the source of holiness, from the Torah, and from discernment with which God has endowed him in a generous

measure? Who dares challenge pronouncements he delivers to us
with his mighty hand, with certainty, after deep study and profound
understanding, especially on matters affecting the laws applicable
to the Holy Land in which he is immersed with heart and soul?
At all times he is ready to demonstrate to everyone the sources
of his decisions and to make clear to those who wish to study Torah
from him, principles of equity, and to guide them toward the truth
by his broadmindedness and sensitive intelligence.

And now a few people, residents of Jerusalem, who should
stand in humble awe in the presence of a great scholar and *zaddik*
as he is, especially before they have reached the depth of *halakhic*
[legal] study, to comprehend its sources, have come out publicly
with their petty statements and their baseless prohibitions. They
have dared to challenge this great scholar without substantive basis
for their position. What he declares permitted, they declare
prohibited. We are heartsick and consumed by pain to see these
depressing incidents which hurt the honor of the Torah and of
Judaism generally, and are calculated to damage the entire fabric
of the Jewish settlement in the Holy Land . . .

And you, rabbis and scholars of Jerusalem, raise your voices
like a *shofar* against these people that they cease their destructive
work . . .[14]

Rabbi Kook was embarrassed by this type of defense, as he made
clear in a note to his brother Samuel: "Such assistance which involves
an attack on the dignity of others, is altogether repugnant to me. They
did what they did independently, without consulting me, though I know
that they were motivated by good intentions."[15]

An attempt was made by Rabbi Abraham Mordecai Alter, the Gerer
Rebbe, to conciliate the differences between Rabbi Kook and his
adversaries in the Jerusalem religious community. He reports of his efforts
in a letter he sent to his family while on his way from a visit in the Holy
Land. It is dated Iyar 7, 5681 (1921) and it is an important descriptive
document of this controversy. It is noteworthy that according to this
letter the opposition to Rabbi Kook appears to have been limited to a
relatively small group in the extremist Orthodox community in Jerusalem.
The greater number sided with him, but the extremists waged an aggressive
campaign which made the controversy a *cause cél èbre.* We quote several
selections from this letter:

It is to be noted that outside of Eretz Yisrael the conception
of this controversy was quite different from what it is in reality.

According to the prevalent information, Rabbi Kook was seen as a rabbi who had succumbed to the 'enlightenment' and was looking for bribes, and that it was because of this that the others came out against him with excommunications and denunciations. At times the newspapers *The Jew* and *The Way* brought such one-sided news reports, but this is not the way, to listen to only one side, no matter who it is.

The learned Rabbi Kook, may he be blessed with life, is distinguished in his mastery of the Torah and unusual qualities of character. Many also claim that he hated underhanded payments. But his love for Zion goes beyond all limits, and he declares what is unclean as clean.

This is responsible for the strange statements in Rabbi Kook's writings. I engaged in many arguments with him, for while his intention is good, his behavior is not, for he supports transgressors while they remain in a state of rebellion and desecrate everything that is holy . . .

It is difficult to elaborate in a letter, and I will therefore state briefly that I began an effort toward conciliation. I induced Rabbi Abraham Kook, may he be blessed with life, to promise me in writing, to which he appended his signature, that though his intention was for the sake of God, nevertheless, since he heard that some of the expressions in his writings result in a profanation of God's name, and a lessening of His honor, he renounces those expressions and those statements.

Then I met with the aged rabbis, the eminent Rabbi Hayim Sonenfeld and the eminent Rabbi Joachim Diskin, may he be blessed with life, and urged them to withdraw the condemnatory sounding of the *shofar*, the excommunication and the denunciation, and they are prepared to sign a commitment to this, since the eminent Rabbi Abraham Kook stated in writing the commitment mentioned earlier. But they add that all they did was to write to rabbis asking them to judge those expressions, whether they may be tolerated in a religious community. But a storm was stirred up about them, and, without their knowledge, a report began to circulate as a result of their letter that the *shofar* had been sounded and an excommunication proclaimed. However, they refused to condemn those reports as long as those strange and bitter expressions had not been withdrawn.

Even before full peace has been established, if only the insults would stop! It is to be noted that the eminent Rabbi Abraham Kook recognizes the *Bet Din* of the eminent rabbis, Rabbi Hayim Sonenfeld and Rabbi Joachim Diskin, may they be blessed with life — and he even thinks that this may be helpful. Since he is in contact with the non-religious as well, as Chief Rabbi, it is good that there be someone to challenge him on some matters. This must obviously be done without abusive language and denunciations, but only in the way of peace.

From the above words of his eminence, Rabbi Abraham Kook, one can discern his qualities, for although most of the people in the holy city and many of the rabbis are on his side, he, nevertheless, shows his respect for the elder rabbis.[16]

These polemics must have been a source of great sorrow to Rabbi Kook. In one of his letters he confessed openly that "the work of the rabbinate is contrary to my disposition and my strength, and I am most anxious to live in the Holy Land without the burden of having to serve as a dispenser of legal decisions."[17] In this letter he asked a friend, Rabbi Joel Mikhal Tikazinski, to recommend him for a position that would enable him to leave the rabbinate. Nothing came of this, and he remained in his post and continued to bear the verbal darts that were directed at him from various adversaries.

When Rabbi Kook finally decided to accept the position of chief rabbi and to establish his residence in Jerusalem, it was his hope that the controversy would abate and that there would finally be a spirit of reconciliation. In a letter to his friend Rabbi Zeev Yavitz he wrote:

I hope that the inclination to controversy and hostility which has been intensified in some circles will be like a passing shadow. Ill-will will eventually give way and the righteous path which is the way of peace. . .will assert itself with ever greater force. All acrimony will then recede, and in place of hostility and competitiveness, there will emerge a flowering of brotherly love, and true friendship and mutual helpfulness.[18]

But this was not to be. While the original issues lost some of their early bitterness, peace was not to be his lot.

Toward the end of his life, in 1933, Rabbi Kook became embroiled in a new controversey, in this instance involving an issue of criminal justice. Chaim Arlazaroff, one of the leaders of the labor movement in Jewish Palestine, an important figure among the Zionist pioneers, was assassinated on a Friday evening in 1933 while walking with his family at the seashore of Tel Aviv. Many saw this as a political action on the part of the Revisionists, a rightist group that was bitterly opposed to the labor movement, condemning it for its embrace of the socialist philosophy and for softness to excessive moderation in the struggle against the British Mandatory power for a free Jewish state. Three leaders of the Revisionists were apprehended and brought to trial before a British tribunal. Two were freed, but one, Abraham Stavsky, was found guilty and sentenced to execution.

Rabbi Kook had been on warm personal terms with Arlazaroff. On the day before the festival of Rosh Hashanah (the New Year) of that year Arlazaroff had visited Rabbi Kook to extend greetings for the new year. But Rabbi Kook was convinced that Stavsky could not have committed the crime, and his execution would be a gross miscarriage of justice. He now began a campaign for his liberation.[19] He issued a proclamation which he asked to be distributed publicly in Palestine as well as the diaspora. It stated:

> I find myself in a situation which forces me to awaken the conscience of the Jewish people, and of all the right-minded people of all humanity against the great peril that innocent blood may now be shed in the holy city of Jerusalem, God forbid. This will happen unless all of us act with all our might, in the name of holiness, justice, and honor, that an innocent life shall not be destroyed, and that we not be guilty of this bloodshed. I can testify out of the clear prompting of my conscience before God and man that Abraham Stavsky is altogether innocent of the murder of Arlazaroff. The court decision was issued on the basis of imaginative conjectures, which only outside influences and the prevalent mood in the environment caused some of the judges to cast a vote of guilty. The truth is absolutely clear to me in this instance that the minority of the judges were right in finding the accused innocent. Therefore, it is wrong for us to stand aside. Whoever, Jew or non-Jew, in whose heart there is a spark of the divine, must protect this fearful wrong, and do everything possible to save Abraham Stavsky from this miscarriage of justice, and to restore to him without delay his right and his full freedom.

This proclamation was issued on a Friday and some of the Stavsky champions distributed it the next day, which was the Sabbath. A friendly visitor came to him with alarm, protesting that this was a desecration of the Sabbath. Rabbi Kook defended himself that he had never been consulted as to whether it would be permissible to post the proclamation on the Sabbath, and that he had never authorized it. However, to one of his critics he added: "But, it would be wrong to forget that what is involved here is saving a life. The saving of a life takes precedence over the Sabbath. It is true that they did not consult me, but perhaps those who decide to be zealous in posting the proclamation on the Sabbath knew the gravity of the situation, and therefore they chose to ignore the Sabbath restrictions for the sake of Abraham Stavsky."

"But the zealots will use this as a weapon in their bitter war against your honor," the visitor said. "This," Rabbi Kook replied, "is of no consequence to me. I fear the Sovereign of the universe, and it is to Him that I will give account for my actions. The zealots I am not afraid of. My zealots are Maimonides and the *Shulhan Arukh* [the code of Jewish law]. I live according to their teachings. I fear no one in the world but God alone."

He preached on this theme that Saturday to a large congregation and mobilized all whom he could reach for this task of saving a person from what he was convinced would be an execution of an innocent man. He took the issue personally and it affected his health. The poet Hayim Nahman Bidlik, who met him during that period, said of him: "He looks as though he himself is standing in the shadow of the gallows."

The partisans of the labor movement were troubled by Rabbi Kook's defense of Stavsky. Arlazaroff was their respected leader. Stavsky belonged to a party that had opposed everything to which Arlazaroff had dedicated his life. The will to avenge his death was strong in them, and they were willing to overlook some of the niceties of juridical procedure which had not been followed altogether at the trial. An anti-Stavsky partisan wrote in graffiti on the wall of Rabbi Kook's house: "Woe unto the generation whose priests cover up for murderers."

A higher court reviewed the case and Stavsky was eventually exonerated. Two years later, in 1935, Rabbi Kook died after a bout with cancer.

Rabbi Kook's independent spirit brought him many adversaries, and he was a center of controversy throughout his life. But this was mitigated by the adulation of followers who understood and admired the bent of his mind, and appreciated his remarkable contributions as a rabbi, a scholar, and a creative spirit, through whom many precious new insights were introduced into Jewish tradition.

NOTES

1. The essay "The Road of Renewal" appeared in Hebrew under the title "Derekh Hathia" in the periodical *Hanir* in 1904. It appears in English translation in *Abraham Isaac Kook*, ed. Ben Zion Bokser (New York: Paulist Press, 1978), pp. 287-302. The passage cited appears on p. 296.

2. Rabbi Kook's letters are published in three volumes under the title *Igrot Harayah*, and they are identified by number. This passage appears in *Igrot*, vol. II, Letter 375.
3. *Igrot*, vol. I, Letter 194.
4. Ibid., Letter 43.
5. *Igrot*, vol. II, Letter 473.
6. Ibid., Letter 555.
7. *Igrot*, vol. I, Letter 522.
8. This appeared in *Moled*, March 1975: 251-262.
9. P. 301.
10. *Igrot*, vol. II, Letter 602.
11. Cited by Rivka Shatz, ibid., p. 253.
12. Ashre Haish, pp. 56f.
13. Pp. 57f.
14. This letter is reprinted in *Igrot*, vol. I, pp. 353f.
15. Ibid., Letter 307.
16. A. M. Alter, *Osef Mikhtavim* (Warsaw, 1937), pp. 66-70.
17. *Igrot*, vol. I, Letter 84.
18. *Igrot*, vol. III, Letter 966.
19. Rabbi Kook's involvement in the Stavsky affair is described in detail in *Haish Neged Hazerem*, by Shmuel ha-Kohen Avidur, Orot (Jerusalem, 1962), pp. 269-296.

II.
Essays

A Call for Unity

Three forces are currently contending among us. The conflict between them is especially discernible in Eretz Yisrael, but their activity derives from the general life of our people, and their roots go back to human nature itself. These three forces need to be united among us, so that each will help the other and seek to perfect it. Left to itself each one will present the distortion of extremism, which is diminished when each one challenges the other. We shall be most unfortunate if these three forces should be left in their separateness and their mutual hostility.

These are the three basic claims to which our life and the life of all humanity must relate in some form: the call of the holy, the call of the nations and the call of humanity. The combination of these three claims varies. Among some individuals, or in some societies, one claim may play a greater role than the other. But we shall not find any form of human life where these three will not be in some interrelation. The harmonization of these three great claims must be achieved in every society that cherishes continuity for its life. When we assess our condition and note that these three forces which are meant to be harmonized are moving farther apart, we must come to the rescue.

This fragmentation is engendered by the negative aspect that the partisans of one force see in the other. But these negative elements in themselves do not justify this destructive response. For in every separate force, especially every spiritual force, there are bound to be negative aspects, especially if it extends its sway over other forces. In this respect there is no difference between the forces in the domain of the holy or the secular. Every thing must be within measure and balance [weight]. "Even the holy spirit which was bestowed on the prophets was bestowed within a limited measure." As fragmentation occurs when unification is called for, then there is a gradual impoverishment of the spirit. The positive content in the position of the fragmented force, at least as far as the particular individual or society is concerned, continues to decline, because of the narrowing in that force which wages a solitary war against the nature of the human spirit to find unification with other basic forces that complete it. In place of unity there develops a tendency to nourish life with negativism, and the partisan of each force becomes filled with fiery antagonism as he rejects the other force or forces which he refuses to recognize. In such a lifestyle a fearful condition sets in, the spirit becomes barren, the concern for truth — its inner recognition, together with its love — declines, and continues to diminish as we become divided into separate camps.

We now have three noteworthy factions among our people. The first is Orthodoxy, as we are accustomed to call it. It champions the cause of the holy; it speaks with vigor, with zeal and with embitterment on behalf of the Torah and the commandments, of religious faith, and of everything sacred to the Jewish people. The second is the new nationalism that battles for everything toward which the national spirit aspires. It embraces many of the characteristics of a nation seeking to renew its national existence after a long period of submergence because of the miserable state of exile. It also seeks to include many elements deriving from the influence of other nations, to the extent that it judges them desirable and appropriate for itself. The third is liberalism, which was an advocate of the Enlightenment in the recent past and still has a following in many circles. It does not confine itself to the domain of the national but demands general human enlightenment, culture, morality and much else.

It is understandable that in a healthy setting there is need for each of these three forces. We must always seek to reach this healthy state, where these forces will act in our lives jointly, in all their fullness and their goodness, in harmonious integration, with nothing in excess or in diminution. The claims of the holy, of the nation, and of humanity will be joined together in a spiritual and practical love. Individuals and parties will be in agreement that each one is to find the fulfillment of his unique disposition by pursuing one of these three causes, with appropriate friendliness, that each is to recognize with goodwill the positive service of the other. This acknowledgement will then develop to a point where each one will recognize the positive role in every cause, that it is desirable, and that it is in order to pursue it for the general good of spiritual harmonization as well as for the enhancement of the particular cause with which he himself is identified. He will go even further in recognizing a positive dimension in the negative aspect of every cause, within its proper delimitation. He will know that it is to the benefit of the very cause of which he is an advocate to be influenced to some extent by the negation, because by its challenge it sets his beloved cause within its proper sphere and saves it from the perilous detriment of excess and exaggeration. This was the symbolism in one of the exacting rites in the Temple service: the measurement of the meal offering where care had to be taken that there not be "too much or too little".

If we shall examine carefully the tension which we suffer in this generation we will know that only one course is open to us. Everyone, the individual or the community, must take to heart this admonition: that together with the need to defend the particular position to which one is attached by natural inclination, habit or training, one must know how to utilize the positions that have found a following among other people and other parties. Thus one will perfect oneself and one's party, both through the positive aspects in the position of the others, and through the beneficial aspects in their negations, by safeguarding one's own position against the defect of exaggeration which produces weakness and destruction. Thus we may hope to attain a way of life appropriate for a people of high stature.

It is obvious that by having included the holy among the three forces, each of which must at times confine itself in order to allow the expression of the other, we referred only to the technical and practical (the institutional) aspect of the holy, and to the ideational and emotional aspects associated with it.[1] But holiness, in its essence, is a comprehensive ideal, and one of its endeavors is to sensitize us to the need of confinement, like all the endeavors for the perfection of the world and of life, in all these dimensions, which draw their inspiration from the ideal of the holy. The ideal and sublime thought, the thought of holiness itself is, therefore, free of all confinement, and the nearness of God is always abounding with breadth of vision which transcends all boundaries. "For every purpose I have seen an end, but Your commandment is exceedingly broad" (Ps. 119:76). When a person or a nation walks in the way of justice, in practical affairs and in thought, each within its proper boundary, peace is sure to reach out to the widest domain of the spiritual life. "From narrow places I called to the Lord, He answers me in a broad place"(Ps. 118:5).

Orot, pp. 70-72.

A Call to the Scholars of Israel

The philosophy of determinism, itself an offensive conception of man's nature, has won wide following in the world, and it will be the very force of determinism which will accomplish the great wonder of proclaiming that the earth is the Lord's.

The dialectic of determinism, the compulsion governing life and its anguished burdens, will evoke the divine light into the world. Necessity will condition the human heart to be receptive to the great light of faith in all its splendor.

It appears as though the world is tottering under the burden of an aggressive atheism . . . A divine flame burns within the heart, in every sensitive person . . . but an atheistic creed has kept it from finding expression . . . But the more it chokes the soul, the more it impedes the divine spirit in every living soul, the more will the human soul gather its inner strength and, in due time, emerge to claim its own with a mighty force . . .

A day will come, and it is not far off, when humanity will bestir itself to visit retribution on the despicable creed of atheism for all the evil caused by it. All at once it will seek to discard its oppressive hegemony. Angrily it will seek to avenge itself for having been robbed of purity and peace without receiving from the atheistic creed even a fraction of those blessings in return. The confusion with which atheism filled the world . . . , alienating man from his Creator, will pass. An ideology, clear and moderate, which does justice to life and thought, which knows the art of equanimity as well as of enthusiasm, and a divinely inspired valor which knows how to establish a people firmly and consecrated to holiness, will replace it. The rod of stern criticism will exact its due from this slave who sought to usurp the place of his royal master, while the sign of his servitude remains branded on the forehead of his soul.

Freedom, which jubilantly marches side by side with necessity, will emerge from its own confinement and trample with contempt on atheism. The yearning for freedom will rise to its ultimate height, and man will recognize that he can live in accordance with his authentic nature, according to the prompting of his soul, and his soul thrives only in God. Without a deep and luminous faith, the soul is without life and without light; it is restless and anguished, beset with cruel thirst. And who impedes it, who keeps it from living in God, who has banished this bird of heaven from its nest, who has imprisoned it and keeps it from soaring in the broad expanse of the heavens, where there is brightness and a refreshing atmosphere full of light and life? Man's own soul will soon recognize its foe, and look on it with scorn, after it will have been exposed in all its sordidness, after the mask woven by an erring imagination will have been torn away from its foolish and despicable face. "The new grass is ready to break through the surface of the earth"; this recognition is drawing near. Asia, America, enlightened Europe, the entire civilized world in general, is already exhausted from bearing the hard yoke of atheism that oppresses man's spirit, more than the most exacting discipline of a religious faith — but yields nothing in return.

In this condition of thirst, man will throw himself into the spring of faith; avidly he will drink from the delightful store of heavenly light. But man knows from experience what the result has been from sating himself with the water of faith, with all the mud and dirt which this mighty ocean has thrown up in the course of time by its seething waters. Therefore will he seek with all his being clean water from the divine brook.

The trend that embraces all mankind has also affected some of our children, though we are closer to the source of light, closer to the source of life, we are fuller with divine soul force, which has nourished us since our youth as a people to the time of our maturing. Although the Jewish people are largely spared this veritable affliction, the servitude of atheism also appears to have embraced great numbers of our children. They are moving convulsively between life and death, denied contentment and peace, and they are thirsty to sate themselves with the waters of faith. But their eyes are soon due to be opened. They have grown impatient with atheism which has become, in a short period of time, an intolerant and arrogant creed, and they are knocking on the gates of pentitence, which only seem shut but which will open to them widely with one push. "Let the gates open that a righteous people that has kept the faith may enter" (Isa. 26:2), with their elders and their young people, a mighty host, like the host of God.

My dear brothers, sages of the Torah, and writers who exert influence, we, too, have sinned; we engaged in dialectics and relished new insights in the *halakha* [the legal dimension of the Torah]; we wrote and we sketched, but we forgot God and His might; we did not heed the admonitions of the prophets of truth, of the best of our sages through the generations, of the saints, the scholars in the field of ethics and mysticism, who insistently warned us that the study of the practical aspects of the Talmud by itself is bound to run dry, unless we add to it from the vast domain of the *kabbalah*, the domain which deals with the knowledge of God, the domain of pure faith which stems from within the soul and emanates from the source of life.

At this time, when our nation is being revived, the call comes to us to heed the claim of the whole man, the claim of the divine soul, which we must develop and strengthen, the divine living soul which must radiate its influence throughout the world, to illumine it and to revive it, the claim of the light which emanates from the Torah and the prophets, which is directed to bringing life to all. This claim presses on us mightily, at this time of our national revival.

In the course of our revival, we will be moved to turn back to the life of enlightenment. It will liberate the light of religious faith from its confinement and return it to the original wisdom of Judaism, which is free from every servitude to alien ideologies, the teaching of the living God which is an essential element in our treasury of life. It will bring us to regular study in the wisdom of religious faith in all its aspects, the revealed and the mystical. By its light we shall live, and with a mighty voice we shall cry out, from the land of our rejuvenation, the place where God revealed Himself and which He has chosen forever as His abiding place: "O house of Jacob, come let us walk in the light of the Lord" (Isa.2:7).

Orot, pp. 99-101

On the Art of Criticism

Every book, by itself, reveals only a limited and partial aspect of feeling and thought. One can only know its true value by finding its link with the larger theme.

When the contribution of one important volume is joined with another important volume which seems in opposition to it, then is the theme revealed in its greater fullness. It is only when these opposing elements are brought together that we reach completeness. One complements the other.

We must always bear this principle in mind when we discuss our books which deal with the inner life. We shall see Judaism in its fullness when we shall regard every book as one of the building-blocks of a great palace, that all join together to form one huge and complete edifice. Although Judaism has many diverse aspects, it is in truth one entity. "These

and also those are the words of the living God" (Ber. 63b). It is only
then that the influence of those books will bestow their great blessing.

But it takes talent to achieve this unification and harmonization. It
takes spiritual discipline and, particularly, hard work and a tranquil mind,
which develop through regular and habituated good training in the love
of knowledge, the love of the Jewish people, the love of Torah and the
love of God.

In general, in the order of our studies, broad, comprehensive
knowledge must come before the work of innovating originality. "A person
should first study Torah, and then engage in speculation" (Ber. 63b).
Especially when it comes to harmonizing clashes resulting from opposition
and criticism, this can be undertaken only after attaining profound and
clear knowledge, which can be acquired with great patience and much
labor. "Keep silent [*basket*], and hear, O Israel" (Deut. 27:9). By a play
on the word *basket*, the rabbis coined the aphorism: "Listen [*bas*] and
then analyze [*katet*]" (Ber. 63b). But even great knowledge in itself will
not be sufficient if it is not also accompanied with the other ethical virtues,
without which it is impossible for the truth to be disclosed.

All these qualities cannot be found by those who come to the spiritual
banquet hall of the Torah like wayfarers, wayfarers who do not dress
appropriately when they enter because this spiritual, honored and holy
banquet hall is regarded by them as some inn that every crude person
can enter, with the dirt on his shoes, and the stain on his garment, and
all life's filth on his body and soul.

Thus the failure to set a fixed discipline of study and preparation
in the spiritual dimension of the Torah has brought about a fearful crisis!
The limited and only occasional attention to this pursuit has resulted
in the fact that these diverse subjects are not joined to each other, and
there is no relationship between them, which is essential for a
comprehensive spiritual outlook. The thoughts proceed, alone and
straying. Each person is influenced by some solitary aspect of a particular
book, or, to be more exact, by parts of a particular book, while the book
itself loses its lustre with the decline of its ideas and the rejection of its
thinking when it enters the realm of the spiritual. "One who says, This
tradition is beautiful and that is not beautiful, concerning him does the
verse say, 'He who associates with harlots wastes his substance' (Prov.
29:3) — he wastes the substance of the Torah" (Erubin 64a). This has
happened in our time, in the fullest sense of the term, in regard to the
spiritual dimension of the Torah.

And those who are accustomed to the ways of religion, of the Torah and the commandments, do they know how to enjoy and to spread enjoyment from the splendor of this banquet hall? From among them should have come those worthy to be the intimates of this chamber. But they look at it with excessive fear, not like intimates of the chamber who are familiar with its significance, but like a watchman of the courtyard who enjoys the exterior of the chamber without it ever occurring to him that it is in order for him to enter inside. Thus the entrance to the chamber is left to those presumptuous ones who enter with all the filth and ignorance, their defilements and their arrogance. And they are the ones who show our people, as it were, the light of Judaism!

Who can speak to such arrogant people concerning the enhancement of one outlook through another, concerning the higher embrace of all conceptions of Judaism, how they harmonize, and that it is precisely from all the shepherds together that will go forth Torah and enlightenment?

They know, for example, that Maimonides speaks in praise of reason and perception, while Rabbi Judah Ha-Levi spoke in praise of feeling and poetry, and therefore they see this as a case where "two texts contradict each other" (Mekhilta on Ex., Jethro). They see no alternative but to downgrade one and extol the other, obviously with the trivial praises with which these petty people can extol. In truth their praise is full of embarrassment and insult, and its benefit is minimal.

Such criticism is of no help to understand the profound thoughts of those *zaddikim*. It only dims the splendor of their light. If, for example, one conception is offered to us in the *Guide to the Perplexed* (by Maimonides) and another in the *Kuzari* (by Rabbi Judah Ha-Levi), each is indeed a complete and luminous world, when taken by itself. But it is only possible to understand their full greatness when "they receive from each other" (Targum, Isa. 6:3), and are included in a comprehensive whole. This is true not only of those two great luminaries, but of all the great and lesser teachers of light, those who focus on the mystical. It is necessary that they shall shine together like the brightness in the sky over the whole embrace of Judaism. Only then will we know their light. Only then will we be able, with bigness of spirit, to add what it is within our power to add, on the basis of our perspective and the level of our culture. Then will our contribution in the work of literature serve to enhance the great edifice built by our prophets and our scholars throughout the generations.

Maamore Ha-Rayah, pp. 11-13

The Nearness of God

The pure, natural state of man's soul can be recognized with a profound and probing analysis when the person is still small, in the period of his childhood, when his soul has not yet been contaminated by the fermenting passion of the tumult of life. On careful study we note how easy it is during those years to experience a divine feeling and how prepared one is to be influenced to the love of the holy and the fear of God, on reaching any capacity for comprehension. The best thinkers in the field of pedagogy have therefore come to the conclusion that the pure religious training, which is illumined by good sense and reinforced with refined feelings, comes most naturally in the state of childhood.

Among grown up persons it is a rare phenomenon, because of the many confusions in life, to find one whose divine soul shines in him with its full natural force and purity. But whenever man's spirit will be truly and fully liberated, when he will not be disturbed by upheavals, good or bad, and he will not be unduly troubled by their fierce distractions, we will see a disposition for the divine, inspired by a natural inner pressure, forging its way in his heart. Without uttering a word, he will feel a longing to raise himself toward the higher realm, and he will also find in himself a mighty desire to feel an inner rest and peace of mind through being close to God.

Similarly, in the life of society, there is no significant human community of even minimal cultural advance in whom the feeling of faith and religion has not had some significant effects through the aspiration for the nearness of God which is astir in its people, even if they are not conscious of it. As for the life of humanity as a whole, the expression, the channeling of the aspiration for the nearness of God, in whatever form, is the connecting thread that links all the religions that are followed by every society of historic significance.

Thus it becomes clear to us, through the diverse circumstances of man and his outlook on life, that of all the spiritual inclinations, yearnings, and aspirations which are revealed in human nature, the strongest and the most sensitive is the inclination to seek the "nearness of God".

Moreover, as our outlook develops we shall find, on the basis of psychological assessment, that this force is the vital center of all the other forces and aspirations of man, that it has a more significant impact on the inner workings of the human psyche, and that the other forces are auxiliary to it. They receive from it, and they aid it. On this basis we must conclude that the aspiration for the nearness of God, in its full force, is the core factor in all inclinations, longings and aspirations of the whole human soul. They all draw from it, and they return to it. It is so in the collectivity, in the general psyche of society as well as of the individual person.

And after a continued examination of different manifestations of life under diverse circumstances, it is also established that many of those forces which impede and oppose this aspiration, as a result of complications in the physical and spiritual life, will be able to hinder only for some time its emergence and its dominant role over man's actual thought. But under no circumstances will it be able to annul it, to subdue and suppress it altogether. And though at times this basic phenomenon (the aspiration for the nearness of God) may fail to appear in many particular individuals, this should not lead us to doubt the nature of the central reality of the human psyche. We have identified the rule that governs the life process of man generally, of nations in their constituent historic communities, as well as in the life of particular individuals; the general nature of humanity testifies concerning the nature of the individual who is part of the whole...

The aspiration for the nearness of God will not cease to act with its strong and constant stirring in the hearts of people. The inclination to freedom, which comes so naturally to the developed sensibility of humanity, will always safeguard the fundamental freedom of the psyche, enabling its forces to expand in the direction to which it is disposed, for which it aspires, by its very nature. Since the aspiration for the nearness of God is a central fact of human nature, it will not be possible to imprison this spirit in any iron walls with which it may be surrounded by the imaginative speculations of narrow-minded people.

We may thus conclude that the freedom of the human spirit presses for the aspiration for God's nearness in all aspects of life, that in the fullness of its expression this is the highest ideal of freedom, to which the best people are drawn and to which the human soul, generally, and social life, in all its aspects, yearns so avidly. When Jacob prayed that his blessings of Joseph may reach "the utmost bounds of the everlasting hills" (Gen. 49:26), the Zohar interprets this as referring to the world of freedom (Zohar II 22a, 109b). We thus see that man's spiritual goal is to perfect that inclination which embraces everything within him, that acts within him at all times and is at the center of his being. What embraces everything does not change its thrust whether many be involved, or few, whether great or small. The general laws of existence are alike in all their particularities. The laws of gravitation embodied in a grain of sand also act upon the most immense planets of the heavens. The laws of life which prevailed at the inception of creation are the very ones which act on the most developed and perfected form of life.

Similarly, the inclination to aspire for the nearness of God, which expresses the soul of humanity as a whole, is the same in its diverse manifestations. It is dominant as a general law which is the same and does not deviate in the psyche of the tender child or the uncultured adult. Among them it is revealed in a rough, unfinished, blurred and uncouth form, while among the choicest individuals of humanity it is discernible as the source of "light for the nations, and salvation to the ends of the earth" (Isa. 49:6).

Here we have reached a point where we can clarify our position. What we said previously, that the inclination to aspire for the nearness of God is the mightiest and most central of the inclinations, yearnings and aspirations of the human psyche, was only to make it comprehensible to the human ear. A central force in the psyche, which conveys its thrust in so significant a form among all the inclinations of life, of the individual and society, can, under no circumstances, be regarded as a *particular* force or a central force or even *the* central force, in a general way. This would make it possible to regard the manifestation of this force as a separate phenomenon, and the essence of the psyche itself also as a separate phenomenon. We sum up our position by saying that this (the quest for the nearness of God) is the essence, the nature, the basis of existence of the psyche. In other words, this is the general nature of the psyche itself, the essence of its life, which is revealed to us as one basic reality with diverse expressions, with many endless inclinations, yearnings and aspirations under one umbrella. They all play some role in life, but life itself, all life, the essence of life, is this and nothing else, and there cannot be anything else — only the foundation, which is the aspiration for the nearness of God.

This formulates for us the definition of man's uniqueness. His life shares with all other creatures the inclination to feel its autonomous nature, together with the aspiration for perfection, which appropriately stems from the profound influence reflected from the perfection of God. The inwardness of the soul has its source in the absolute and eternal perfection in the *En Sof* [the Infinite]. The process works to satisfy our aspiration for the nearness of God, in all its aspects. Thereby the soul becomes a faithful reflection of the absolute life of absolute divinity. "In the image of God made He him" (Gen. 1:27).

Maamore Harayah, pp. 32-34

Morality and Faith in God

The ideological conflicts in the human race, among all people, and particularly among Jews, are based on the issues of morality. Everyone knows that wisdom and talent refer to capacity, to strengthen the intellectual or practical capacities. Morality seeks to perfect the human will that it seek the good. If man's capacity should increase but his will for the good remain undeveloped, then the increase in his powers can only lead to disaster. When the love of self rises beyond the equitable through the loss of moral sensitivity, it is bound to make life more difficult to the extent that one's powers increase, and this love itself, being without a proper base in the spiritual, eternal life, will degenerate progressively to crude and ugly desires. On the other hand, with a good moral state, which engenders refinement of soul, a higher sense of holiness and a love for people, it becomes possible for man to structure the limited forces operative in his humble capacities in such a way that they will engender good and blessing for him and the world.

It is true that the full benefit will surely come through the complete union of these two forces, the capacity and the will, in their full state of excellence. When these join together they will become as one, like all the forces which manifest themselves to us in the wide domain of creation, that are united in their source. And the more a person will grow in knowledge, the more will he recognize the unity of the forces which manifest themselves in diverse forms . . . This is the most significant perception of the full unity of capacity and will, as the highest expression in man's development. But the decisive force in the continuing development of man, from stage to stage, from generation to generation, and from epoch to epoch, to the end of time, despite intervening periods of retreat, is the force of morality and justice. This is the *will*. It also stimulates the development of wisdom and talent, which is the realm of *capacity*. "The world rests on one foundation, and his name is *zaddik*" [the righteous person] (Hagigah 12b).

The rise of atheism which has emerged in the world generally, and has spread like an unnatural disease among the Jewish people, could not have occurred without support from some argument based on the issue of morality.[2] The only basis for this was the occasional deficiency and weakness on the part of those who represent the positive (religious) beliefs. They also furnished some excuse for the atheist position which bases itself on scientific claims. Both are nourished by a shallow scientific and moral perception. It is only at a later period, as this trend continued, that atheistic literature pretended to be a scientific literature, which it could never be according to its own character. With all its pretensions, it is a morally-based literature inspired by a distorted fantasy.

It never occurred to the great thinkers of the human race, even those who are regarded among the atheists, like the Greek Epicurus himself and others like him, that they could argue for the disparagement of the belief in God solely on scientific grounds. They argued against "the knowledge of God in the land" (Hosea 4:1), that is, against the moral influences exerted by the teachings about God. In their opinion these had an evil effect on the human race and served as a detriment to its moral and natural development... In any case, the atheism based on moral concerns is always the basis for the atheism that presents itself as grounded in science, for it does not have any rationale on its own terms. Therefore, the more the champions of the Torah and of religious faith will improve their behavior and their character traits, the more will morality-based atheism decline and, as it declines, so will its scientific appendage and "iniquity will shut its mouth" (Job 5:16), "and God alone will be exalted that day" (Isa. 2:17).

We can sense this readily. Every intelligent person knows that the maintenance of religious faith, whether it be the general concept of God, as rationally defined, or the practical fulfillment of the holiness of the Torah, is not affected by any aspect of astronomical or geological teaching. In general, the revealed teaching of the Torah which is of significance is the knowledge of God and morality, and their derivative applications in life and in action, in the life of the individual, the nation and the world. Truly this knowledge, which is crucial for all of life, is the basis of everything and it embraces everything. But concepts based on scientific research and feeling, which are but faint sparks of light as compared to the knowledge of God and the holiness of life, are irrelevant as far as the teaching of the Torah is concerned. There is no difference whether we follow the views of Ptolemy, or Copernicus, or Galileo and others, or the latest of teachings that have been or may yet be developed, or any views that are promulgated by way of research from time to time.

The view has been sufficiently explained that prophecy draws the illustrations for its teachings concerning human behavior from the prevailing views of the idiom current at the time, to make it comprehensible for people of that period, to transmit to the ear what it can listen to in the present. "A wise man's heart knows time and judgment" (Ecc. 8:5)... Human perceptions of the nature of existence, whatever they be, have *some* impact on man's moral development, and his other lofty goals. Each generation formulates this according to these perceptions, which change continually. But the objective is to harmonize everything with the purpose of the general good and the mercy of the eternal God. The inner concept, the pure knowledge of God, and the practical and rational levels of morality will endure always. "The grass withers, the flowers fade, but God's word will endure forever" (Isa. 40:8).

Eder Hayakar, pp. 36-38

The Lights of Faith

Faith in God is not an expression of reason or feeling, but it is the most basic self-revelation of the soul's essence, which needs to be directed according to its own disposition. When we do not destroy the path that is natural for it, it needs no other substantive resources to support it. It finds everything within itself. At a time when its light is dimmed, then reason and feeling come to clear a way for it. But even then it must know its worth, that its aides — reason and feeling — are not of its essence. And when it will remain fixed in its position, then will reason and feeling succeed in clearing the way and in finding rational and moral means of removing the stumbling blocks from its path.

Religious faith — which is a response of God's presence — is illustrated in the illumination of prophecy and, on a lower level, through the influence of the holy spirit, though these sometimes also join with reason and feeling on the path of their manifestation.*

It is well to know that one cannot turn to God with reason and feeling, and certainly not through the experience of the senses. One can turn to God but with faith alone. Prayer is an expression of faith. Love and fear (awe) are also expressions of faith. We sometimes speak of "faith based on sense experience", or "the feeling of faith", and certainly when we say "the knowledge of faith", and "the rationale of faith", these are all borrowed terms. Faith in its essence is none of these, but higher than they. It is not deficient in anything. It embraces in a higher and perfect unity the most significant and strongest substantive elements in all of these.

The faith that is established as an inference from the world, that is, the faith based on contemplating natural existence, and the faith communicated by the Torah, that is, the faith rooted in the miraculous revelation conveyed by tradition, and the faith that is rooted in the inner life of the person and communicated from the depths of the soul – these are the three great lights each of which has distinctive conditions and claims distinctive functions. At times they are merged and fuse their power, and at times one comes with full force and seeks to take full control of the heart, of all life. It is then essential, when the one has full control, that we know how to deal with the other factors which are then in a dormant state, and which then ascend to their higher source, to be renewed in power and to return with new blessings and new vitality.

The perfection of faith is attained when its body and soul are well linked to each other, that is, the faith based on the inner life and the faith based on tradition. This link between body and soul yields many treasures of light and life. But at times this beneficial state is impoverished; the link between the tradition-based faith and the faith based on inner experience is severed. Then religious faith appears to be in a state of crisis (sickness). The degree of peril it faces is to the extent of the dissolution referred to earlier. At times, as a result of the profuse flow of light from the inwardly based faith, it rises above the faith based on tradition. Though this occurs through a spiritual rise, it is destructive and represents a diminu—tion of power.

The healthy state is always represented by harmonization, and as the spiritual (inwardly based) faith rises, the faith based on tradition rises with it. It ascends with it but does not descend with it. Through a higher wisdom and a wholesome moral flexibility the two dimensions of faith are fused, and they become more potent. They are adorned with holiness, and they convey to the person eternal life. When this process is at work in society, it stimulates a higher revival and activities luminous with light eternal are revealed. This fusion is the inner objective in the performance of each of the commandments. Happy is the person who pursues this goal of unifying these two dimensions of faith, the one focused on the inner life, and the other on tradition. Great lights will shine for him, and a higher splendor will illumine his brightness. "Happy is the man who listens to me, watching daily at my gates, waiting at my doorpost, for he who finds Me finds life, and wins favor from the Lord" (Prov. 8:34-35).

Faith offers the ultimate purpose of existence, and science, the means for identifying it and comprehending it. If a person should be negligent in attending to the *means*, the purpose will be hidden to him. And if he should cease aspiring for the purpose, all the means will lose their significance, and in the end they will be of no avail. The contribution of science to faith is always in the exploration of the ways for attaining the purpose, and the contribution of faith to science is in the quest for purpose as a motivation for the means.

When the world reaches the erroneous thought that it has already attained the purpose of faith, one will at once begin to turn away from it, for the purpose of faith is very elusive to us, and in the higher unknown (hiding place) good and light, truth and riches are hidden. By neglecting the search for purpose, the scientific endeavors begin to lose their value, and the wisdom of scholars declines; and the person feels that he has suffered a decline in his precious spiritual possessions. The higher purpose in the divine realm whence his soul is hewn releases a force that presses him to return. He continues to purify himself, he proceeds to return, until he comes back to the heights of faith.

Maamore Ha-Rayah, pp. 70-71.

Our Separate Paths

We stand at the threshold of a new year. May it bring blessings to us and all Israel. We are bestirred with hope that all the depressing conditions we experienced in the past year will pass from us. And from the depths of our hearts let us say: May there be an end to the old year and its troubles and may the new year and its blessings commence.

We are called upon to examine our actions and draw closer to the light of penitence which brings redemption and healing to the world, to note the special objective which it is for us to emphasize toward this basic goal.

It appears to me that we are divided into two camps. We are accustomed always to invoke the two names which embrace our general community, the "religious", and the "secularists". These are new names which had never been heard of in the past. We were aware that people are not alike in their characteristics, especially in their spiritual disposition, which is the basis of life. But that there should be a special name, limited toward this objective of designating tendencies and parties — this we never knew of.

It seems to me that on this subject it is appropriate to say that the former years were better than these. Would that it were possible to purge from ourselves, in general, these two names which stand as an obstruction to the path of a strong and pure life. May it return to us, with the light of God that He will release for us. The emphasis placed on these two names and the imaginative consensus that links particular individuals so that each one can say: "I belong to this camp," and the others also can say: "I belong to that camp," with each one being satisfied with his position – this blocks the road of mending and perfection on both sides. The one who regards himself as belonging to the camp they call the "religious" looks down on the other camp they call "secularists". As to giving any thought about mending, of taking stock of oneself and engaging in penitence, he at once fixes his view on the other camp which he sees as standing before him stripped of Torah and the commandments; and he thinks to himself that the call to penitence, in its fullness, applies only to them. It is directed to them, but not to himself. On the other hand, the "secularist", that is, the one who belongs to the camp that is designated with this modern name – he certainly thinks that the entire concept of penitence is part of the lifestyle of the religious which does not apply to him. It thus turns out that we are defective on both sides, and whence will come the healing for our inner affliction?

This is one impediment. There is a second impediment which is no easier than the first. The two camps are separated from each other, as by an iron wall. The light which should shine on the entire people of Israel, emanating from the holy source of divine unity, is as though hidden from us, and we stray like blind people in the dark.

There is no alternative but to remove these idolatrous names from our camps.

In truth we have long had not two but three camps. It is an old tradition that the term community [*zibur*] includes "righteous ones", "middle of the road ones", and "wrong doers". But this is only a collective designation. As to each particular person we have been taught that "even if the whole world tells one, You are righteous, you are still to see yourself as a wrong-doer" (Nidda 30h). It is very helpful for a person to be absorbed in self-assessment, and to probe his shortcomings, while viewing others charitably, for there may indeed be in their hidden self a goodly treasure that eludes the eye.

It is for us to decide that a hidden force directing our steps toward the good exists in each camp, and in every person, especially among all to whom the general worth of the Jewish people and its hopes are precious in any measure.

Let us be known by the general name of the people of Israel, not by the name of a party or a camp.

Let us know that in each camp there is much to be mended, and much light and good that one can receive from the other. Then there will dawn on us the divine light through which we will find eternal deliverance. There will then be realized in us the holiest of our prayers which we are summoned to recite with all our strength: "And they shall form one fellowship to do Thy will with fullness of heart."[4]

Maamore Ha-Rayah, pp. 76-77

The Call of God

In the depths of the human soul the voice of God calls ceaselessly. The tumult of life can confuse the person so that most of the time he will not hear this voice. But under no circumstances will it be able to uproot the source of this voice which, in truth, constitutes the essence of human life. We therefore see in all human history that, like the tides in the oceans, the ebb and flow of the currents of life are always related to this voice of God which calls without ceasing.

This awesome voice takes on various forms. The individual and society, collectively or in its fragmented constituencies, continues to seek ways how best to listen to this voice. Some try to run away from it, and to silence it, but this reveals all the more the attachment of the self to this mighty voice which does not cease to reverberate in their hearts and to have sway over them. Indeed every effort to free oneself from it and every effort to silence it are futile. God's voice will not stop, nor can it ever be forgotten. It will always rebuke us in our inner being. "The voice of the Lord speaks with might, the voice of the Lord speaks with majesty" (Ps. 29:4).

The basic cause for the great movements in the spiritual history of mankind, which reflect man's relationship to God's voice in its diverse forms, both positive and negative, is the fact that we encounter God's voice in two fundamental phenomena, which appear opposite in their nature. These never stop prodding the human heart to follow them and live life according to their promptings. One is the inner longing of the self for nearness to God: all existence, all currents of life, all human consciousness continually testifies that only this is the good, this is the happiness, this is the eternal life, the source of light and joy. The other is the refining voice that purifies this yearning for God's nearness, that raises it from its darkness and brings it to the clear light. These two tendencies together establish the pattern of the holy, of holiness in a state of purity.

Even in epochs when the human spirit was on a very low plane and no expression of moral refinement and noble feelings of purity could penetrate man's heart, the voice of God did not cease to speak within him. That voice then robed itself in frightful coverings that brought confusion, impurity, evil and folly to the entire spectrum of life, the collective and the individual. Through this voice, in its distortion, there emerged the idolatrous cults, all forms of idolatrous service with all their perversions. But even under this vast domain of darkness the mighty voice, which in its essence is God's voice, did not cease to do its work, despite the fact that the multitude of the ignorant had transformed its manifestation into a form that spelled confusion and destruction.

The course of the human spirit does not change the character of this mighty force which includes within itself these two contending tendencies: the basic call to draw closer to God, and the process of refining the forms of this closeness. From the time when man began to invoke God's name, from the time of father Abraham until now, the voice calling for the cleansing of the nearness of God in the feelings of the human heart did not cease its activity. However, only the great giants of the spiritual life, that arose among mankind, and especially among Jews, had the strength to join these two principles in their wondrous unity. They brought life to the soul of man, generally, and especially the soul of the Jewish people by hewing a wide path for the cultivation of the nearness of God, which gives vitality to the world, and for the process of cleansing the expression of this nearness, which is the light of the world . . .

In the heart of the people during the generations these two trends were active: the positive force of the desire for nearness, and the negative force which seeks to refine this desire for God's nearness. Nothing could impede the constant fluctuation which results, as is customary, in the wake of these two stormy forces. At a time when the positive force gains ascendency, the challenging, refining force is weakened. Necessarily they also attach themselves to the positive aspects elements that dim, to some extent, the state of purity. And, on the other hand, when the cleansing spirit is strengthened, and asserts its critical elements, the positive spirit necessarily suffers weakness of strength and will, to some extent, decline in status.

Only the great giants of the spirit have the double virtue in their souls. All the positive sensibilities which derive from the impulse to seek the nearness of God in all its strength are in harmony with the tendencies to cleanse the spirit, and they are pervaded by every refining influence of the negative. Their expression of the nearness of God is refined by all the cleansing therapies and is imbued with the fullness of its strength, and they are the true saviors of the spiritual life of the people and of its individuals. They establish the community and the individual on the heights of their spiritual perfection. They are the elite, from the fruit of whose spirit will live many generations, and their light will illumine the darkness which continually hovers over life, in all its dimensions. Their remembrance will not cease in all the generations forever.

Maamore Ha-Rayah, pp. 113-115

The Torah and Human Culture

When we ask ourselves the general question: "What has the Torah of the Jewish people contributed to the culture of humanity?" we must begin by making it clear that the concept "the culture of humanity", as a well-defined phenomenon, cannot be the basis of our inquiry. The reason for this is simple. We do not as yet have a complete and perfected human culture, so that it might form the criterion and the identifying measure to judge what is good and exalted. Then we would have been able to explore what the Torah contributed to it. All we have is some glimpses of the cultural ideal of which the contemporary culture reflects only tiny sparks. These are mixed with much dross which the fully developed culture will have to refine, and raise them to a higher perfection.

We must also make the preliminary statement that when we use the expression "the Torah", we must liberate ourselves from everything that narrows this all-embracing concept. We shall not be able to envision the luminous scope of the Torah by selecting some part of it, which, because of well-known historic circumstances, is more familiar to us. We must include the whole embrace of the Torah, together with its underlying principles, which are related to the meaning of general existence and to the specific meaning of the Jewish people, its past, its present and its future. We must remember, when we speak of the Torah and its relations to human culture, that we are dealing with the word of God, in the light of which humanity is an integrated part of all existence. In the light of this conception we can evaluate the cultural contribution of the Torah, which does not confine its perspective to the limited sphere of the human. It is precisely by broadening its perspective to the underlying aspiration of all existence that it offers us a well-defined conception of the central role of humanity.

The Torah can then appear to us as the soul of human culture, the basis of its existence, and the inspiration for its development toward its ideal form. It is linked firmly with the divine soul, which is at the heart of man's being, because of the image of God which abides in him.

When we glimpse in the Torah the soul of culture, in its most refined, its most perfect and highest sense, we are saying that there is a cultural force hidden in the soul of humanity, which derives from the nature of the divine creation that pervades the world. This divine soul which comes to illumine culture and perfect it, to ennoble it and refine it, when it is manifest, confirms and leaves intact whatever has true cultural value, which brings humanity true happiness, both to the individual and society. It eliminates from human culture those defective parts, the elements effected by corruption that developed in humanity as a result of various material and spiritual factors. When it becomes clear to us that the impact of the Torah is discernible in the outer expressions of culture through elimination and additions, there is acting on us the spirit of the living God which hovers over all existence, over all the work of creation, from beginning to end, to direct it on the long and eternal road toward perfection, toward completion and elevation.

I have already explained elsewhere the ensemble of the different elements which we find in the spirit of humanity, that, in general, they are four in number, embracing four eternal aspirations, and that all other aspirations represent only their branches and derivatives: 1) a sensibility for the divine; 2) a sensibility for the moral; 3) a sensibility for the social; and 4) a sensibility for faith or religion.[5]

Man's refined sense of beauty always fashions various integrations of these four sensibilities, whether he is conscious of it or not. At times one of these forces may become obscured in some philosophy of life, or in some part of the world, or during some epoch of history. But though some aspect of these forces is then hidden, their activity is constant, even below the level of consciousness, and the hidden aspect enters into fusion with those that are openly discernible. Together they perform their function of cultural regeneration, until the preparatory period of spiritual creativity is over, and the aspect which has been concealed emerges into open awareness, embraced in splendor, and its activities and influences become visible on the horizon of general life.

The sensibility for the divine reveals itself in the realm of the holy — in prophecy and in the secular realm, in philosophy and in the highest dimension of poetry. The sensibility for the moral is manifest in the norms of life, in the juridical systems, in mercy and justice, and the like. The sensibility for the social reveals itself in the establishment of countries, nations, and governments, and from those is derived the spirit of a particular nationality, and the institution of the family. The sensibility for faith reveals itself in the institutions of the different religions, according to their distinctive characteristics.

These four forces do not stop for one moment beating upon the strings of the human soul, and they bring about the vast, diverse activities in practical life, and the disposition for thought and human creativity which continues to proliferate in the world in the different epochs that define the mark of the generations. It is true that when these four forces begin to crystallize in the life of a person they are like compressed seeds, small in scope and crude in appearance, but it is they, with all their crudeness and smallness, that constitute the basis for the cultural life that is destined to develop.

The Torah, with its influence, comes to clarify these four forces and raises them to the highest vistas which the different branches of humanity will attain in the end. This will be accomplished through the full purification of these forces, which perfect the general spirit of man. Both the narratives and the commandments of the Torah are directed toward this great end, which is explained through the Torah and the teachings of the prophets of Israel, and which is elaborated and fulfilled in life through the influence of the history of Israel on the general history of humanity.

We must recognize that the sway of these four forces was always important in the human sphere, but in ancient times these forces were cast in the mold of the natural, primitive, strong in essence, and linked with primitive life and the puerile conceptions of the multitudes of early people. The Torah, with its divine light, comes and develops these four forces, refines them, ennobles them, and places the human foundation on a basis that is strong in its spirituality. Then the thought about God, about morality, about society, and about religion rises, through the influence of the Torah in the world, to a high and noble level.

We also affirm this simple proposition. In the thought about God, even when it is in its simple, natural form, there are hidden the thoughts about morality, society and religion; and similarly in the thought about morality there are hidden the thoughts about God, society and religion; and in the thought about society are hidden the thoughts about God, morality and religion, and similarly so in the thought about religion are hidden the thoughts about God, morality and society. As culture develops, there will be spelled out the vast riches of the particular forces hidden in each dimension of the human spirit, and every dimension of the human spirit will be enriched through the influence of the other dimensions.

The special contribution of the Jewish people in the realm of the spiritual, the divine, the moral and the religious, establishes its significance in the realm of the societal, in whose midst it stands pervaded by these three great forces: the divine, the moral and the religious.

The inner dimension of the Torah is directed toward the one people with whose essence and history the whole Torah is concerned. This is the community of Israel. It acts with a gentle divine force which places its stamp on this people, bequeathing to it, through this eternal Torah, long life and eternity. The people of Israel has lived from the days of antiquity and continues to march toward the latter days, from antiquity when culture was at its infancy, to its time of maturity. Its mission is to serve as a channel for bringing the early cultural values which are so deeply imbedded in the primitive and natural life of ancient man to their mature state, in a refined form, fit to become the inheritance of all humanity to the last generation.

The seed from which was to emerge the higher faith in God, which has been refined toward genuine unity, and which is continuing to be clarified through all the sciences and all the practical and intellectual experiences in the course of many generations, was planted in its natural but immature form in ancient man. The power of the imagination, the energy of the will, the sincerity of life were present in the mighty bloodstream of the human family, but it had not yet been subjected to the new cultural challenges that arose to weaken its power with their many claims. It was when humanity attained its full strength that it was purified and refined, and it is continuing to be subject to the process of refinement through the power of the Torah, all of which proclaims the honor of God and the splendor of holiness, of morality and refinement of spirit. These are all released from the source of the divine attributes which are ascribed to the exalted God, the God of Israel, who launched creation with mercy, with justice, with compassion, with strength and with righteousness.

Through the appearance of the Torah, the future culture of humanity is destined to be built on the basis of science, equity and justice. Its continuity for all generations is assured through the knowledge of God, the lord of the host of Israel, which He bestowed to the human species through this people that is the bearer of the wondrous Torah. From it alone, through the streams which emanate from it and branch out to many nations, it is appropriate that cultural highways be established for the world, and that the inner fountain shall always remain in its pure form with this distinguished people that has been entrusted with the divine prerogative to release many additional streams, mighty religions and faith, that will win the hearts of many nations in the near and distant future.

Through the revelation of the creative potency of the Torah and its influence on the spiritual and practical life of the most significant portion of humanity in the past, we can understand how to contemplate what is hidden in its treasury for the future, especially what this treasure will accomplish in the world when its central basis, the full spiritual fountain in the soul of the people, to whom the Torah is linked so intimately, will be restored to its dignity and authenticity. How mighty will be the spiritual influence which will be released in that future time. Part of it is already discernible in our time in the commencement of the realization of God's promise on behalf of this remarkable people, and on behalf of His land with its wondrous characteristics, and its destiny, which fascinate nations and kingdoms. And how it will penetrate the hearts of mighty nations and the backbone of the human community and their culture in the future!

The mission of the overall purpose, hidden in this concealed truth, is to pave a way for the eternal success of man and all existence. Human culture, on its high level, will reach this with only a very slight effort. However, this is the ideal of ideals, and the ultimate yearning of all life's yearnings. It is a program for the renewal of culture and for the perfection of society with all its broad needs that deserve to be looked upon as the crown of creation, from which all branches of culture reach out.

All this is found in the people of Israel and it continues to be disclosed in humanity despite all the stumbling blocks on this bafflingly long road. It is all an illumination from the Torah, in the past, the present and the future. We are thus surrounded by all existence, above and below, with bundles of answers to the great question asked of us: "What has the Torah contributed to human culture?"

Maamore Ha-Rayah, pp. 101-104.

The Inner Dimension of the Torah

The sages of Israel, our highest authorities, were the advocates of unity in the realm of thought, which always illumines the dark places of the world. They stated long ago: "Some [masters in the academy] rule that a given item is unclean, and others that it is clean,[6] some forbid it and others permit it . . . but one God gave those teachings, one leader spoke them, they all emanate from the Lord of all creation, praised be He" (Hagigah 3b). They also said: "These and also those are the words of the living God" (Erubin 13b). This is the great testimony to the unity of thought, which validates the seemingly contradictory expressions in the realm of thought and of the spirit, acknowledging how they bear a blessing for the world. There is no better therapy for the sickness of fragmentation of forces, especially the spiritual forces of the Jewish people, than this lofty rule which embraces in its sweep worlds without end. But the stronghold where this true principle must manifest itself among us is particularly in the realm of Jewish ideology, in contrast to the realm of action, which has a unitary character, including in its spectrum diverse shades of thinking.

The fragmentation of thought produces a decline, a weakening of thought. For how can one engage in thought if he believes that whatever is outside his own skull is nothing but a profuse confusion and that the [meaning of the] world and life is only what is found in his own tiny mentality? . . .

The lack of effort to bring together all the worthwhile ideas of the house of Israel, to harmonize them and to develop them, resulted in the fact that those ideas which were indeed the product of confusion, which could not be united with the full inner life of the Jewish people, rose like dark clouds and brought darkness upon the world. They took away especially from the young people the dignity of understanding themselves on the basis of the healthy and authentic sources. They were misled by the shallow ideas engendered by myopic vision and lack of faith in the mighty unity of God, which is the source of Israel's strength and dignity. "He rules by His might forever, His eyes keep watch over the nations, let not the rebellious exalt themselves!" (Ps. 66:7), "I weep in secret for her pride" (Jer. 13:17), "for the pride of Israel which has been taken from them" (Hagigah 5b).

In our world of thought which focuses on action, the study of *halakha* [law] and Talmud, the experiment has worked well. All opinions, those that won agreement and those that did not win agreement, were gathered together. Together they enriched our knowledge, they broadened our concepts and strengthened our mental faculties, by enabling us to confront every subject which focuses on action-centered problems with new reflection, in a clear and successful way, according to our circumstances. The benefit experienced through the wide domain of study, which was structured by bringing together diverse opinions and weaving them toward unity, blunted altogether the feeling of controversy and dissension which could have been engendered through differences in thinking and in resolving the issues under consideration. Instead this brought us unity, love, and feelings of respect without end of all the different and conflicting ideas as well. It is this, too, which enabled us to see the positive results [from this diversity of thought] in all their splendor and forces.

This is not what happened to thought in the realm of ideology. Despite all the efforts of the masters of *aggadah* [the nonlegal element in the Talmud], the masters in the field of *musar* [morals], research and the speculative Cabbalah, at least to popularize and raise the esteem for the ideational centered studies, we have not been privileged as yet to establish fixed study groups whose goal shall be to bring together in aggregate and harmonization all the diffused body of important thinking of the house of Israel, which came to light in different form, in different generations, under different circumstances, from different groups, in varying specialties of theme and style, but all contributing toward one goal — toward Israel's fountains of wisdom.

And all those wonderful books in which the great scholars of former generations invested so much effort in writing and spreading them lie neglected or they are regarded as recreational reading, which one looks at occasionally. Such reading cannot effect the general sought-after goal: to bring together ideas, to interrelate them, to develop them. Those whose general intellectual development has brought them to a state of being thirsty for thought and avid for new and vital ideas, being unable to find agreeable and healthy nourishment in Judaism, rich in varying ingredients, prepared by workers living in our midst, and acceptable to the new generation — they become alienated. Impoverished, they stray in every direction, following the ideas prevalent in the nation where they reside. The influence this exerts among us, in turn, brings about sorrow and enfeeblement.

All this has happened to us because of the exaggerated fear of reflection and thought in that dimension of the Torah which is directed at the heart and mind. The great masters of the past, especially the Cabbalists, cried out against this. This fear is itself a product of a lack of study and understanding of the general attribute of the higher level of the fear of God [awe]. When this grows unrefined in the heart it is turned to panic and terror, which is altogether different from the awe before the majestic splendor of God. The latter shows to what extent studies focusing on divine themes work or the good of general culture, and to what extent the name of the God of Israel releases a light of peace and justice in the world.

It is surely our duty at the present time to write about the God of Israel in books, pamphlets, essays, imaginative tracts, poems, commentaries, and homilies, in all the forms of literary expression that can communicate our thought to the public. And it is for us to state our beliefs and opinions in comprehensible terms, for ourselves and for the generations to come.

Eder Hayakar, pp. 13-15.

Assyriology and the Bible

When Assyriology made known its findings, our hearts were troubled because of some dubious similarities between the teachings of the Torah and some cuneiform texts in beliefs, morals and norms of behavior. Is there any basis in reason for this concern? Is it not a well-known principle that there were individuals in antiquity who were knowledgeable about God, prophets, and great men of the spirit, such as Hanokh, Shem, Ever, and others?[7] And is it possible that they had no effect on their generation, though their work did not receive the recognition of the work of our father Abraham? And how is it possible that there should be no traces of their influence left on their generation? There is bound to be a similarity between these and the subjects treated in the Torah!

As to the similarities in teaching, it was already made clear in the days of Maimonides, and before him in the teachings of the Talmudic sages, that prophecy reckons with man's nature, for it is its mission to raise his nature and his disposition by divine guidance, as is implied in the statement that "the commandments were only given so as to refine the nature of people" (Genesis Rabbah 44:1). Hence, whatever educational elements there were before the giving of the Torah, which gained a following among the [Jewish] people and the world, if they only had a basis in morality and it was possible to raise them to a high moral level — the Torah retained them. In a more enlightened outlook, this is the sure foundation for the acknowledgment of a good cultural element deep in the nature of man. This is conveyed in the statement that the most all-inclusive teaching of the Torah is the verse: "This is the book of Adam's descendents. When God created man, He created him in God's image" (Gen. 5:1,2), and that this is even greater than the verse: "You shall love your neighbor as yourself" (Lev. 19:18), which was cited by Rabbi Akiba.

Such and similar explanations should have occurred to every understanding person, as a basic outlook, and then there would have been no basis for the nefarious heresy to spread in the world and to find support through such incidents.

However, [this heresy] is bolstered by moral claims, because of the unbecoming behavior by some people who are devotees of the Torah and religious faith, which, according to the advocates of heresy, brought weakness and a stumbling of spirit to the people. Then they sought support for their position in some inane scientific references. There are many who do not realize the true psychic motivation which brought them to this lowly state of disdain for the Torah. . . But the true cause for all the confusion, which has brought evil to the world through wrong beliefs, is the sin of desecrating the name of God. On the other hand, great is the power of hallowing God's name which is effected by "a scholar whose business dealings are equitable, who speaks to people gently. Of such a person the verse states: 'You are My servant, Israel, through whom My glory is made manifest'" (Yoma 86a, Is. 49:3).

Only the good moral behavior in good deeds and good attributes of character, on the part of Torah devotees, of *zaddikim*, and people who fear God, is the surest guarantee for the rejection of the erroneous basis of the heresy caused by moral failure; and when this will disappear, there will be revealed the weakness of the heresy based on teachings of science. Then the iron yoke of negativism which weakens the children of Israel will be broken by itself, and the divine light will automatically shine once again in their lives. The various forces of the people will then grow toward unity, and the blessings of life and peace will draw closer to the people of Israel.

Eder Hayakar, pp. 42-43

The Service of God

The concept of serving God, when it is defined in lowly terms, corresponds to a person's limited understanding of what he means by God. It is the service of a slave. It rises in stature to the same extent as his understanding of God will rise. If a person should reach a state where his moral and intellectual powers have been duly developed, in accordance with his potentialities and the cultural climate of his time, yet his understanding of God remains on a low plane, then there will necessarily emerge in him a fierce opposition to the whole idea of serving

God. The only remedy to overcome this is to elevate his concept of God through deep feeling and comprehensive understanding of ever-increasing scope, at least paralleling his other perceptions of the great and the sublime. The affirmation of God, however, is preliminary to everything else. "When I invoke the name of the Lord, declare you the greatness of God" (Deut. 32:3).

As long as the concept of serving God is defined as a service directed to a particular Being, dissociated from the acknowledgment of the ideals which are an integral part of the very essence of the service, it will not free itself from the immature outlook which is always focused on particular beings. This will remain the case even if the concept of the divine being be defined in metaphysical-spiritual terms, through all kinds of philosophic and speculative elaborations. The mature outlook calls for the formulation of divine ideals, to refine them, to try and strengthen them, and to actualize them in the life of the individual, of the nation and of the world . . .

This is the unique position of the people of Israel whose maturity is attested to in the verses: "Israel is My first-born son" (Ex. 4:22); "like grapes in the wilderness I found Israel, like the first ripe fig on the fig tree" (Hosea 9:10). This is the profound outlook of "a people that is wise and understanding — that has righteous statutes and judgments as this entire Torah" (Deut. 4:6,8), that abounds in exalted ideals and mighty and dependable strategies for translating them into practice throughout the generations. It is indeed well-known that, according to a deeper understanding of the Torah, even the names of God do not designate the *essence* of the divinity, but rather the divine ideas, the ways of God, His will, the divine emanation, the *sefirot*, the attributes, the paths, the gates [through which one may come close to Him], the personifications.[8] To some extent the substantive content of these ideals is also written in man's nature, for God has made him upright. The mightiest desire imbedded deeply in man is to translate this hidden light from the realm of potentiality to action, to bring that unlimited perfection of the divine ideals ever closer into the structure of life itself, of the person, of society, in the realms of action, will, and thought. This is the enlightened service of God, the service of [mature] children who feel within themselves an inner relationship to their Father, their Creator, the source of good, of life, and of light.

This ideal concept will always broaden the spirit and elevate it while the concept of the slave-like service, which involves service to a particular being, detached from the ideals, can fall to the level of idolatry, as the anthropomorphic and limited and changing characterization [of the deity] are prone to have this effect. It narrows the spirit and lowers it. The concept of service to a particular *being* without the affirmation of ideals which emanate from the divine source is the most primitive concept because it emerges from a childish stage of reasoning, at a time when a person does not yet distinguish between a particular being and its attributes. All his relationships seem to him, therefore, as directed only to a being in its aspect of particularlity [detached from its attributes]. But after a person acquires the mature outlook, he realizes that every being in the world is to be comprehended only on the basis of attributes and one's relationship to them. The concept of serving God, when conceived in this manner, also becomes more exalted. It invests the person with vitalizing energy. God's relationship to him will become more profound, more exalted and more vital than any other relationship. The full truth of the higher humility, which is higher than wisdom, will then crystallize for him: "What wisdom has fashioned into a crown for its head, humility has turned into a heel to its shoe" (Yerushalmi, Shabbat 1:3). Only then will it be made clear that a person's own existence is to be defined in terms of a relationship to attributes, and that the relationship of the divine to him is the essence of his life and the truth of his existence . . .

The differentiation between the two conceptions is not dependent on one's ability to affirm the profound metaphysical truth about the unity of God. This can be asserted by any people. What is critical is the divine disposition in the inner life of the person to love equity and justice and the firm aspiration for these divine ideals in all their force. These abound with an unreserved love for truth and the light of peace, and the desire always to advance them in the life of the nation, especially in its *national life*. To attain these goals there must be a favorable disposition in the nation's psyche itself. It is for this reason that not only the mental outlook of Judaism needs cultivation, but also its nature. Its nature cannot be safeguarded and blessed unless it pursues a suitable way of life, which is available through all the commandments of the Torah . . . to love them and to honor them in thought and feeling, with the aid of all the educational strategies needed for this purpose . . .

The Jewish people is unique in that its natural characteristic, the deepest yearning of its nature, is the mighty desire for divine justice and its development. This desire came to us as an inheritance from our ancestors — the history of our race. Particularly now, after the passage of a long time, this vision stands and flashes before us its call from the light of history, from our forefathers, who made this the highest ideal of their lives, to establish a people in the world, among whom the divine ideals, the highest norms of morality, will find a place, not only in the private lives of its individual members, but also and especially so in their national life. These ideals, moreover, were to be not an auxiliary interest, but the substantive essence of their national being. Thus when the people of Israel will rise to its full stature, and achieve full self-realization, it will also be able to serve as a model for all the nations of the earth, to raise man's dignity from the depths of his lowliness to the intended heights of his creation.

Eder Hayaker, pp. 145-149

NOTES

A Call for Unity

1. Rabbi Kook refers here, no doubt, to institutional religion which is a channel of service for the holy, but at the same time narrows it and limits it. Holiness, in its essence, is a vision of universality which affirms the need of all dimensions of thought to be given free scope for development.

Morality and Faith in God

2. Elsewhere Rabbi Kook sees a certain positive role for atheism, even on the ideological plane. It is a necessary protest against religion on a low level when it becomes subject to superstition and anthropomorphic conceptions of God. It is when religion reaches its full maturing that the challenge of atheism has lost its validity. But the credibility of atheism is enhanced by the moral failures of its representatives. (See the essay "Pangs of Cleansing," in *Abraham Isaac Kook*, ed. B. Z. Bokser, Paulist Press, 1978, pp. 261-269.)

The Lights of Faith

3. Rabbi Kook regards the holy spirit as the prophetic faculty before its full emergence from potentiality to actuality (*Lights of Holiness*, vol. II, p. 27). This is essentially the view of Maimonides (*Guide* II 45).

Our Separate Paths

4. This prayer is part of the Amidah recited during the High Holy Days.

The Torah and Human Culture

5. Rabbi Kook distinguishes between a sensibility for the divine and a sensibility for religion. The former refers to the divine as the mystical reality underlying all existence. The latter refers to institutional religion.

The Inner Dimension of the Torah

6. The conditions which render certain objects, animals, and even persons Levitally unclean are specified in the Bible, principally Lev. 11-13.

Assyriology anf the Bible

7. These were Biblical characters described in the Bible and in the rabbinic tradition as having led virtuous lives.

The Service of God

8. God does not want adulation directed to Him, as a specific Being. Indeed, His Being, in itself, is beyond our knowing, and beyond our characterization. What we can know are His ways in creation, and in His providential ordering of the world. The attributes that characterize His creation and His providence are models for man to emulate. They become what are here referred to as divine ideals, and we serve God by affirming those ideals and seeking to realize them in life. The *sefirot* refers to the ten divine emanations released by God to bring a concrete world into existence. The most important of these is love. This concept was developed especially by the Jewish mystics.

III.

Letters

An Open Letter

To our young brothers in the Holy Land who are dedicated to the study of Torah, greetings.

I write not because I have the strength to write, but because I no longer have the strength to be silent. . .

Praised be the Lord, we are engaged in the study of the Torah, in the area of *halakha* [law]. But we must bear in mind that this is only a prelude to the study which focuses on the inner life, the hidden treasure of piety in its purity. This is the beginning of enlightenment and the source of wisdom.

The great spirits of our past left us the important treasure of thought concerning the inner life, the deep dimension of the soul. This is the wisdom they always sought after, and they always added to it in every generation. But we only draw on what has been previously prepared, through inferences and the inferences from the inferences. We do not even reexamine the old, and we certainly feel no need to add, to broaden and to create anything new, to give expression to the stirrings of the heart, in some form appropriate for communication.

This complaint is old, but it must be restated with renewed seriousness. The holy spirit cries out, saying: "The masters of the Torah do not know Me," therefore is the Torah in a state of decline; "the wisdom of scholars has degenerated" and "the common people continue to grow in ignorance". No one says anything, no one lifts a hand to help. But this is not a time for us, the leaders in God's cause, to sit with folded hands. The therapy for this condition is in our hands, thanks to Him whose presence abides in Zion, for He brought us to the beloved land, the place of vision whose air restores the soul to life, where the people are again renewed in wisdom, life and spirit.

But we on our part must bestir ourselves to listen to the divine voice that pulsates in us in the inner recesses of our hearts. This is a time to act for the Lord. We must commence to walk on that path which will enable us to acquire the pen, to establish for ourselves a healthy position in the world of literature, whose different expressions serve a beneficial purpose. Thus will we be able to hallow God's name, and reflect honor on the Torah, and win praise for our beloved land, and glory to our holy city, Jerusalem.

The pen is the offspring of thought, and thought is engendered by study. Therefore must we bestir ourselves with firmness, with confidence and inner resolve, to arrange a broad program of study in all subjects that deal with the heart and thought, with all philosophical aspects of the Torah, from the lowest and simplest level of morals to the most sophisticated inquiry into the mystical dimension of the Torah.

But we must be careful to watch that this be structured in an orderly fashion; we must not skip over even a tiny element. All must be done according to order, with a clear mind and largeness of spirit, diligently and with patience. It must be done in such a way that it will enable us to express our thoughts with clarity and precision of language, and God will endow us with wisdom, knowledge and understanding.

The subjects of study I advocate should be pursued some part each day, in a programed fashion, but only a part, for the world of *halakha* [law] is the foundation, the life-giving force on which everything is built. This, too, will grow and flourish, as the philosophical study to which we are not challenged is revived, to open up for us the spiritual riches, the precious treasure, the treasure of the true fear and knowledge of God. The dormant powers will be awakened. Our ability to think will once again become alive, and with the help of God, the pen, and the literary talent will return to us. The pen will work wonders, with the help of God Almighty, to declare the greatness of the Lord, the God of Israel, and to acclaim those who love His name and contemplate His Torah.

This call is directed especially to the Yeshivah scholars whose fixed vocation is the pursuit of Torah study, who are free of the yoke of rendering legal decisions, and of the burdens of public responsibility, whose only goal is Torah scholarship, regardless of what branch of Torah scholarship they pursue. They have the obligation to honor God and the holy city of Jerusalem by setting a fixed schedule of study in the subjects that have to do with a broader knowledge of God. Thus from their collective efforts we will acquire authors, innovators, thinkers, advocates of ideas beneficial to the people of Israel, its Torah and its land. In the course of time, the entire people of God, that is very thirsty for God's word, will know that out of Zion comes forth Torah and light.

Even before the time when authors of books will arise, good writers will bring us fine articles, and they will stimulate each other in exploring the duties of the heart. This also embraces the entire subject of "the scientific study of Judaism",[1] which is presently in the hands of harsh masters. Our task is to break the iron gate, to release this branch of Jewish study from its confinement. But we must not be frightened and alienate ourselves from life. We must work on the side of life and on behalf of life, to hallow life, to exalt it and edify it.

We must avoid gloomy and depressing thoughts that foster stupidity and grief. These only result from casual study and shallow understanding. But a fixed program of study which aspires to enlarge the domain of knowledge, especially in the aspect of the spiritual, must necessarily stimulate the spirit and rejoice the heart. A person who meets this mandate is called "a beloved companion, a lover of God, a lover of people, who brings joy to God and joy to mankind" (Avot 6:1).

Let us hope that these few words which come from an anxious and impassioned heart will reach other hearts and bear fruit. We shall be content with a slow beginning. Let us speak, let us bestir, let us write "a song each day, a song each day" (Sanhedrin 92b); even "stones yield to the continued inflow of water" (Job 14:19).

But give us the heart, "give us the hidden light" (Introduction, Hovot Halevavot). "Let us say to Zion, Come, shine for the time of your illumination has come, and the divine light will shine on you. And those who know Your name will trust in You, for You have never abandoned those who seek You. It pleased the Lord, because of His righteousness, to magnify the Torah and strengthen it. For out of Zion shall go forth instruction and the word of the Lord from Jerusalem. The Lord will never abandon His people for His great name's sake, since it pleased the Lord to make us a people dedicated to Himself." (Isa. 60:1, Ps. 9:11, Isa. 42:21, Isa. 2:3, I Sam. 12:22)[2]

Your servant, who is committed to hope, for the sake of Zion and its environs, and for the peace of those who are learned of the Lord, who are her children and her builders.

> Abraham Isaac Hakohen Kook
> Servant of the holy people that resides in the
> holy land, the holy city of Jaffa and its environs,
> may it be rebuilt and established, Amen
> Igrot I, Letter 27

By the grace of God

To my dear son, may he be blessed with a long and good life, Amen.

You brought me joy with your delightful and precious words. May your strength increase.

I wanted to write you at length various details, especially concerning the norms of behavior. But you know the nature of my work, and the burdens I carry, in addition to my lack of energy due to ill health. May God, praised be He, grant us strength and firmness for the sake of the Torah and His service.

I was pleased to note in your letter that you have agreed to make your permanent quarters this semester in the holy city of Jerusalem, may it be rebuilt and established. Be strong and resolute. What matters most, my beloved son, is that you try to cultivate good qualities of character, the fear and love of God and the diligent pursuit of the study of Torah. It is important that you study and understand and review your studies regularly, so that the teachings of the Torah will be familiar to you in all their profundity. You must try to improve yourself with every kind of perfection in behavior and in knowledge which are a person's adornment.

Do not minimize even the slightest virtue without trying to cultivate it. Nor should you overlook even the slightest defect in your character, without trying to redress it and to mend it. Always be imbued with an affirmative spirit, and try to be inclined toward cheerfulness and goodwill. Attach yourself to people who are God-fearers and knowledgeable in the Torah, those who are wholesome in thought and sincere in knowledge, and let your conversations be with them, and their ways of behavior be to you also at times a model to emulate, after you reckon with your own thoughts and your own commendable good sense.

Write us, dear son, all the details of your way of life, the minutest of details, for you cannot imagine how interested we are in all that affects you, your rising up and your lying down, when you eat breakfast, and what it consists of, when you eat your lunch and your evening meal; and when you retire for the night, and did you accustom yourself to recite the prayer on retiring for the night with due devotion; and when do you rise in the morning; and in what type of room do you regularly sleep, and is it far enough from a window, for the air in Jerusalem, may it be rebuilt and established, is sometimes cold.

I will close with a blessing, my beloved son, and may great peace be yours, as befits your beautiful spirit, and your father who embraces you and kisses you.

Give my regards, with much love, to your teacher, may he be blessed with life.

The holy city of Jaffa, may it be rebuilt and established, Marheshvan, 5666 [1906].

Igrot I, Letter 28

By the grace of God, the holy city of Jaffa, may it be rebuilt and established, 15 Adar, 5668 [1908]

To my friend, the wise and renowned Rabbi, Shmuel Alexandrov, may the light of his life continue to shine, peace and blessing.

Your precious letter reached me, but I am beset with a multitude of burdens falling on me from the people of God who are settling in the Holy Land, and unable to indulge myself in a serious discussion appropriate for your communication.

In general I wonder why we must draw an absolute distinction between feeling and reason. These distinctions are only subjective. Even the distinction between sensation, perception and conception are not absolute, but relative. It is a simple and common-sense perception of every rational person that everything is pervaded by life and intelligence. We add that this is a phenomenon that goes on *ad infinitum*, and we reach the profound conclusion that errors and breakdowns are a precondition to mending and perfection. This is the wisdom fostered by religious faith.

In general we have no reason to be so addicted to the belief in evolution. Certainly there are many sparks of truths in it, but it also has many untruths and fantasies. It is a clearly established fact that there were people of incomparable greatness in earlier generations, and we have none like them in the present, and certainly we cannot place them on a lower plane of development as compared to us. The slow process of evolution is only one of the myriad paths through which He who is the life of the universe manifests Himself.

I said that there is a relative difference between Abraham and Moses, that in comparison with the latter, the comprehension achieved by the former is as a darkened horizon. It is comparable to what has been said (Tikkune Zohar 70): "The divine emanation, the *sefira* 'crown', though it embodies a bright illumination is dark in comparison with the Cause of all causes."

In general I see the flight [from rational thought] increasing in our generation, out of fear, and this engenders in the heart a fear of God which is weak and on a low plane, but the desire to achieve the higher fear of God [awe] prepares the ground for an understanding that is based on strength and clarity.

There is no reason for a retreat from the practical commandments, for they are rooted in moral considerations, whether they affect the individual or the community. When their moral motivation does not seem clearly discernible, we may still assume them to be moral, in the light of all the possible interpretations that we can associate with them. For we and our reasoning are not a recent creation, and before man was created his thought was already revealed [in the realm of ideas].[3] It is appropriate for every wise man to defend them [the commandments], too, because of a love for our people, which is linked with them with many precious associations.

Igrot I, Letter 117

By the grace of God, the holy city of Jaffa, may it be rebuilt and established, Tevet 13, 5666 [1906]

To my beloved son, my treasure, the light of my eyes, may he live to a long and good life. Amen.

Your precious words in your letter filled me with delight and joy. Strengthen yourself, dear son, in the diligent study of the Torah, in its various divisions, according to your ability, following the method which you know to be my heart's favorite. I trust with good reason that thereby you will find happiness and true success, inner joy, peace of mind and a noble delight. It will bring you a love for Torah and general knowledge, and sound reasoning, and above these a pure reverence for God, which broadens the mind and ennobles life with illumination and clarity.

I find no need at this time to explain once again the basic principles involved here. I have explained them in a previous letter, and I see, thank God, that you have understood the subject, according to your capacity, though there is no end to the degree of understanding and the quality of perception. This is the basis of the endeavor for continued perfection, even in subjects that one has absorbed well. Thus the rabbis observe: "If you have comprehended the old, you will comprehend the new" (Ber. 40a). The whole sickness of this generation is that they think that once a subject has been studied, it is no longer necessary to review it and to understand it properly, and they seek the new without possessing the old. Under no circumstances will they be able to achieve this, for the new cannot be properly established unless it is drawn from the roots of the old, which becomes like new each day to one who studies it with an upright heart; and one who truly serves God is one who reviews his studies one hundred and one times (Hagigah 9b). This applies to all subjects of study. Therefore, my son, strengthen yourself in patiently reviewing your studies, and do it with joy, slowly and with diligence. With the help of God, you will grow in understanding and you will succeed.

I cannot be more elaborate at this time, and, my dear son, forgive me. Be strong and resolute, and write us the minutest details concerning your affairs, clarifying things well. Thus you will bring joy to your father, who desires your success and anticipates your renown.

Igrot I, Letter 29

By the grace of God, the holy city of Jaffa, may it be rebuilt and established, Shevat 14, 5666 [1906]

To my close friend, the learned Rabbi Aaron Hakohen, may he live to a long and good life.

Greeting and may God's mercies be on you.

My burdens and distractions have increased these days, and I cannot satisfy the requests of those who make demands of me that call for research and reflection. This applies to the request made by your honor. I am especially unable at this time to undertake matters that are requested of me with the claim that I am obligated. In general I do not wish to be obligated to any person and bear the yoke of obligations, except those due to God, praised be He. Nevertheless, I am sending your honor the text of the legal decision in the style I agreed to write it. More than this I refuse to be involved in the matter.

Concerning the expenses of the society "Geulah", how can I render a decision with authorization to draw funds, without knowing the arguments of the party on the other side? This is necessarily impossible. Your honor should decide this according to his own discretion.

I close with a blessing, and with great love, as befits your noble self, and your friend who seeks your welfare.

Igrot I, Letter 31

By the grace of God, the holy city of Jaffa, may it be rebuilt and established, Kislev 12, 5667 [1907].

Peace and blessing to the honored, renowned sage, our master, Rabbi Yeshaya Orenstein, may his light continue to shine.

Your important communication reached me. Truthfully, I was uncertain whether to reply to you or not, because I was concerned that your honor might be disturbed by my letter, and why should I grieve an elder scholar like you, may you be blessed with life? I decided, however, to reply to you briefly. Perhaps God will grant it that you will heed my words, and then you would no longer be so troubled about the pamphlets. This would be my reward, to save a precious person like you from pain and worry.

Your honor should know that my primary goal in these pamphlets and in all my writing is to stir the hearts of scholars, old and young alike, to concern themselves with the inner dimension of the Torah. This includes the field of morals in all its dimensions as exemplified in the writings of the holy masters, the works of scholarly research available to us in the holy writings of the masters in research; the Cabbalah in all its dimensions according to early and later masters, according to the method of Hasidism, and according to the method of Elijah Gaon and Rabbi Moshe Hayim Luzatto. The latter must be studied with the text of the Zohar, the Sifra de-Zeniata, the Sefer Ha-Bahir and the Sefer Yezirah. We must also include the Midrashic works of the Talmudic sages. These works need be studied in depth to be fully conversant with their content. To accomplish this one must study with great diligence, like the diligence required in the study of the Talmud and the legal codes.

Because of the bent of their nature, not all people are qualified for this type of study. Whoever is not equipped for this type of study, and his heart is drawn to dialectical analysis, should certainly pursue the analytical study of the Talmud and the codes. But whoever is qualified to engage in the deeper study of theosophical wisdom and Cabbala should arrange for himself regular short periods for this type of study. He can allow longer periods for the study of Talmudic dialectics. With it all, one must not give up altogether the analytical study of the legal aspects of Torah in which the Only One, praised be He, takes delight. The primary goal of one's studies, however, must be to become more knowledgeable of his Creator. Thus it is prescribed in the introduction to the *Etz Hayim* and see also the statement in *Or Neerav* [two Cabbalistic works].

In our time when, because of our many sins, a great number of our young people are lured by the attractions of the literary style of the rebels in our midst, it is also important to show the world that scholars who engage in the holy pursuit of studying the true dimension of the Torah are not lacking in the graces of a good literary style. This was the objective which inspired the saintly Rabbi Moses Hayim Luzatto to write his books on literary style. In my humble way, I aspire to follow in his footsteps, to the extent of my ability.

In order to fully understand the Torah, it is also necessary to possess worldly knowledge in many areas, especially in order to be able to respond to the arguments of heretics, which is most urgent in our time. I cite the statements of our sages, Rabbi Elijah Gaon, may his memory be for a blessing, and our master, Rabbi Loew of Prague in his *Netivot Olam*, Netiv Ha-Torah, ch. 14. The latter calls for diligence in the study of Torah and the cultivation of good qualities of character and behavior, especially the need to avoid anger, pride and depression, the major negative traits. To these he adds the need of programing a daily period for studying the inner dimension of the Torah, each person according to his capacities. And then he declares as a clearly established principle that, after these preliminary conditions have been met, it will in no sense be perilous, God forbid, to cultivate the knowledge of worldly wisdom, when these studies will be pursued for the sake of heaven. On the contrary they will strengthen a person in the service of God, praised be He, with great joy and with a broadened outlook.

If there are some people who err in interpreting what I say and distort my position, this is no reason for suppressing the good from those who are prepared to profit from it. One is reminded of what Maimonides said in one of his letters in a similar situation, quoting the verse: "The ways of the Lord are upright, the righteous walk in them but sinners stumble over them" (Hosea 14:10). By regularly studying the satisfying inner dimension of our holy Torah a light of joy and higher love will shine on the person, with spiritual delights which are intimations of the world to come, and he will have no need whatever to invoke the lower fear, the fear of retribution, except in a very small measure. This will endow him with strength and courage and he will not fear any evil afflictions in this world or the next. For even if one dwell in darkness, the Lord will be a light to him. This is the substance of what I intended to convey, to which your honor reacted. How good and how agreeable it would be if we each judged one another charitably. Thereby the honor of God would be exalted and magnified, as well as the honor of the holy land, and the honor of the scholars in Eretz Yisrael.

As for me, I am, thank God, far from taking great pleasure when people praise me, nor am I unduly disturbed when they insult me. I thank God, praised be He, that my constant pursuit of the study of morals and the inner dimension of our holy Torah has had this effect on me. I therefore see no need to apologize to your honor, only to calm your honor's heart, that you should not suffer anguish; for all my desire is to bring happiness to people and, to the extent of my ability, to fulfill the expectation expressed in the verse: "Those who revere You will see Me and rejoice" (Psalm 119:74). I have therefore said: May these words of mine bring peace to the heart of your honor. And may the Holy One, praised be He, bless you with good old age, you and all that are yours, and may we be privileged to see the rejoicing that will come to Zion and the rebuilding of Jerusalem, when the glory of the divine kingship will be manifest for us, raising us to acclaim and praise among all the nations of the earth, and the whole earth will be filled with the knowledge of the Lord. I offer this prayer, as is appropriate for your noble spirit, and for your youthful friend, the trodden on doorstep, who hopes for light and deliverance.

The lowly Abraham Isaac Kook

I am surprised that your honor criticizes me because of what someone wrote in *Havezelet*. Do I know him, and what can I, or anyone else who releases his writings in public, do if some people will react to them with nonsensical remarks?

I subsequently examined what that person had written in *Havezelet* and it became clear to me that it does not contain those objectionable remarks which your honor attributed to it, God forbid. It is in order that he, too, be judged charitably, and that we love peace and truth.

Igrot I, Letter 43

> By the grace of God, the holy city of Jaffa
> may it be rebuilt and established, Amen
> (5667 [1907])

To my dear son, the apple of my eye, may he be blessed with life. You can imagine without my telling you how pained I am that I could not write to you immediately in reply to your delightful communication. My thoughts were pervaded by your beloved expressions, and I said to myself that I will sit down and fill up a large sheet of paper to satisfy your precious self that is eager for my comments. But I was interrupted by various distractions, and I am grieved because of your disappointment. I almost decided to write you a perfunctory letter, but I was ashamed of myself to offer you this even temporarily. Realizing that I cannot manage to write you at length, I will satisfy myself by writing you briefly.

My darling, write me in detail concerning your situation. What impediments, if any, have you encountered, and what troubles did they cause you, and have you emerged from those difficulties, and have you already set your affairs in order? As to your lodging, it is difficult to agree that you rent quarters for a year. Perhaps you will succeed to find quarters during the renting season which will be close to the yeshivah. That you yourself carry the responsibility for preparing food, even on a temporary basis, will, I am afraid, involve you in a waste of your precious time. It also seems to me that you lack the skills in food preparation.

Extend greetings with much love to Rabbi Harlap, may he be blessed with life . . .

I enjoyed what you had to say concerning Talmudic homilies. It is always necessary to add that with all the progress we have made in our philosophical analysis, we have no understanding of the exalted holiness in prophecy. We can only explain it by approximation, as we view the supernal light of the knowledge of God, praised be He. The clearest and the most vital perception we have of it is in truth what is disclosed to us by a fullness of faith, when our contemplation is accompanied by pure faith, preceding it and following it. This was the characteristic of our father Abraham, in whose footsteps we follow, as it is said of him: "And he believed in God" (Gen. 15:6); he was the leader of the believers.

It is truly impossible to grasp fully any spiritual concept except through the holiness of complete faith. Enlightenment and expansions of knowledge are only an aid to comprehension, not its essence. And whenever a person is privileged to enter the domain of the knowledge of God, praised be He, he grasps more clearly the comprehension wrought by faith. The primary factor in redressing the condition of our generation in general, and in particular cases, depends on this perception, and the salvation of the people of Israel, and their honor, and the salvation of the whole world is only dependent on this. As long as people do not attain an expansion of comprehension through the holiness of faith, all their knowledge will be particularistic and limited. As it is deepened in the knowledge sustained by faith, it will rise to greater universality, reflecting the universality in the word of God, a "kiss from the kisses of His mouth" (Exodus Rabbah ch. 41). A person of your wisdom will understand these words of mine, with the help of God.

If they should publish critical comments on what I say, even if it be the lowest kind of disparagement, I trust in God, praised be He, that no damage will result, not for me personally, nor for the cause which engages my holy commitment, to raise the soul of the Torah among our people in the Holy Land. On the contrary, sharp reactions stimulate keener probing of the issues.

Be strong my son, and firm, in the study of Torah and the fear of God, in diligence, and in reviewing your studies, in good attributes of character, with resoluteness and bravery, and also try to inspire a spirit of joy and purity whenever you can. It is for this that we were created. And may the Lord our God gird us with strength and courage, wisdom and knowledge, the humility which engenders justice and uprightness, for His name's sake and for the sake of His people, His eternal possession.

Convey my regards to Rabbi Uri Michelson, may he be blessed with life, and convey regards with much love to your teacher who is a favorite of mine, may he be blessed with life.

Succeed in your progress toward the truth, with all that is worthwhile, as befits your beautiful self and your father who looks forward to your happiness with heart and soul.

Igrot I, Letter 45

> By the grace of God, the holy city of Jaffa,
> may it be rebuilt and established, Rosh
> Hodesh Shevat, 5667 [1907]

To my honored friend, the renowned rabbi, our Master Rabbi Dover Milstein, may his light continue to shine, peace and blessing.

Your precious letter reached me. As to my advice on how you are to act toward your children, I have already told you when you visited with us that my way is to act with full loving-kindness toward our young people, and to tell them that there are many good elements in their disposition, and that their basic error consists in their belief that the good elements which they have embraced are against the Torah, while in truth they are of the very essence of the Torah.

Therefore, while it is in order to give them the freedom to study literature, and foreign languages, and the sciences, to their heart's desire, it is in order that they, on their part, show their love for Judaism and for its precepts, at least the basic and more important ones, for thereby they perform a kindness and an act of justice with the people of Israel.

It is necessary to explain to them, to the degree that they can comprehend this, that it is meritorious for any person to act charitably toward his people by activating hallowed principles that have been part of its faith from earliest times. A Jew should feel this especially, for even our lowest ones can see that we have some distinction in matters spiritual, in comparison with all the other nations, and it would be wrong for any person with a sense of equity to contribute to a decline of this distinction. It is appropriate, on the contrary, to raise it in significance by acting in accordance with the tradition of Judaism, while following in the way of the enlightenment and the new lifestyle, in accordance with the times.

This is the lowest level of conversation that the parents can hold with their children, which will win them listening ears. But if the parents should attempt by force to raise the children beyond their level of comprehension, through the holy enthusiasm which they feel in their hearts, it will not help at all; it will only prove damaging. Therefore, it is well for a person to heed my advice on this, for he will thereby save his children from descending even lower. Slowly, through love, he will bring them closer to the ways of Judaism, and in the end, in their later years, they will mend their behavior. It may well be that the children born to them may turn out better than their parents. May God, praised be He, help us to turn the hearts of the transgressors among our people to full penitence, and hasten for us the true deliverance, when a redeemer will come to Zion, and to those who have turned away from transgression in Jacob.

As to the wine made in the colony Rehovot, your honor may drink it without any hesitation, for everything is made according to the rules of *kashrut.*

I will close with a greeting, and with much love, as befits your precious self, and your friend, who wishes you in love to prosper in the study of Torah.

Igrot I, Letter 50

By the grace of God, the holy city of Jaffa, may it be rebuilt and established, 16 Shevat, 5667 [1907]

To my honored friends, the inhabitants of the holy city of Accre and especially to the honored City Council, may the Lord keep them in life and watch over them, peace and blessing.

I find it necessary to convey to you my feelings which may perhaps indicate to you how deeply pained I am. It is for this reason that I cannot desist from writing to you. The duty of reprimanding rests on every Jew, especially on a public servant like myself.

I heard, to my distress, that there are people in your community who were presumptuous enough to insult the renowned rabbi who is the head of your rabbinic court. One of them performed the nefarious act of tearing down a notice which had been issued by your rabbi, and he accompanied this evil act by mouthing some vicious words, not fit to be listened to. When this came to my attention, I became indignant, and I was moved to cry out: Alas, what has happened to us! How could it happen that in a decent community in the Holy Land, like the community of Accre, may it be built and established, there should be such a decline of Jewish honor, the honor of the Torah and the honor of a scholar. And what a scholar! A distinguished scholar, like your renowned rabbi, who is crowned with such good qualities of character, with such agreeableness of spirit! If such qualities were found even in an ordinary person, it would be appropriate to draw close to him with love and respect beyond measure.

My dear brothers, give thought to redressing this situation. Consider that the duty to revere the Holy One, praised be He, also includes the duty to revere a scholar (Kiddushin 57a), and that the respect for one's teacher is like the respect due to God (Avot 2:12). The one who sinned by speaking arrogantly, if he wishes to avoid divine retribution, must resolve to come humbly before the rabbi, may he be blessed with long life, to ask his forgiveness in the presence of other people, as it is stated. Let him face other people and say, I have sinned, and let him repent and he will be forgiven. Then it will be possible to say that the offense was committed unintentionally, and, who can be free of unconscious errors? I know how embarrassing these words of mine would be to your honorable rabbi, but in this matter, for the public good, I must not consider his wishes, which are otherwise always dear to me.

And may the Lord, praised be He, bestow on you blessing and much peace, and may we merit together to see that the honor of the righteous in the Holy Land has been uplifted, as God sends deliverance to His people, speedily, in our own time, Amen.

Igrot I, Letter 57

By the grace of God, the holy city of Jaffa, may it be rebuilt and established, 26 Shevat, 5667 [1907]

To my friend, the scholar, the honored and wise Rabbi Israel Dov Frumkin, editor of *Havetzelet,* may he live to a long and good life.

I urgently request that you publish my statement as written in your esteemed periodical.

The sages called for severe penalties for one who is silent when a scholar is insulted, as is mentioned in the case of Rabbi Elazar ben Simeon in the chapter dealing with the hiring of workers (Baba Metzia 84b). I therefore wish to register an open protest before the entire people of God, and especially before our brethren residing in the Holy Land, and before all Ashkenazic Jews living in Cairo in Egypt, because of the frightening insult the leaders of the Ashkenazic community visited upon their distinguished rabbi, Rabbi Aaron Mendel Hakohen, who has served in the rabbinic office of their city for many years.

After examining the complaint of his adversaries, which were published in *Havetzelet,* I am convinced that even if all that is alleged is true, as stated, there would then be reason for the elder rabbis and scholars to make him aware of the need to change his behavior in the future, so as to avoid gossip. But it is wrong to undermine his livelihood because of this. This is an act of cruelty not becoming for Jews who are described as being merciful ones, the children of merciful ones. The action is especially offensive because there is no doubt that their allegations have an element of exaggeration, and with slight exaggeration one can readily turn some slight error, which can be committed even by the greatest and most righteous of people, into a frightful sin and a capital offense. And who is as vulnerable to acting on false charges as our fellow-Jews?

I therefore say openly that the leaders of this community face a great and holy obligation to return to their rabbi, the learned Rabbi Ram,[4] his position and to mollify him in due measure, publicly. They must do this if they wish to satisfy a divine imperative, for they must know that the Holy One, praised be He, protects the honor of scholars.

I hope that they will agree to these words of mine, with the help of God, for their own good in this world and in the hereafter. For one must not overlook a case that involves a profanation of the name of God. And I have faith in the goodness and patience of the learned Rabbi Aaron Mendel Hakohen, rabbi of the Ashkenazic community in Cairo, that he will forgive those who offended him, when they will acknowledge their wrongdoing, as is the attribute of scholars who love peace and disseminate peace in the world. And "when God favors the ways of a person even his enemies make peace with him". He will then resume his position with the dignity due him, as he did until now, before the outbreak of this controversey.

And may God, praised be He, spread His tabernacle of peace over His people, and "those lost in the land of Assyria and those banished in the land of Egypt will return to bow down on the holy mountain in Jerusalem" (Isa. 27:12). May it happen speedily, in our time, Amen. Thereby peace will come to the people of Israel, and to the scholars, and to all who serve the community for the sake of heaven, as befits their precious selves, and him who signs with blessings of peace for the people of Israel and for its scholars.

Igrot I, Letter 61

By the grace of God, the holy city of Jaffa, may it be rebuilt and established, 3 Adar, 5667 [1907]

Peace and blessing to my friend, the renowned rabbi, the highly esteemed scholar, Samuel Alexandrov, may he live to a long and good life.

I was delighted with your precious words. Time does not permit extended considerations and exposition of the important matters raised in your letter. I am only satisfying your request to advise you that I received your highly esteemed letter.

I have already written to you that as far as spiritually advanced individuals are concerned, we do not differentiate between adherents of one people or another, and "a non-Jew who pursues the teachings of the Torah is similar in status to a High Priest" in Israel (Baba Kamma 38a). Our early sages are quoted as having said: "Let us go to welcome our colleague the philosopher" (a non-Jew, Derekh Eretz Rabbah ch. 5). When we speak in praise of the community of Israel generally, this is because of an affinity for the divine which is found in the soul of the Jewish people as a whole, which also manifests itself in some form in each individual. And this is stated fully in Scripture: "We...are distinguished from all the people that are on the face of the earth" (Ex. 33:16).

We are fully free openly to raise our heads and take pride in our love for the community of Israel, which has its imprint on our souls, and we have no reason to deny this love, not for reasons of any scientific findings, nor because of a cosmopolitan spirituality [*hasidut*] When we shall draw water from our own well, the well of Israel, we shall have everything, spirituality and culture. And from the broad perspective of our inner riches, we shall view the vast domain of all mankind, to take pride in the significant part we contributed to the collective treasure of all, and in the distinctive portion which is not shared by others. "O praise the Lord all you nations...for great has been His mercy toward us" (Ps. 117).

Igrot I, Letter 64

By the grace of God, the holy city of Jaffa, may it be rebuilt and established, 9 Tishre, 5667 [1907]

To my beloved friend, wise of heart in the study of Torah and in general knowledge, who is more precious than gold, our master, Rabbi Moshe Seidel, may he live to a long life, may you be sealed for a good year and for all good.

You brought me joy with your writing. My beloved friend, it will make me very happy if you and our dear Rabbi Menashe Levin will become closer physically and spiritually. You are dear to me, you are my witnesses, demonstrating that the teachings of the Torah, which are expounded with a deep analysis of the underlying ideas, to the extent possible, reach their goal, to ennoble and delight precious souls, to raise them and strengthen them in the love of Torah and in reverence for God. And I feel justified in the anticipation that you will continue to make progress in this direction, and the God of Israel will aid you, to cause His light to shine on your way in life.

Tonight will begin the day of Yom Kippur, and were it not for the great love between us I would not be in a position to devote the time to write you even briefly. But you are dear to me and highly esteemed, my beloved one, and from the distance, from the Holy Land, I remember you with unfailing love. I know your good talents, your precious human qualities, and your heart's inclination, to pursue wisdom and to do good. What touches me particularly is that you are sensitive to my style, and can discern the intended meaning of my statements more than others with whom I did not maintain an oral dialogue, even when they are talented with quickness of perception. I hope that you will also glance at this second volume of *Ikve Hazan*, and will find my views agreeable. You will know how to relate the thoughts one to the other, and to draw pearls of comprehension from the thoughts expressed there, to help you attain with a full heart the service of the God of truth, who created us for His glory, to serve Him, and to praise Him, and to proclaim His majesty.

The explanation of my statement "that every attribute of greatness is tied up with defects which correspond to it" is simple.[5] "Heavenly gifts are not given us on a half-way basis" (Yoma 69b). All forces are created to have universal sway, and this is man's vocation: to exercise care in choosing his path so that the general force shall serve the good and not the evil. The great among the ancient masters already observed this, that the remarkable power of memory will recall to a person all the wisdom and the good he has observed, but also all the folly and the evil. This is true of all forces acting in the self. Thus the defect cleaves to them by their very nature. Inevitably, therefore, the greatest thoughts and the most precious dispositions are tied in with defects of corresponding dimensions.

It is only when man rises to the highest level of development, when he sees the divine truth as fully manifest, that evil will not touch him, for evil and filth are included in the truth only to the extent that the divine light is hidden from those who comprehend it and experience it. When "the sun shall be no more your light by day, nor shall the moon give you light for brightness, but the Lord shall be to you an everlasting light, and your God your glory" (Isa 60:19), then will "your people be all righteous" (Isa. 60:21). But much inner preparation is needed to be readied for this, a refinement of the inner being, until the will to live itself will be identical with the light of God's will, who gives life to the universe (Dan. 12:7), the Righteous One who animates all worlds, from whom derive the souls that animate mortals (Zohar I 13a). Then it will no longer be necessary to suppress any force and any human impulse, and there will be no need to pursue an ideal to redress a wrong. Folly and the low level action which reflect the world when the power of evil is ascendent will no longer have any purpose, and they will automatically come to an end. The closer we move to realize God's will in His world we raise life and condition it increasingly to this lofty goal of the universal sway of the good.

Since not only individuals but also nations act in the world, we must also assert ourselves at all times to act in our role as members of the Jewish people, to raise it and to strengthen it, to uplift it and to honor it; and each one must say: "For my sake was the world created" (I am responsible for the state of my world, Sanhedrin 45a), and "when will my behavior reach the standard set by Abraham, Isaac and Jacob" (Tanna Debe Eliahu, ch. 25) who committed themselves to the ideals embodied in the community of Israel even before its full development as a people? Even today, though we are part of the household of Israel, insofar as it has become a reality, we remain attached to the standard set by the patriarchs, which was an anticipation of what was to be realized in the future. We are uplifted with the general level of the people, which is not judged by the values of particular individuals or generations by themselves, but by the nature of their integrated whole. It is similar to the action of the solar system in comparison with the motion of the individual planets. And who of all the nations is like the Jewish people, endowed with potentialities that have not been realized, with all its fine qualities and its high esteem [still in an undeveloped state]? There must therefore be with us great defects. But all will be turned to wonderful virtues, when full realization is attained. "One will see no defect in Jacob and no iniquity in Israel, the Lord his God is with him, and the acclaim for the King is among them"[6] (Nu. 23:21).

I was interrupted while writing you, and this day is full of work. I hope that this letter, though it is brief, will offer some substantive matter as is suitable for a discussion in Torah in which a person always finds meaning when he engages in it.

I close with the greetings appropriate for this season, that you may be sealed for a good year, you and your wife, as is becoming for your precious self, and your friend who anticipates your distinction and success, with fullness of heart, who sends you his blessings from the Holy Land.

Igrot I, Letter 93

By the grace of God, the holy city of Jaffa, may it be rebuilt and established, Tevet 22, 5668 [1908]

To my dear and beloved brother Samuel, may he be blessed with long life. A long time has passed, and I have not written to you, my dear, because of my many distractions.

You know my spiritual state, that I would like to do big things, but, alas, I have not succeeded in anything. There is no one with whom I can have a heart-to-heart conversation, not with older persons, nor with young people, who might come close to what I aspire after. This troubles me greatly.

The manuscripts which I copied with some improvement need more revision and arrangement, according to Zevi Yehuda [his son], and he is right. But this is almost beyond me. He began to copy them again, according to the arrangement he suggested, which may make them more acceptable. But who knows if he will pursue this diligently and not neglect it. I put my burden on the Lord, both in practical and in spiritual matters. I received the volumes of *Dorot Ha-Roshonim*, and I prepared a letter of thanks to the author, with some notations concerning the subject matter of his work. I also called to his attention my own plans which I have in mind. Perhaps, by the grace of God, something good will come, even through one as unworthy as I am.

Write me, my dear, concerning everything worthwhile that is happening to you. How wonderful it would be if you could make me happy with the news that now, since you are alone and independent, you set aside time for the study of Torah. I am sure that is indeed your own inner desire.

I will close with greetings and best wishes of peace, as befits your precious self, and your brother who looks forward to your well-being, and extends to you much love.

Igrot I, Letter 104

By the grace of God, the holy city of Jaffa,
may it be rebuilt and established, 2 Adar II,
5668 [1908]

To my beloved brother Samuel, may he live to a long and good life,
Amen.

Concerning the printing, it is well to begin. There is no reason to
be concerned how the first folio will come out. Perhaps later on, when
I will see the printed text, my perspective will be enhanced, and I will
improve the style.

Concerning the letters of Alexandrov,[7] I, too, was distressed, and
our friend, Rabbi Benjamin Levin, was also distressed by this. However,
there is no need to worry. Those who truly understand will draw a
distinction [between our views] and recognize my position as it is, with
God's help. As to those who do not understand, one cannot take due
precautions, and there is no need to be overly concerned.

I am greatly impeded in acting and writing by the heavy burden
which rests on me in practical and intellectual matters. May God grant
me the freedom to attend to each matter in its time and place, that I
may be able to be of service, with the limited strength God has bestowed
on me. But I must think a great deal before I act or write, even extremely
little, even the briefest summation of my views. Then the result will be
in proper shape, at least from my point of view. But circumstances press
on me to speak, to act, and sometimes also to write in response to pressure
from the outside, and for this I have no talent at all, for I am not
accustomed to such routine and I have never achieved anything with
my own powers. I have been graced by God with a talent for originality
but this must assert itself in the person with a full sense of security, without
any subservience to an outside force. When my writings will take shape
according to this pattern, I can see that they will bear fruit and be of
benefit, by the grace of the Almighty, praised be He. But if I press on
them in a laborious routine I can accomplish nothing, with my limited
resources and lack of knowledge.

I am very eager to know what you are so preoccupied with. May
God bless you with all good, and may you be a successful person,
ambitious and prosperous, as befits your precious self and your brother
who loves you with heart and soul.

Igrot I, Letter 124

By the grace of God, the holy city of Jaffa
may it be rebuilt and restored, Adar II, 5668
[1908].

Peace and blessings from the Holy Land to my dear and precious brother,
the renowned rabbi, who is celebrated and honored, our master Rabbi
Dov Hakohen, may he be blessed with a long and good life, and his
faithful wife, may she be blessed with life, and their sons and daughters,
may they be blessed with a long and good life, and bring you much good
and satisfaction.

After waiting a long time to read a welcome communication from
you, my dear brother, we received your letter. Considering our habit
of being among the affluent ones who are miserly when it comes to
writing, this itself is a happy event. Thank God that all is well with you.
I ask you, dear brother, and I include myself in this request, that the
time has come to turn away from this negligence. It would be better
that we each enjoy helpful support of the other, in lengthy or brief
communications, depending on the time, and to encourage one another
with friendly, brotherly letters, and not the kind of letters which casual
acquaintances write one another. Though there is ample room to excuse
myself with extenuating circumstances, I do not want altogether to justify
myself. A good deal is caused by physical weakness, and more than this,
by mental weariness, which is a moral defect that can be healed through
the exercise of free will, simply to put an end to this denial of the good,
may God forgive us for this.

But do not think, dear brother, that the complaint about my burdens
is exaggerated. I am truly weighed down by heavy pressures, pressures
of work and pressures of thought. How my mind is stirred when it
contemplates the vast field waiting for dedicated labor, a labor in the
service of God, to bring enlightenment for our people and our land, for
the enlightenment of the world. But much of the good is impeded by
lethargy, due to tiredness of the body and tiredness of the mind. Recently
there has been a change for the better in our office, through the addition
of another member to our Beth Din [a religious court of law], a good
scholar in the law who also gets along well with people. It is my hope
that as a result of this my own responsibilities in practical matters will
be alleviated to some extent.

I have begun to have closer relations with the "Shomre Torah"
[Guardians of the Torah] organization, which I did not pursue previously,

because I suspected that there would be ideological disagreements between us. I hope that our relationship will turn out to work smoothly, with the help of God. Under my authorization there has been added a vocational department to the curriculum of the Talmud Torah Shaare Torah, which is now growing. I hope that it will bring honor to the religiously faithful in Israel, showing to all that we are interested in the practical upbuilding of the land. They are now involved in making iron boxes for granaries, which are not inferior to those imported from Europe, and they bear the imprint of the firm "The Vocational Section of *Shaare Torah*". It is my opinion that there is cause for rejoicing over this development.

As to my proposal for the establishment of a yeshivah [to be based on his philosophy of education], there have been various reactions. It has made a deep impression in the religious circles of Germany. Rabbi Isaac Halevi, the author of *Dorot Harishonim*, has promised to lend his support, and he has much influence in the West. The Mizrahi organization there also would like to have a share in this, and help can also be secured from other sources. But the matter must be launched on an impressive scale, as befits the honor of the Holy Land, and the advanced state of the Torah in its midst.

I am anxious to know if the rabbis in Russia [this was written in 1908] are doing anything to save the state of Judaism in their country, and what approach do they take in their efforts, and whether it is possible to establish a link with them. It seems to me that the time has come to wake up from the lethargic sleep of passivity, and to seek ways, ways of life, new as well as old, to help the Jewish people. I wonder if anyone can exempt himself from this task. One dare not be humble in this. Everyone who does something, whether much or little, contributes to the rescue, and together this becomes of much significance. But this work must be done with discretion and good sense, and not merely by the release of emotional feeling in which there is an admixture of unrefined dross.

Perhaps you can tell me what was the impression made by the pamphlet "Binyan He-Umah" [the Rebuilding of the Nation] by Rabbi Pinhas Lintus, may the light of his life continue to shine. Despite its errors in grammar and other technical infelicities, it has much merit. But I doubt if there are people to listen and to be stirred.

Write me in detail concerning good things that have happened in your life, the state of your studies. It seems to me that one can become accustomed to review the study of Maimonides in an orderly fashion, a chapter or two each day, as is possible, at times without the commentaries and at times with the basic commentaries. But it is most important to pursue regular review. In the unfolding future it seems to me that the "Yad" [the fourteen sections of the Maimonidean code of Jewish law] is destined to become the basic fountain of knowledge for scholars, in the system of study which is surely destined to have a revival.

Our brother-in-law, Rabbi Joseph Rabi, long may he live, has written me that there is a possibility that a position may become available for him in a yeshivah in his own city [Vilna]. I would be immensely pleased if he could earn an honorable livelihood from this, though I would prefer it if we could all join together, at the earliest opportunity, in the Holy Land, to serve in unison the great cause that waits to be served there. May God extend his help to us.

You surely are aware of the tragedy that has befallen my brother-in-law Rabbi Maragola [his wife died], may he be granted life. May God comfort him. It would be appropriate to befriend him and to comfort him. He complains of his loneliness. At times through a letter and friendly contact one brings to life and strengthens a troubled person in such a state.

You will undoubtedly receive letters from Samuel [another brother], may he be granted life. He is more diligent than I. Thank God, he studies Torah regularly and is beloved by people in the holy city, may it be rebuilt and established. May God bless him with success. I repeat once more my suggestion that we now begin to plan, with God's help, in a more intimate manner, to exchange regular letters. We will derive from it much satisfaction for ourselves, and more so added strength for any general cause, through our spiritual collaboration, God approving our purpose. . .

I sign with a greeting in faithfulness, with much love, as befits your precious self, and your brother who is attached to you with his whole being, and who sends you best wishes for success in your studies form the holy mountains of the land of Israel.

Igrot I, Letter 125

By the grace of God, the holy city of Jaffa, may it be rebuilt and established, Iyar 5, 5668 [1908]

To my beloved friend, the distinguished scholar, a treasure of Torah and the pure fear of God, Moshe Seidel, may he live to a long and good life, peace and blessing.

I enjoyed your precious words which reached me some time ago, but I did not find the appropriate time to enjoy the pleasure of responding to you, my dear friend, with words of peace and truth. Even now I am beset with burdens and distractions. However, I will rise above the impediments and write to you briefly, with the help of God.

I find it necessary to explain to your noble self how we are to respond to teachings imparted to us through recent scientific research which for the most part tend to contradict the simple meaning of the texts of the Torah. It is my opinion that one who is of sound understanding must know that though it does not follow that these new teachings are necessarily true, we are not at all under the obligation to deny them categorically and to oppose them. It is not at all the intent of the Torah to tell us stories about past events. What is primary is the substantive content, the inner meaning of the subjects discussed. The latter will become even clearer whenever it is challenged by a negating element.

This basic principle was already stated in the writings of early masters, and principally in the *Guide to the Perplexed* [by Maimonides, in I 71, II 15, 16, 25, and cf. III 3]. At the present time we must extend this principle even more. It is of no consequence to us if there was once in the world a golden age, when man enjoyed much good, materially and spiritually, or that existence began by developing from a lower to a higher state, and that it continues to evolve. What we must know is that there is the definite possibility that even if man should reach a higher state of development, and be in line to enjoy all the honor and delight life can offer, if he should corrupt his behavior he may lose everything, and injure himself and his descendents for many generations. This inference is suggested to us by the experience of man in the Garden of Eden, his sin and his banishment. And the Lord of all souls knows how deeply this warning against sin must be felt in the hearts of people. The text in the Torah of truth testifies to the need of this deeply-felt warning.[8] Once we reach this conception we no longer need to resist the conception which is promulgated by the new scholars, and since we no longer have an ulterior interest in the matter we shall be able to judge equitably. And now we shall be able to refute their positions confidently to the extent that the truth shows us the way.

The core pride of our life is the truth about the universal unity, in all its eternal majesty and splendor, the eternal claim of justice which is inseparably associated with it. This is the soul of the Torah, and from this perspective one may also glimpse its body [its precepts] and its robes [its narratives]. In general the concept of evolution is itself in the early stages of its development. It will undoubtedly change its form, and it will come up with perceptions which will acknowledge that there were also leaps in the world's development. This will help to complete the vision of existence. Then will the light of Judaism be understood in its substantive brightness.

This is the very opposite from the conceptions of the non-Jewish thinkers, and of those Jews who follow in their footsteps: they view the Bible from the perspective of Christianity which sees this world as a prison. But the clear perception of the joy of life and its brightness which is embodied in the Torah is based on the assurance concerning the past, that man was very happy and that it was only through the accident of sin that he strayed from his course. It is obvious that an accidental stumbling must necessarily be open to mending, and man will return to his high station. The theory of a development without the aid from the past has frightening possibilities, lest man halt in the middle of his path, or retreat backward, since we have no definite assurance that happiness is a fixed destiny for man, especially for man who is a material being, an amalgam of body and soul. Thus it is only man's having been in the Garden of Eden that assures us of the world of light, and it is therefore appropriate to be read as a factual and historical truth, though this is not critical for us.

In general this is an important principle in the conflict of ideas, that when an idea comes to negate some teaching in the Torah, we must not, to begin with, reject it, but build the edifice of the Torah above it, and thereby we ascend higher, and through this ascent, the ideas are clarified. Then, once we are free of ideological pressure, we can also actively resist the idea that challenges us. There are many illustrations of this, but it is difficult for me to elaborate. For a person as wise as you, the brief statement will suffice, indicating how we may affirm with pride our loyalty to the name of God, above the changing winds of the times blowing about us, at the same time drawing on everything for our true good, which is also the universal good.

As to the vocational choices you have made, may God grace you with success, and illumine you with the light of His wisdom and grant you His many kindnesses, so that you will be privileged to be among those who hallow His name, praised be He, in His world. And you will be a source of pride to the Jewish people, to strengthen those of faltering faith with the love of Torah and true reverence for God, which is so urgently needed in our generation from all who are firm of heart and of a spirit of truth.

I will sign with good wishes and much love, as befits your precious self, and your friend who wishes you success in your studies, with much love.

[A brief reference to a legal matter in this letter was not translated. The letter is also followed by a note from Rabbi Kook's son, Zevi Yehuda, who edited this collection of letters: "My master, my father, may he live to a long and good life, wanted me to add that this letter was written under many distractions, which did not enable him to reflect peacefully, and he was therefore unable to explain the subject properly and to express all that was in his heart, and this grieved him."]

Igrot I, Letter 134

By the grace of God, the holy city of Jaffa, may it be rebuilt and established, Iyar 7, 5668 [1908]

To my dear and beloved friend, renowned for his knowledge of the Torah and for his piety, whose whole life proclaims his honor, our master Rabbi Avigdor Rivlin, may he live to a long and good life, peace to you with much love, and all good always.

It is a long time, my friend, that I have not written you. I also owe you an answer to many letters to which I did not reply. You can blame all this on my many preoccupations and on my frailty which causes these preoccupations to make me weary. Many times even a minor effort at writing becomes an immense undertaking. Believe me, my honored and beloved friend, that the remembrance of your goodness and your sincere love will never leave my heart and I shall always remember you with true endearment.

It seems to me that I forgot to thank you for the volumes of *Dorot Hareshonim* which the learned author, may his light continue to shine, sent me, undoubtedly through your initiative. On the basis of my exchange of letters with him I have the impression that his spirit differs from mine, and I see from the style of this work that this is indeed the case. He is pervaded by combativeness from head to foot. It is true that he fights the battles of the Lord, while I am a man of peace who seeks peace, even in places where most people would not envision that it may be found. But this is my character, especially since I am a descendent of Aaron, who was committed to the covenant of peace.[9] It therefore seems to me that I am not a fitting person to establish links with his outlook and his lifestyle. However, his work and his personality are very important to me. Would that many walked in his footsteps. Then, through the cooperation of all, each walking in his own path, would the truth be established to illumine the horizon above our heads.

Your honor's thought of coming for a visit to the Holy Land to see it, and to see our people as they have begun to blossom on our ancestral homeland, is sound. This will also enable you to see the institution for which you work, and its prospects, if the proper forces should be influential in it. Obviously its officials will not go to court with you concerning the travel expenses. If they should request that you share in the expense, it will not be difficult to reach a compromise. The thought is worthwhile and it would be far from involving any loss. It would surely yield a spiritual reward of seeing our beloved land, may it be rebuilt and established, speedily, in our time, Amen.

I will close with a blessing, and with all good wishes, as befits your precious self and your friend who is devoted in his friendship for you, and wishes you well in your studies of the Torah, with much love.

P.S. I am surprised that I did not receive the typewritten material you mentioned in your letter.

After I wrote my letter, the authorities of Shaare Torah [the institution Rabbi Avigdor Rivlin worked for] mentioned to me that at this time it would be wise to defer the visit, because of their difficult financial situation. When the difficulties ease, they will advise you.

I finally did receive the typewritten letter. There is no need in this case to annul the marriage. Where the wife has become insane, it is simple legally to end the marriage.

Igrot I, Letter 136

By the grace of God, the holy city of Jaffa,
may it be rebuilt and established, 12 Iyar,
5668 [1908]

Peace and blessings to his honor, the great and esteemed Rabbi, fountain of wisdom, and crowned with glory, our master Rabbi Yizhak Isaac Halevi, may he live to a long and good life. Amen.

I feel obligated to call your honor's attention to the true facts which are at the root of our efforts on behalf of our Holy Land.

I note that your honor cautions the rabbis of the Holy Land not to swerve even one iota from their position, as though they were in the habit of retreating from their views because of external influences. It is well for you to know that this is not so. If we should seek through all the world, we will not find people who are so set in their views, with inflexibility and punctiliousness, as the rabbis in the Holy Land, in whatever has to do on issues of religion. There is no need to urge them toward such a disposition. Indeed, it is our duty at the present time, on the contrary, to consider the after-effects, and to be concerned about the state of religion in Eretz Yisrael which, in a certain sense, embodies the religion of the entire Jewish people, so that it may retain its vitality for future generations. But this will not be possible unless we draw new forces into the camp of those who represent the cause of Torah and religious faith. We need people who will be firmly rooted in life, by being suited to participate in the life of society, by being educated in the knowledge of the world and the more important languages.

In addition we must also draw on the divine light which is embodied in Judaism, in its highest expression, which extends to the most advanced knowledge of God, by expanding Jewish culture in all its branches. Toward this end we must revitalize the program of yeshivah education, and this innovation will elude us under all circumstances if we begin with the existing institutions. This approach can only yield deceptive pronouncements from both sides but it will not prove efficacious in yielding a continuing flow of divine light on the people of Israel, for which we hope.

At this time we must establish a new Yeshivah, and particularly so in the center of the new settlement, which is more in need of spiritual revival. Here we will be able to unite toward a common goal. The goal of this Yeshivah will be, firstly, that the most gifted of those trained there should be able to serve as rabbis in the colonies, because they will know well the state of the world and of life, and they will be able to inspire a spirit of the knowledge of, and love for, Torah and true reverence for God in the colonies. The others will also be people who will gain for themselves that grace and dignity suitable for disciples of the Torah who are involved with people. The most talented will be able to serve as competent authors in all those subjects of Torah and wisdom, which call for serious study in our generation in order to restore the honor becoming the name of God, for Eretz Yisrael and for the people of Israel. Those fit to serve as educators would be able to serve as good and respected teachers, abounding with the light of a healthy life, a sacred spirit of Judaism and a firm faith. They will be able to stand up against the breaches wrought by the new pedagogy, which is engaged in undermining everything that is holy to the Lord.

Together with this we must establish vocational and agricultural schools that will be pervaded by the spirit of Torah and religious faith, with culture and sound common sense, with a pure desire to revitalize the Jewish body and soul. However, this must come after the establishment of the major Yeshivah.

When by the grace of God our efforts will succeed, all will see in the light of experience that the right course is indeed the one which is deemed honorable to the one pursuing it and which brings him honor from his fellow-man. When they will realize that all those imaginary fears felt by the leaders of the old institutions, of any change for the better, even if mandated by the Torah and common sense, and based on sound reasoning — they will realize that they feared where there was nothing to fear. They will realize that, on the contrary, their passivity bears with it a more pronounced danger. When those educated by masters for Torah and piety have not been prepared for life, neither by the content of what they studied, nor by their behavior and their manners, then when they grow up they become weaklings, depressed in spirit and dependent for support on the community. Anyone who is clear-eyed can readily see that those who support this approach are paving the way for absolute destruction. In the light of all this I want to bestir you to the realization that only when we have something positive to which we can point, only then will the advocates of the old way, whose motivation is for the sake of God, make concessions to us. Automatically the improvement will then spread to all the schools and the yeshivot in the Holy Land, and this will result in added strength for the holy people. This is the true way, destined to endure and to yield us a noble harvest that will bring joy to God and man.

Why then should we dissipate our strengths in a futile endeavor by proposing that we, together with select members of our Orthodox brothers in Germany, demand a reformation in the *yeshivot* of the old order? It would be preferable that we begin by establishing the new institution to serve as a test, and we can be sure that God will establish our way. When our effort succeeds, we will have a proper foundation on which to base the necessary reforms throughout the Holy land.

With P. Nathan [a leader of German Jewry then visiting in Palestine] I spoke guardedly concerning the establishment of a Yeshivah to train rabbis for the settlements of the new immigrants. I could not explain to him more, considering the state of his sensibilities. Obviously I pointed out to him, not once, that the internal leadership must necessarily rest with religious individuals who reside in the Holy Land and are familiar with its conditions and know its needs.

I hope that your esteemed self will honor me by reacting to my practical suggestion without undue delay. The problems are continually pressing us to begin with practical steps to carry out what we have thought of for a long time.

I will sign with a greeting and best wishes, as befits your esteemed self and as is appropriate for me who feels honored through your friendship, and wishes you success in your study of the Torah, with much love.

Igrot I, Letter 137

By the grace of God, the holy city of Jaffa, may it be rebuilt and established, 21 Iyar 5668 [1908]

Peace and blessings without end to the precious organization "Kehillat Yakov" and all its supporters, blessings forever.

My heart was stirred with joy on seeing the pamphlet which, in your goodness, you saw fit to send me. Because of your important objective, the holy purpose which inspires you, you deserve thanks and blessing from all who love to see the goodness of the Lord in the land that is being restored to life. I would like to hope that all the great Torah scholars among the people of Israel, from near and far, will extend to you a helping hand. The time has come, dear brothers, when all who are truly zealous for the love of God and look forward to the spread of His holy word shall reach out to win the practical world in the Holy Land, not by quarrels and controversies, not with denunciations, but with practical efforts to establish opportunities for a livelihood, through work and constructive projects, especially for our scholarly people.

Only through this method will those most qualified to become the great scholars of their generation be able to concentrate on the study of Torah, developing breadth of vision, much talent, and true wisdom. The entire community of those dedicated to the service of God will enjoy added honor and esteem. Their lifestyle, based on the Torah and religious faith, with a commitment to worldly progress and an expansion of the practical upbuilding in the Holy Land, will serve as a model for all our brethren who are taking root again in the new settlements, now and in the future generations. As our zeal in pursuing these practical efforts increases, so will the success with which God blesses those who follow in His ways. An involvement in the affairs of the world, and commitment to productive labor, sweetens life and brings health to body and soul. This noble effort will enlarge its sphere, and it will link the concern for the service of God and a life of Torah and the commandments with the practical restoration of the nation in our beloved land, which in truth is the basis of the hoped-for salvation for the house of Israel.

Therefore, beloved brothers, hold firm this holy and exalted banner of the desire to engage in the practical upbuilding of the Holy Land, on the basis of the love of Torah and the commandments, and their expansion in the practical life of Eretz Yisrael, which continues to progress before our eyes. Do not abandon this banner. This external goal, which stems from the Eternal One, praised be He, will endow you with strength, so that you will be able to realize your holy purpose. Even if its beginning should be small, there is hope that its latter end will be very great.

Your brother who greets you with a full heart and wishes you a renewal of spirit and a life of fortitute, for the sake of the people of the Lord, the pride of Jacob the ever beloved.

Igrot I, Letter 139

By the grace of God, the holy city of Jaffa, may it be rebuilt and established, 27 Iyar, 5668 [1908].

To my friend, the revered rabbi, the distinguished sage, our master, Rabbi Samuel Alexandrov,[10] may the light of his life continue to shine, peace and blessing from the Holy Land.

Some time has passed since I received your important letter, but I have not had the opportunity to offer an appropriate reply because of various impediments. I ask your forgiveness. Even now I do not know whether I will be able to clarify the issues which divide us, so that we may move from one subject to another and not become embroiled in an endless polemic on one theme which keeps on recurring. To the extent I can, I must, however, comment on this subject, about which much has been written by others as well as by yourself.

Your honor has focused on the issue of the obsolescence of the commandments in the days to come, and you seem to imply in your statement that I challenge this, because I follow the view which holds that the commandments will not become obsolete in days to come. Not so, my friend. On this issue, as on all issues where there is a divergence of opinion, it would be appropriate to apply the adage: "These and also those are the words of the living God." We all realize that the term "days to come" is so unlimited, so broad and all-embracing that it does not deny the inclusion of both opinions, in an ordered progression. There is a category of "days to come" when the commandments will not be obsolete, and there is a category of "days to come" when the commandments will be obsolete.

Those who seek to probe the concepts of religion, in all its purity and profundity, must define the conditions that differentiate the two categories of "days to come", and to understand with a rational and mature comprehension the conditions which appropriately define the two categories of time. It is my opinion that on this subject there need not be any disagreement among thinkers. What I feel the need to emphasize in my communication to your honor is that you seem to hurry the time when we may say that the commandments have become obsolete. You seem to set this condition in our own age, when moral breakdown and failure are so rampant, when there is a decisive need for practical steps to shore up our values. With this I disagree.

It seems to me that it would be appropriate for every sensitive person to abandon this view. We encountered similar situations in previous epochs of history when people decided that the world had already progressed morally so that it no longer needed any refining discipline, any guidance of religion, or obligation to tradition, from whatever source, whether prophetic-spiritual masters or national-sociological experience. We can see no sign of this. What we see, on the contrary, points in the opposite direction.

This error of regarding the world as already "perfected" when it is still full of defects has been very costly to us. It has already happened in many epochs of history when some noble individuals, who were indeed of superior moral stature, judged the world by their own standard, or they took a particularly enlightened incident when the nation rose to great heights and judged it as though it was a permanent condition. They sought to "hurry" the end, to abrogate the fixed disciplines in convention and tradition, as set by the great seers of the world. But always this error showed itself through much pain, and the world returned to revolve in its circle, and the practical and spiritual life-process returned to its customary forms, to gather strength and rise in its values by keeping customs and traditions, by cultivating religious faith and keeping the discipline of the commandments, to rise through this slow process to a higher level of development.

Common sense teaches us otherwise. We cannot assess the world by the standard set by some individuals of superior moral stature who, thanks to the influence of the fixed moralizing disciplines, may have risen to the highest level of moral sensitivity. Nor can we assess the entire span of history by some special period that proved particularly suitable for spiritual progress. On the contrary, it is well to know always that though the individual may ascend to a higher level of life, he remains linked with a thousand attachments to the general community, and all those moral afflictions which dominate continually or through sudden eruptions in the community may yet have their effect on him as well, in some measure. And the idyllic time (looked upon as though it was the culmination of historic development) even when it appears to be in full force, may yet be affected adversely by the currents of history, of periods past and future.

It is therefore always appropriate not to jump toward the undoing or the weakening of the established disciplines, even for the elitist individuals and even during the passing periods, when the world seems in an ideal state. It is well to bear their yoke with a general love, and to extract from them the vitalizing energies for the better days whose dawns will come in due time. Then will the illumination be so diffuse and shine with such brightness that there will no longer be any doubt whether the ideal time has come or not. The entire configuration of life, in its outward as well as its inner form, will testify that the hoped-for day has arrived, and the world and all its fullness will be robed in joy and song. But as long as evil exceeds the good and darkness the light, everyone who studies the pulse of events has the duty to caution the people, as well as its elitist elements who have risen in light and intelligence, to love the established commandments and disciplines that are directed at the community as a whole, the general moral obligations which are directed to all humanity, as well as the obligations which refer particularly to one's own people, whether young or old. The people will then reach a state of perfection when the inner light of the free and higher moral sensitivity shall shine within it with greater splendor. It is this which we seek.

We are familiar with the results which followed the renunciation

of the commandments by the sons of Aaron,[11] and, in another form,
by the Alexandrians,[12] and by those wholly steeped in evil, the followers
of Shabetai Zevi. These should serve to us as a warning of the likely
consequences of a premature utopianism.

Your honor finds in Judaism some intimations of the ethical views
of liberal anarchism. Good; one can find intimations of all ideologies
in any teachings which embody truth. Truth is not fragmented. Truth
must embrace everything, but its distinctive role is to transform everything
to the core of true illumination embodied in it. Not only the anarchism
which is modified with liberalism can find a supporting source in Judaism,
but also the version of anarchism which declares the self-sufficiency of
the physical self of each individual. However, it, too, is to be purified
before it is admitted into the domain of purity.

The higher perception of universality, when seen in its highest
dimension, must judge that the entire process of individualization is a
deceptive phenomenon of short-sightedness. Our bodily organs are linked
together in one organic whole, and therefore when ne part is damaged
all others feel it. Thus we have a fragmentary anarchic self-love; but it
spreads out to its constituent elements. One part of one's body suffers
for another [lit. "skin for skin", an allusion to Job 2:4], through those
channels that transfer feelings from the parts to one another. The same
relationship exists on a spiritual level in the links of love between persons,
which forms the basis of the family. If we can only free ourselves from
habitual thinking, we shall realize that there is little difference between
the spread of pleasure or of pain from one bodily organ to another and
their spread from a son to a father or from lovers to each other. When
the channels are enlarged these feelings reach out further. When the
national entity is fully developed, and is in a state of perfection, it will
pattern itself after the manner of the family. The development only hinges
on the broadening of the channels, and when the unity of the individuals
is extended to reach the domain of the nation. From the nation to
humanity as a whole is only a step, and from humanity to the embrace
of all living being is another step. From a concern with the fate of a
planet in all its fullness, to an inner serious concern for all existence,
in all its vastness, is only a distance — a big distance, it is true, but eternity
need not be in a hurry. Thus the development continues until all the
constituent individuals of all existence rise to their fullness.

All we need, therefore, is an "anarchism", a great and mighty, fully
developed self-love. But all the paths which lead to it are the ways of
life which emanate from the source that proclaims the unity of the One

who is the life of all worlds. That source is Judaism. When such mighty sparks of light fall downward, they descend and sink into the mire of life; these are the fallen ones from on high (Zohar I 37a). What we must repeat then is that Judaism has within its treasure everything in its broadest and noblest form, and that it leads us in practice toward it through its own distinctive way, which remains relevant for us and for our children. If only its inner light should break out of its concealment, we shall not need to go searching for anything, but "the night will shine as the day" (Ps. 139:12) for us and "the sun will shine for us as in the dawn of morning" (II Sam. 23:4).

I remain your friend who wishes you well in the pursuit of your studies.

Igrot I, Letter 140

By the grace of God, Rehovot, 4 Menahem Av, 5668 [1908]

From narrow places, He who illumines the world and all its inhabitants will raise a light of deliverance. To the renowned rabbi, our pride and source of strength, whose name is adorned with holiness, our master Rabbi Yizhak Isaac Halevi, may he be blessed with a long and good life, peace, peace, with much love.

Your honor's esteemed letter, written on 20 Tammuz, reached me, to my great joy, and I note that we are drawing closer in our goal. Most of the differences between us do not touch on substance, but have to do with the terms of designation. This leads me to hope that the matters where we still disagree will also be clarified so that as far as action is concerned we shall reach a consensus, to engage in the holy work for God and for His people in the land of its inheritance.

I shall offer some explanation of my words: I see from your honor's statement that you also agree that there is a great need at this time to make sure that our children, who are educated in Torah and in the fear of God, shall be equipped with auxiliary training which has to do with the necessities of life. Thus when they grow up they will not be the weakest part of our people, but will be able to stand up, with their right knowledge and good deeds, to defend our faith with dignity against the destroyers who are undermining everything holy to us. The difference between us is then only in terminology. I call the grades where we shall offer the students auxiliary subjects, together with the basic foundation in Torah and the fear of God, "the lower classes of the yeshivah", on the broadest level possible, while your honor would call them "Lower Schools" or "Talmud Torahs". With full heart I agree to the change in name, provided the matter be arranged in the initial plan, that these grades shall serve as preparatory to bringing the best students to the Yeshivah, which is our primary objective.

As far as the primary purpose in establishing this Yeshivah, I have stated in my previous letter that my entire objective is that it be a center wholly devoted to Torah, but Torah in its broadest and most embracing scope, which includes all its branches, both the practical as well as the ideational and the spiritual. Here apparently your honor does not agree. Subjects which I call the essence of the Torah, and which I yearn to introduce as a permanent element in the curriculum of study, your honor seems to regard as an "old-fashioned type of scholarship which is of no consequence in our time". I feel it necessary to clarify my position on this matter, so that we may achieve a consensus on this subject as well.

When I say that we must study the spiritual dimension of the Torah as a regular subject in the curriculum, and that this offers the promise of deliverance for our generation, I do not have in mind confining my objective to some specific texts of later or early masters. My intention is not to study the "Beliefs and Opinions" of Rabbi Saadia Gaon, the "Guide to the Perplexed" of Maimonides and the like, as they are in themselves in order to master their views, so that we draw from them the armor with which to fight our battles. I, too, am aware that most of the issues those books focus on have become passé. Many of them have become obsolete because their philosophical assumptions have become obsolete. However, a great many of them still merit study and teaching because they included eternal ideas which cannot be disregarded because of any change in the cultural climate of the world. The world has turned its back on this vast intellectual domain because it has abandoned all spiritual concerns and has chosen in their place the study of subjects which deal with the practical side of life. The lack of a spiritual anchor in the world's thinking will surely turn out to be troublesome and destroy what endows life with grace and delight and, in the end, it will turn back and eagerly seek the spiritual treasure it has abandoned in its over-anxiety to grasp the material aspect of life. This, however, is a perception that only a chosen few can realize, and we cannot as yet go out to discuss it among the common people.

It is for this reason that I am not now projecting a goal with a specific practical focus, but rather an obligation to study the Torah on its highest level, with the confidence that its beneficent results are due to come in the end. In this objective I do not exclude any of the components we possess in the spiritual treasure of the Torah, the written and the Oral Torah, the early and the later masters, the philosophers, the researchers, the Cabbalists, the exponents of *aggada* and homeletics, the moralists, and the pietists. All of them together make up what is for us the vast specialty of Torah, which scholars in our time are obligated to know. Obviously included here is also all aspects of modern historical scholarship, the primary works of which are your honor's own writings. And just as the riches of *halakha* [the legal material] are more fully established by knowing all positions, whether they become the norm in law or are rejected, so the knowledge of the many and diverse positions enlightens the student and helps him grow toward self-realization: to become a person with some originality, one who knows how to differentiate, to evaluate and to create what is new — this is also true with the riches in the field of *aggada* [non-legal material].

I do not refer to shallow study, as this has been done by scholars in Germany, and as is the practice among the "Seminarians", but in its profound sense, with a focus on the inner dimension. This can be acquired through hard work, and a fixed regimen of study, which is also linked with a sensitivity to the holy and a pure fear of God, as is exemplified by those who pursue the study of the Torah for its own sake. It is this which prepares the person to live a life of spirituality and holiness, so that he is enabled to create many exalted new paths, to release the light of the Torah in all the ways that are needed by our generation, similar to the creative achievements of the great spirits of early times and the important later figures in their own time.

We cannot ignore all the bitter complaint voiced by the great spirits of the world, the Cabbalists, the philosophers, the moralists and the pietists, over our neglect of the spiritual dimension of our faith. The essence of this complaining is already found in the Torah, in the prophetic and the later writings, and among all the sages of the Talmud. The knowledge of God, His love, and the higher level of His fear, which are merged with a responsiveness to life in its fullness that is renewed each day — this is the foundation of all life. It is the basic objective of the Torah and the commandments, of the entire Talmud, and the *halakha* [the corpus of law]. When this is present everything is present. What inspired the heretics to reject the principles of our faith and to subvert its teachings by repudiating the Cabbala, is in its essence the fact that the world has grown even darker, from generation to generation, through the withdrawal of the inner light that is transmitted through the spiritual channels. The decline in knowledge [of God] has led to a decline in love for Him; because feeling has run dry, love has ceased; and because there has been a decline of love, heresy has emerged to undermine the expressions of piety that have become a burden. It could only accomplish this by sinister rejections and ignorance. If the love had continued through the holy sensibilities of the person and his attachment to the light of the Torah, through the power of spiritual reflection, which is joined with the broad and profound domain of the practical *halakha*, this state of affairs would never have come to pass. . .

I am not saying that all the students of the Yeshivah are to be great scholars in all fields. This is impossible. Some special individuals may be born with such talents, that they can absorb everything, but the majority divide into specialists and a person can only master that to which his heart is drawn. In its general orientation, however, the Yeshivah must give our people all that it lacks. And since in our time, among the subjects to which people are drawn and which have a great impact on life is literature and poetry, we must also see that in this field, too, we shall have our own, and it shall no longer be a fact that every talented person in the field of literature and every prominent poet must automatically be a heretic and a sinner. We must destroy this false assumption and show the world that the beauty of poetry and the delights of literature will flower when they are rooted in the life of our people, in its natural state, when it is faithful to a past whose source is the living water of faith in God.

The substance of the matter is that I do not find a wide divergence in our views, and where "a righteous person will smite me in kindness" (Ps. 141:5), to heed his counsel, I herewith advise your honor that I am far from insisting on my views arbitrarily. Especially on public issues that are of a subtle nature, I decide only after careful weighing of all sides, and with the intention of serving God, with no ulterior considerations, God forbid. But even after all this I remain prepared to bow before all the leaders of the people of God who are also devoted with heart and soul to the pursuit of ways of strengthening the Torah of God and His covenant with Israel, in order to strengthen the foundations of God's deliverance for His people on its beloved land. . .

I repeat again my statement that the primary task we face for the mending of the Holy Land in our time must begin particularly with the establishment of a new, important Yeshivah, central to the new *yishuv,* and He who has chosen a Torah which fosters life will show us the revival of His Torah and His holy people on the holy land, and will truly exalt His people and those who fear Him.

May your honor enjoy the blessings of a long and good life, and may he be enabled to illumine the eyes of the people of Israel with his precious books for a long time. May he enjoy the goodness of the Lord, in the only land, at the head of the exiles returning to Zion in song and joy, when a redeemer will come to Zion, with their king before them and the Lord ahead of them, as befits his great spirit and as is the wish of one who esteems his exalted worth and extends his blessing with much love from our beloved land.

Igrot I, Letter 149

By the grace of God, the holy city of Jaffa, may it be rebuilt and established, 5 Iyar, 5669 [1909].

Peace and blessing from the Holy Land to my friend the rabbi who is wise and abounding in Torah and the fear of God, our master Rabbi Benjamin Menashe Levin, may he live to a long and good life. Amen.

A long time has passed and I was not free to write to you even a few words. I ask your forgiveness. I am most anxious to know the state of your studies in the Torah, accurately and in detail. May God prosper you.

I hope you will satisfy my request to inform me through frequent letters concerning everything I am eager to know.

Concerning the expression I used,[13] this was deliberate on my part. At a time like this we must repair the breach from another side. Everyone who seeks God knows that there is a common element in all religions, which is the quest for the knowledge of God and His ways. The clarity of this element depends on the condition of the world, especially on the moral state of those who are particularly committed to the quest for God and to the extent that their spirit is oriented toward all that is good in life. To establish this principle is the talent of our people, which is truly dedicated to God, without any exaggeration. At a time of decline, especially when our people is impoverished from many sides, this element becomes blurred. Then a hatred for the concern with God becomes a hatred for religion and its disparagement, not merely for any particular religion, but for religion generally: "What is the Almighty that we should serve Him?" (Job 21:15).

It is obviously easier to attack another faith, but whenever the attack is inspired by hatred for the quest for God generally, it is an abomination, and it is bound to end with a damaging effect on one's own faith. "When you sit and speak ill of your brother, your brother who is not the son of your mother, you will end by slandering the son of your mother, the son of your own people" (Ps. 50:20, as expounded in Tanhuma, Pekude 7). Therefore, at a time like this we must clarify the general elements of religion, according to its diverse expressions, and not be intimidated by the total disdain and unmitigated hatred which is hidden in the soul against everything alien. Thus will the light of the quest for God assert itself triumphantly, according to its diverse levels of expression, and then it will be possible to distinguish between the dim and weak light, which is as darkness in noonday for those who walk by it, and the light which is as bright as the dawn, from which all the shining lights in the world receive their illumination, the light of God that shines on His people forever. And the thoughts which will emanate from this source will serve as our aid when the time comes to evaluate all the effects wrought by the alien faiths. For among them, too, will be found sparks of light, and it will be well to know how to react to thoughts engendered by their type of literature. Praised be the Lord who trained my hands for combat.

I close with much and faithful love from the mountains of Judah where is the pride of Jacob, the ever-beloved.

I send greeting with much love to my friend Rabbi Moses Zeidel, may he be blessed with life. The feelings I expressed here also apply to him.

Igrot I, Letter 194

By the grace of God, the holy city of Jaffa, may it be rebuilt and established. 8 Adar 5670 [1910].

Peace and blessing to my friend, the renowned rabbi, who is wise and learned, a treasure of Torah and the fear of God, our master Rabbi Barukh Meirs, may he live to a long and good life, the head of the rabbinic tribunal of the holy city of Haifa, may it be rebuilt and established.

Your precious letter reached me. Rabbi Joshua Burak has undoubtedly informed you of our conversation concerning the general condition, and that I wrote him an encouraging letter. May it be God's will to prosper his efforts to strengthen the knowledge of God and His laws among the people of Israel in the Holy Land.

My dear friend, you called my attention to the state of religion at the present time. What can I say to you, my friend? My heart suffers grievously because of the general situation. There is no one left who represents with dignity the cause of God's name and His Torah in the Holy Land. The more I brood on this thought, the more troubled I feel in my heart and I cannot see an effective way to begin some corrective action. For it is very difficult for me to come to a meeting of minds with most of the leading religious figures of our time, may God watch over them. They desire to follow the old path solely, to keep themselves at a distance from every creative talent and from all current trends in life. In my opinion, this is altogether against the way of God. By their attitude they strengthen the hands of the rebels and support the wrongdoers. Alas for the sins of these people, though they are well-intentioned.

I have no alternative but to support the educational efforts which make room for the knowledge of the world and of life, and that trains the children to find joy in life, to be strong and brave, to cultivate hygiene and personal dignity. When this training will be combined with training in the Torah and the true fear of God, it will become their adornment and enhance their vitality. In the end even the nonreligious forces will have to acknowledge the validity of our position.

But what can I do when this approach, which I have no doubt we must follow, has embroiled me in the entanglements of a war from the right and the left? However, I place my hope in God, may His name be praised, that He will strengthen me to hold on high the banner of truth, that the holy cause be vindicated. And you should know, my friend, that these important issues are all interrelated. Most of the scholars of our generation, even the greatest among them, pay no attention to cultivating the principles of the fear of God, in a spirit of broadmindedness, as would befit the leaders of the generation. They cannot pursue new paths appropriate for the needs of the times, to direct them toward holiness. In their opinion, they must not veer from the old pattern, refusing to draw on any good element in the new ways, thereby to mend the condition of the generation. They will not acknowledge, under any circumstances, that they have neglected a basic principle which embraces the whole Torah and all religion.

It is for this reason that we stumble in the daytime as the blind man stumbles in the dark, and the multitude is astray; they are increasingly alienated from their faith. But they are in no sense at fault. Since there is no one to show them the right course, to join the holiness of the Torah and religious faith with life, they are losing their faith. But there are many good elements in them and much sensitivity of spirit, and many among them desire with a full heart the salvation of the people of Israel and the revival of the Holy Land. No matter how low is their conception of this, their basic goal is rooted in holiness, for the salvation of Israel truly embraces all aspects of holiness. It is for us to judge charitably even the most offending among them, if only he is not willing to defect from our people and join our adversaries.

The more we add positive elements to our educational program and teach our children the subjects which help a person earn a livelihood and gain self-respect, together with the study of the Torah, the foundation of the Torah will be strengthened and gain in vitality.

But with whom shall I speak, who will agree with me, who is prepared to jeopardize his own honor for the honor of God, praised be He, and of His Torah, and for the holiness of His beloved land?

Let us hope that God will act for His own sake, and inspire the hearts of all the Torah scholars to comprehend the pure way of God and that Israel and Judah will soon find deliverance. And this will be my reward.

My greetings to you as so befits your precious self, and with much love, and in anticipation of God's help.

Igrot I, Letter 274

By the grace of God, the holy city of Jaffa, may it be rebuilt and established, 28 Iyar 5670 [1910].

To its precious rabbi, who seeks God with all his heart and soul, our master, Rabbi Zevi Hirsh Meisfish, may he be blessed with life, peace and blessing.

Your precious letter reached me. As to your request for advice how one can strengthen his spiritual life so as to serve God with joy and courage, it is difficult to explain in few words even one principle of the divine service in its purity. To me and others like me, the basic concern is to set aside fixed periods of time in an appropriate measure for the study of the spiritual dimension of the Torah in all its branches, so that it not be left aside for occasional reading. Then, automatically, the light of the soul will shine and a spirit of joy and courage will be astir in the heart of the person who peruses the truth without equivocation. But I will not refrain from formulating one important principle. Though it, too, will not be grasped in all its depth without considerable study, it will, nevertheless, offer us an aid in our quest for the love of God, praised be He, and the light of His holy Torah.

This is a simple truth, that even the lowest type of person — if it be made clear to him that he is at all times in a position to bestow beneficence upon the entire world, which embraces within itself so many beings, beyond number — will be aroused with joy and courage to do good. All our negligence and weakness results only from the lack of faith in the great good that one bestows on all existence by pursuing the study of the Torah: the performance of the commandments, the divine service, and the refinement of one's moral character. This is the reason that God enlightened us through the holy teachers, the masters of Cabbalistic truth, who elaborated on the greatness of the divine service and how one raises through it the whole of existence and all its constituent parts. But this concept must be made comprehensible rationally, so that the zeal be firm and the joy be soundly established.

This explanation is based on the understanding of the spiritual unity, that is, the realization that each individual soul is linked with the universal soul of all existence, from which all that has being, in all its constituent elements, draws the light of its perfection. It is within our power to enhance the light in our own souls through the Torah, through wisdom, through the commandments, the divine service, and through our moral virtues, at all times, in every moment. And every moment we seek to enhance the light in our souls, it is well to bear in mind that we are concerned not with ourselves alone, but with all existence, that "everything which God created is for His sake" (Prov. 16:4), and that we add perfection and life to everything. The righteous person strengthens us through his service, and the wrongdoer redresses some of his wrong-doing, and thoughts of penitence come to him. Even animals become more refined, according to their capacities. Even creatures that have a disposition to damage and destroy become more gentle through the added light of holiness which is released through one soul that is truly concerned with the state of existence as a whole. There is no need to add that there will be an increase of light in the domain of splendor where the souls are and in all the spiritual domains that are of endless beauty and holiness and preciousness. This is understandable to each person, especially if he is a child of the holy people, and more so if he lives in the Holy Land, and especially if he is in the luminous world of the city of David, to which all our material and spiritual existence is linked as are the branches to the tree's trunk and roots.

This principle will be clarified and accepted rationally and in full faith the more a person pursues the study of Torah for its own sake, especially the spiritual dimension of the Torah, that is, those books which focus on the illumination of the knowledge of God, whether through human reason or through the mystical contemplation of the hidden meanings in the Torah, which are granted to those who truly revere Him. And to this extent will joy and courage grow in heart and soul to love God, to zealously perform the commandments, and to study the holy Torah. But one should add to this that the full enlightenment in all existence will be effected especially through the influence of the Jewish people when it is renewed in the Holy Land. The hope for liberation will therefore always be linked with the life of the soul. When the heart releases the stream of sensibilities with holy words appropriate for this, at the appropriate time, a new and delightful spirit will emerge which will soften all the severities. The person will then be able to pray at favorable times for his heart's desire, first, for spiritual objectives, and second, for material objectives. And the Lord, may His name be praised, will not deny the good to those who walk with integrity. But one must also be careful to attend to one's health of body and mind on a natural level, and to avoid thoughts of fear and depression, but to always draw strength and joy on oneself. For "strength and rejoicing are in His place" (I Chr. 16:27).

May the Lord, praised be He, open for you and all who zealously seek Him the doors of grace and good will, true satisfaction and gladness with full blessing, as befits your precious self and your friend who hopes for your happiness and enlightenment, and the enlightenment of all who love God and hallow His name among His people.

Igrot I, Letter 301

By the grace of God, the holy city of Jaffa
may it be rebuilt and established, 15 Sivan
5670 [1910].

To the editors of *Hamoriah*, Jerusalem.

I find it necessary to express my great distress over the article by
some rabbis in the holy city,[14] may it be rebuilt and established, which
appeared in the periodical *Haor* without my knowledge and consent.
Though I am aware that its authors, who are renowned scholars and
sincere in their piety, acted for the sake of God, my view is nevertheless
that this is not the proper procedure when we face a divergence of views
in decisions of law. It is for us to judge charitably each advocate whose
intention is to serve God and to advance the truth.

I am especially distressed over the exaggerated praises expressed for
me in their writing which, alas, are even partially untrue. God forbid
that I deem myself a great scholar, even in comparison with any disciple,
and certainly not in comparison with well-known rabbis. May God protect
me.

It is only when an issue of truth is involved, and the welfare of the
Jewish people and the Holy Land is at stake — then even a weakling
like myself is prepared to play the part of a strong man, and I will defer
to no one in battling for the Lord, by defending the upbuilding of Eretz
Yisrael, which, by the grace of the Guardian and Redeemer of Israel,
has begun to develop, enabling our people to return to the place of their
beginnings. I find myself obligated to confirm and to strengthen the
decision by the elder rabbis in favor of the new settlers on the holy land
[by suspending the rule to cease all agricultural labor during the Sabbatical
year], for the sake of the people of God and His inheritance. And blessed
be all right-minded people who love truth, who anticipate God's
deliverance of His people and cherish the signs of our redemption
discernible on the mountains which have begun to yield their harvest
for the returning people of the Lord. They will support me with a firm
hand.

I express peace and blessing with all my heart both for those who
agree and those who disagree with me, provided they are motivated by
the sincere desire to serve God.

Igrot I, Letter 308

> By the grace of God, the holy city of Jaffa,
> may it be rebuilt and established, 23 Tishre,
> 5671 [1911].

Peace and blessing, in continuous abundance, to his honor, my close friend, the renowned rabbi, a treasure of Torah and the fear of God, our master Rabbi Zevi Hirsh Jaffee, may he live to a long and good life, and may his entire family, and all that is his be blessed from the Holy Land, with all that is good. Amen.

I received your greeting with great joy, and in reciprocity I send you greetings with love, and with best wishes for all good, and may we merit to witness the rejoicing wrought by God for His people, to effect deliverance for all who fear God and revere His name, for all who are upright of heart, for all the people of God.

Concerning the ruling on *shemitah*,[15] the matter has become more complicated then it should have, to my distress and to the distress of all who truly and sincerely fear God. Rebels on one side, and ignoramuses on the other, have raised a tumult, where there should have been quiet and trust in the help of the Lord, may He be praised. I, on my part, cannot find that I did anything to cause this storm which erupted. The substance of the ruling is old, but its implementing details were my responsibility. To whatever extent possible, I sought to satisfy all opinions, and to take into account the restrictive view of the *Mishnah*, as is appropriate for anyone charged with legal decisions, who is guided by the fear of God.

I did publish the small volume *Shabbat Ha-aretz* [*The Sabbath of the Land*], with a condensed version of the laws of *shemitah*, as a supplement to the basic teachings of Maimonides. While doing so, I added some notes to clarify the subject as is the way of the Torah and to stimulate scholars to study these laws, particularly those applicable to residents in the Holy Land. I cannot find that there is anything here to justify the upheaval in the world. In fact I was anxious to help in the fulfillment of the commandment, to gather aid for all who feel moved not to void the holiness of the Holy Land and prefer to keep the law of *shemitah*, in all its regulations. But I told them that we cannot issue a prohibition against all who circumvent the *shemitah* ordinance, who follow a ruling of old masters, among whom was also the renowned and holy Rabbi Joshua Leib Diskin, may the memory of the righteous be for a blessing. To do so would endanger the new Jewish settlement, which would veritably imperil lives.

To me the very love for the holy, the fact that the development of the Holy Land would be impeded through the suspension of the permissive ruling on *shemitah*, and that this would encourage rebels openly to break with all discipline and to renounce all tradition — this was a major consideration which moved me to embrace the lenient interpretation of the Torah. I acted against the advice of my friend, the renowned Rabbi Jacob David [Ridvaz], may he be blessed with life, who, on the contrary, sought to eliminate the permit altogether. It would not have helped to proclaim that the permit was granted with the support of Rabbi Joshua Leib [Diskin], may his memory be for a blessing, because the other side would have issued a public denial, and since there is no written record of his concurrence in the permit, the denial would have been easy. My learned father-in-law [Rabbi Elijah David], may the memory of the righteous be for a blessing, also suffered from this denial, but he could dissociate himself from the matter to some extent. For in the end he did not bear the responsibility for the future of the *yishuv*, and I therefore could not act as he did.

I am surprised that your honor attacked me because the free-thinkers declare my praises. It is true that their praises grate on my heart and spirit, more than the insults from the other side. The latter at least are our kindred spirits in a commitment to the Torah and the commandments, and one should judge them favorably, for their motivation is for the sake of God. But as to the substance of the matter, what surprise is it that they praise me? Surely Jewish blood flows in their veins, and they see with their own eyes that a group of people have arisen to undermine the settlement of the land, to lower its honor to the ground, and to hem it in against future development. To them this is the essence of their Jewishness, and they see that I alone among the rabbis who are known to any extent have stood up in disregard of my own honor and status to battle for the preservation of the *yishuv* and all its interests, and for no ulterior motive whatever. How can they not be moved by all this to praise me?

As to your question, who are on my side? In general they are people who fear God, accomplished scholars who are upright of heart, all of whom are outraged by the new tumult, especially because of its dishonorable tactics, and particularly since its principal agitators cannot at all be sure that they act for the sake of God, even according to their own opinion. However, I did not ask anyone to support me. I regard it as an insult and betrayal of the dignity of truth to receive help through agreements and supports from uninvolved people. I trust in the grace which the Lord, may He be praised, has thus far shown me and, in His great mercy, has brought me here to the Holy Land, and has deemed me worthy, with my limited ability, to lead His people, who are returning to the land of their inheritance, to be the pioneers of the redemption. I trust that He will also be with me in the days to come, and the entire people of God and its great scholars will recognize my sincerity and the rightness of my efforts, and they will support me with their sense of justice and their knowledge of the Torah.

Igrot II, Letter 335

> By the grace of God, the holy city of Jaffa, may it be rebuilt and established, 1 Marheshvan, 5671 [1911].

Peace and blessings with much love from the Holy Land, to his honor, my beloved and precious rabbi, the great and renowned sage, the scholar and logician, who releases light in the chambers of Torah study, our master, Rabbi Selig Reuven Bengis, the head of the rabbinic court in Bodki, author of the precious work "Lepalgot Reuven", may he be blessed with a good and long life, and with much good to all that are his.

I was filled with joy by your precious letter of greeting which reached me, and I reciprocate greetings with love to you, may you be exalted with the strength and heroism that emanates from the glory of the Torah. And may He who is girded with strength satisfy all the wishes of your noble heart in full measure.

As to my condition, I am, thank God, pleased that I have settled in the Holy Land, for there is no limit to the advantages of Eretz Yisrael, and I shall always be thankful that God was gracious to me and enabled me to dwell in the place He has granted us as our inheritance, and to lead a holy people who are returning to inaugurate the beginning of the deliverance of God's people on its holy land.

As to the controversy which followed my ruling concerning the Sabbatical year, obviously I was grieved, not that some people arose to challenge me but, in general, that the matter led to insults for a scholar. The matter should have been passed over quietly and in dignity. But I acted and will act in good faith, with the help of God, and will be an advocate of peace among the people of God and the pious ones among them, and among all who regard themselves as Jews and are dedicated to their well-being. And may it be God's will that we merit to be among the builders and settlers of the land of our inheritance and thus to raise esteem for the Torah in the holy land and throughout the world.

It was good news that you sent me the second part of your important book. My dear friend, please accept the small volume I sent you and let this be a token of good wishes and much love, as is becoming for your noble self and your friend from the Holy Land who wishes you well in your studies.

Igrot II, Letter 338

By the grace of God, the holy city of Jaffa,
29 Marheshven, 5671 [1911].

Peace and blessing to the learned rabbi, a treasure of Torah and the fear of God, Zeev Markan, may he live to a long and good life, Amen. I begin with good wishes for your well-being, with much love.

Many thanks to your honor for the precious gift with which you saw fit to honor me, your esteemed pamphlet, "From Our Ancient Literature."

Because of many preoccupations, I cannot offer a detailed reaction to your writing, but your general approach is certainly sound. As to the behavioral characteristics of the Sadducees, it would have been appropriate to cite what Josephus Flavius said about them, which later historians have also mentioned. However, according to the *Tanna Debe Eliahu*, the concept *derekh eretz* [the way one acts in the world], refers in most cases to a general attitude to the world, and this may involve a protest against the Essenes, who dissociated themselves from society and from the political order.

One of the sources which proves the antiquity of the *Tanna Debe Eliahu* is its first statement that a minor *sanhedrin* [court of law] consisted of thirty members, which is not mentioned elsewhere. Graetz [the historian] depended on this in describing the minor *sanhedrin*, without citing the source. The author of *Dorot Hanshonim* challenged him on this, without justification.

May your honor be strengthened in his holy work to disclose for us precious items in his research into the culture of our ancestors, whose spirit continues to sustain us. And how precious are such scholars for us in these days when the sickness of innovation distracts us from the ancient treasure, the treasure that holds out life for the people of God, His beloved for all time.

And thus I send you greetings and blessings with much love, as befits your noble self, and your friend who wishes you well in your studies, with heart and soul.

Igrot II, Letter 341

By the grace of God, the holy city of Jaffa, may it be rebuilt and established, Tevet, 5671 [1911].

Dear Sir, editor of *Moriah*, peace!

I am greatly distressed over the tendency to attack [those with whom one differs] which has become a continuing affliction, especially among those who pride themselves on bearing the banner of the ultrareligious. I cannot, on my part, forgive you for your offense against the editor of the *Hamodia*. An Orthodox editor should, above all, be sensitive to the law, and according to the law, it is forbidden to insult a scholar. Certainly a rabbi in an important Jewish community, and a well-known leader in the affairs of Judaism, meets the standard of a scholar in our time. There may be some doubt as to whether the rule of compensation for the insult by payment of damages applies, but there is no doubt that he comes under the category of a scholar, whom it is forbidden to insult, surely when it is without provocation, and publicly. You committed a grave offense under the banner of Orthodoxy, which your newspaper claims to represent, even as you sinned in your role as a pious Jew, who must exercise restraint in the use of offensive language.

Why should the sin committed by speech, when expressed in writing and circulated in a newspaper, not be governed by the meticulous admonitions of the law as are all other commandments of the Torah? And I will not hesitate to tell you, my dear friend, that even after you regretted it, you did not mend the inequity in a manner appropriate for a serious offense of publicly insulting a scholar. It is incumbent on you, in my judgment, to correct the matter with wisdom and dignity.

In the sphere of doctrine, according to my way of thinking, I have not found anything significant in your newspaper. Some expressions appear occasionally, but they must be more closely directed to the inner dimension of piety and the genuineness of religious faith. These subjects must, however, be touched on gently, as wise men are always admonished to speak.

In general, however, I tell you, my dear friend, don't be discouraged, be resolute in your work, and if you have erred at times, does not a person come to a clearer perception of the teachings of the Torah after he has stumbled over them (Gittin 43a)? In an overall assessment, no one can deny that the periodical *Moriah* is generally an asset to the religious community in Jerusalem, in its present condition.

Public opinion continues indeed to develop, and good literature is certainly the channel for its development and perfection. The newspapers that are concerned with raising the level of public opinion must always seek to be on a higher plane than the general public and to issue material that will influence the public and gradually raise it to the height which the general character of the newspaper has already attained. Obviously we are not referring here to the state of mind of the editor himself, but to the spirit of the newspaper and the circle of its most influential writers.

The cultural level of "Orthodoxy", to justify this designation, is to be assessed according to the state of its spiritual perfection, the depth of feeling and the breadth of understanding in the fundamentals of the knowledge of God and the holiness of religious faith as rooted in the divine illumination. These are surely the soul of "Orthodoxy". But now the quest for God is abandoned altogether, and the multitude of Torah scholars, for the most part, are not even sensitive to its need. The aim of Torah scholarship is regarded by them as consisting of contributing a casuistic addendum [*pilpul*] to some aspects of law, which is surely holy and precious — but this cannot illumine our souls. Therefore, honorable editor, instead of focusing on the need for administrative improvements in the *Yeshivot*, which cannot always meet our true goals, and from which may come perils more than improvements, choose the path of always challenging and stimulating the talented and dedicated Torah students to shed light on the soul of the Torah, in all its breadth, with sharpness and erudition. Then their hearts will be illumined and their path will become upright. The public, within and outside the religious community, will begin to recognize that we have people who, instead of being experts in some form of legal dialectics [*pilpul*], with some astuteness, whether straightforward or contrived, are girded with the strength of the Lord, pervaded by a holy fire, and the true Torah of the Lord is in their hearts.

These students will of themselves be suited for their tasks. The light of the Torah, pursued as an end in itself, will release on them its light and its splendor. "Whoever studies the Torah for its own sake will attain many virtues. Yes, such a person justifies the world's creation" (Avot 6:1). The strength of the spiritual life, which becomes firmer each day, will hew its path, and as those who wage its battles increase, so will its resoluteness increase. The slumbering talents will awaken and will begin to bring forth their blossoms, and from the great spirits of the elitist elements among the Yeshivah students there will begin to spread a spiritual soul-force even on middle level disciples and on the inferior ones. Each one will then be better equipped for some occupation in the practical or spiritual life of the community, in areas that are directly or indirectly suitable for those educated in the *Yeshivot.*

Such reforms, honorable editor, will make their way through constant pressure for them. They address themselves directly to the spirit and, moreover, they are not overly dependent on the personal approval by the supervisors and administrators of the institutions. This many-faceted advocacy has a wide zone of relevance. In itself it prepares the ground for the pursuit of spiritual labors, and as it develops it will contribute many gains to the holy cause; its end will be most fruitful.

My preoccupations are many and I cannot elaborate. But at the end of my letter I cannot fail to call your attention, as many others beside me have done, that the title you have added to your newspaper as "official" [the "official" Orthodox organ] is in bad taste. The term "official" can only be applied where there has been a general authorization on the part of the people who are within some corporate body, and the authorization has to be announced publicly. All these are surely lacking in the case of your newspaper in Jerusalem. How then can you continually tolerate the shame of a designation which spells "falsehood" on your "Orthodox" newspaper, whose chief characteristic should always be truth.

Igrot II, Letter 344

By the grace of God, the holy city of Jaffa, may it be rebuilt and established, 11 Adar, 5671 [1911].

To my devoted friend, the rabbi distinguished in Torah, wisdom and a pure fear of God, of distinguished ancestry, and abounding in good deeds, our master Rabbi Meir Berlin, may he live to a long and good life.

You brought me joy, my precious friend, with your important communication, full of personal feeling and true love. There is no need for you, my beloved, to apologize for your delay in writing me. I am familiar with the person who is burdened with work, as you are, my dear. I, too, cannot meet my obligations in letter writing, and I continually look upon myself with a sense of guilt toward great people whom I also love. But this does not derive from a rebellion against or a betrayal of love of good people, but from preoccupation and weariness, due to various tasks each of which claims its attention mightily. Nevertheless, I would like to hope that, with the help of God, our exchange of letters in the future will be more regular in connection with your holy labors for the *Haivri*[16] from which we can rightly expect great and mighty things for the unity of our people and for the upbuilding of Eretz Yisrael, in accordance with the light that God has revealed to His people.

As to the suggested change in the title of my article, I say to you my friend unreservedly: I agree. I did not choose this title. It was my son, may he be blessed with life, who had copied the article from the notebook and set it up in its form. I did notice some minor changes where my intention would have been expressed more clearly if the text had remained in its original version, such as "He illumines all the dark areas of man," instead of "He is exalted above all." I was particularly troubled by the omission of the verse, "And the stability of the times shall be made secure with a wealth of salvation, wisdom and knowledge — and the fear of the Lord which is His treasure" (Isa. 33:6). This sums up the whole thought in the article. However, in general it remains true to its original spirit.

I have no doubt, my dear friend, that the *Tahkemoni* [a High School] and the *Haivri* [the periodical] are twin projects whose beginnings are small but that will in the end prove of immense significance, with the help of God. Since my coming to the Holy Land I became aware that we must hew a new path for the renewal of Judaism, which is truly the renewal of our people in Eretz Yisrael. I saw the weakness and the decadence in the institutions which are the pillars of Torah and Judaism in the old *yishuv*,[17] and, on the other side, the emptiness and the filth of that alien element, whether it calls itself "Hebraism" or whether it no longer so calls itself, in the institutions that have developed in the new *yishuv*. I was anguished at the crisis of our people that has come to light, particularly at the time of healing, when the displaced are returning, when the exiles are coming back. I then decided, in spite of all impediments that might confront me, whether from the right or the left, that it was my mission to combine what is good and healthy in the two communities [*yishuvim*], and to battle against what is decadent in the two. It was my resolve that I would not do so with words, or with any negative actions, but through strengthening positive forces and by the establishment of institutions, which will unite the elements wherever they be found. Then, automatically, the shadows will lift. If the [existing] institutions should wish to maintain their autonomous existence, they will compete with us, and they will also embrace the good and the fruitful from both camps. They will also become a source of blessing to Israel and to Eretz Yisrael. If, on the other hand, they will stubbornly insist on remaining in their previous state, we can rightfully hope that they will not be able to hurt in any way our good objective, which will bring to realization the most important demands of the best of our people, the people of mind and heart who are stirred by the spirit of God.

And praised be the Lord, it did not take long and the *Tahkemoni* school was established, and it continues to grow, to progress. It still has a long way to go. We must wage a battle of competition against the schools which are destroying Judaism, the most serious being the Gymnasium, which has been established here. It captures hearts with the beauty of its buildings and the ordered curriculum of studies, but with all this it stultifies the vitality of what is the authentic life of the Jewish people, and makes seductive gestures to the spirit of aliens, in the Hebrew language and style; and "an inciter to heresy who speaks in the holy tongue becomes a seducer" (Yerushalim, Sanhedrin 7:12).

However, even concerning this I say unreservedly that God intended it for good so that we would be forced to compete with the most beautiful and modern programs to adorn, with them, the institutions which are inspired by the holiness of God in the Holy Land. And now when the time has come to build the edifice of the *Tahkemoni*, we must mobilize our strength that the building shall not be inferior to the Gymnasium in form and beauty, design and construction. It is also necessary that we add at least two classes so that it be comparable with the program of studies in the Gymnasium, and to include classes for girls, so that we may have Jewish mothers in Eretz Yisrael who are adapted to the ways of life, girded with the strength of knowing the love of Torah and true faith. It is obvious that the whole national spirit which is prevalent in the nationalist schools, among them the Gymnasium, with all its cultural expressions, must be introduced in our institutions, obviously reworked and reshaped in the spirit and the holy light of the Torah, with true love and with a spirit of self-sacrificing zeal, and with a clear recognition of the great work we are doing to revive our nation for future generations on the land of its beginnings.

The goal of the Tahkemoni must clearly be to raise the banner of true Judaism in Eretz Yisrael, to include all that is good and fruitful, all that is strong and pure in all the different parties and to evolve a formula for harmonizing these different parts through the spirit of God which pervades His people in the Holy Land. The national spirit, the hope of the rebirth of our people, the renewal of the land, the nation and the [Hebrew] language — all is alive and is freely astir in the halls of the *Tahkemoni.* The voice of Jacob in the study of Gemara and its commentaries resound, to the rejoicing of all who fear God and truly love His Torah.

The best of its students who will choose to excel in the knowledge of the Torah, in Gemara, with the commentaries of Rashi and the Tosefot, and the codes, with agility and erudition — they will, I hope, enter the Yeshivah which has recently been established, with the help of God, and which is the primary objective of my efforts. There our talented young people, while pursuing the customary practical studies in the profound domain of the law, with the conventional dialectic [*pilpul*], with proper concentration, will also familiarize themselves with the inner light of the Torah: that is, the aspect of the Torah which directs itself to the heart and mind, the rational basis of faith in all its branches, the broadening of concepts and the systematic exposition of all aspects of morals, of beliefs and thoughts. Thank God, I see that the experiment is succeeding, and the atmosphere of Eretz Yisrael is working here also for good. The students are few in number but those few who number now about twenty are continuing to develop. They are becoming scholars, mature in thought and feeling. They recognize their life goals, as people knowledgeable of God in general, and particularly as scholars in Eretz Yisrael, especially at this time of renewal and upbuilding of our people. Obviously, I do not wish to speak about a Yeshivah of few students as something already completed, but it deserves to be spoken of as a plant of the Lord on which eternal hopes are centered, with the help of God.

Now I am reacting to your inquiry about Petah Tikvah. I cannot decide as to how to advise you, because you did not indicate what would be the fate of *Haivri,* if you, my dear friend, should accept the responsibility of the rabbinate in so distant a place. In any case, with the help of God, let us hope we will discuss in detail this important question in forthcoming letters. Because of the usual and special preoccupations at this time I must be brief.

Your firmly committed friend, tied to you in spirit and soul with full heart, who hopes for your personal well-being and the renown of your activities for the sake of God and His people.

P.S. For the time being the Yeshivah does not draw its expenses from the funds of the *Tahkemoni*, but it would be most important to secure the position of the Yeshivah so that it should be able to expand physically and spiritually. I hope that in the course of your travels, my friend, you will be able to speak to some people of means on behalf of the Yeshivah specifically, obviously in a manner that will not hurt the *Tahkemoni*, for both of them together are of special merit.

Igrot II, Letter 349

By the grace of God, the holy city of Jaffa, may it be rebuilt and established, 25 Adar, 5671 [1911].

To my dear friend, the rabbi who is distinguished in Torah, in the fear of God, in wisdom and knowledge, the man of many deeds, our master — Rabbi Meir Berlin, may he live to a long and good life, peace, with love always.

My dear, I find myself constrained to express to you several reactions concerning the *Haivri* [the periodical], vol. 10, whose appearance indicates that it was published without your honor's supervision. All of it lacks that unifying spirit that generally permeated the *Haivri*, with which only an editor pure of heart and uprighteous of spirit, a person of distinguished talent like you, my friend, could endow it.

The past is past. But because of my deep love for you, my precious one, and out of respect for this highly esteemed organ, of which we can justly be proud and from which we can expect great things, with the help of God, through the diligent work which you have shown thus far, I find myself obligated to call to your attention your great responsibility as editor of a periodical which represents authentic Judaism, guided by the light of wisdom and knowledge. This is an invaluable source of hope for the Jewish people, to bring forth a light of life out of the darkness of our time. In a task of this kind one cannot be "a watchman who transfers his responsibility to another watchman". The pages of this issue testify that you did not assign to the editorship a person who can maintain his independence in judgment, as you do, my friend. Thus the opening article by Rabbi P. remained trite, without any idea to expand one's thought.

We no longer need poems of praise for Rabbi Levy and Mr. Yavitz [Yizhak Isaac Halevi and Zeev Yavitz, two historians who expressed a traditional day for the two authors whose characters are well-known, with their light and their shadows, as though the entire world depended on them. Special articles of critical evaluation of those two distinguished authors, even if all favorable, may be accepted, but when one always focuses on their documentation of the riches of our spiritual life, it appears like a confession of poverty. Though we have no other good and traditionally acceptable works of history, we cannot deny that there are many good elements in writings that we regard as tainted with a nontraditional bias. Moreover, those two historians were not always right in their tendentious criticisms, and the truth is to be preferred above all else, and only through it can God's praise and our faith be enhanced. The rebuke to Bible critics and to nonreligious writers, when it is uttered only in generalities, does not mean anything and makes no contribution. Among the young people whom we are trying to win over, this style of writing does more harm than good. I am certain that if you had reviewed this article you would have made it more acceptable. You would have added to it a more scientific tone, and you would have reduced its size to enhance its quality.

This is my criticism because of an excessive tendency to the right. Now my criticism because of a tendency to the left. The article "From Eretz Yisrael" should not have repeated the boasting of a writer that "I am not religious." The meaning of this statement hurts deeply at a time like this. And what would the article have lost if this subjective declaration — which is repeated twice, contrary to the spirit of our *Haivri* — had been omitted?

As to the obituary on R. Eliakim Getzel, may he be blessed with life (that it was based on a false report one cannot blame you, since other newspapers stumbled over this, even *Hamodia*, which is known to suspect news reports), it is not dignified for the *Haivri* to reprint a tribute to one so distinguished in piety from the *Hed Hazman*, as though the *Haivri* does not have enough to say in tribute to this beloved person, and has to follow the style of the *Hed Hazman*. What hurts especially is that in the reprint, even the troubling epithet, "the last of the Mohicans", was not omitted.

The poem, "Stories", though it has some lyrical qualities, is too empty and it gives the impression of triviality, to a point where it should properly have been rejected by the *Haivri*.

And how "free" to a point of nausea is the style of the article "From the Beauties of Ever in the Tents of Arav." To my regret I lost vol. 5 before reading it, and I do not know the content of the first installment of this article, or its style [see Rabbi Kook's postscript below], but I am confident that when you were at the helm of the editorial work you did not approve of a style so inappropriate, especially a style that reflects such a narrow faith. Incidentally, it is not in keeping with our spirit to spice up the impressions of a trip by noting "the attractive faces with the red cheeks of many of the girls in the land". When it comes to expressions such as these, we need not imitate the modernist trend, but to resist it with all the strength of our pure spirit. Similarly, the sketch "The Kiss", especially in describing the kiss of Hannah, is not suitable. I am certain that all these things occurred because of your absence, my friend, from the editorial office. See to it, my dear friend, for God's sake, to mend the situation for the future and do not allow the publication of any material, small or big, without your critical review.

I will tell you the truth, my dear friend, that despite my great distress over this issue, I was also delighted in recognizing more fully your faithful labor in the editorial work. This recognition fills me with hope that, with the help of God, this beloved organ will be perfected for the spread of the light and honor of the holy faith and true Judaism, that follows on the path of our early sages, the mighty men of faith and knowledge in whose light will the Jewish people see light.

I hope that in your goodness, my dear friend, you will forgive me for these words of mine, and you will believe me that I am distressed over the distress which I imagine you must also feel because of the characterization of the aforementioned volume. I am confident that this stumbling will guide you to be cautious in the direction of the right way which is appropriate for our precious *Haivri.*

I close as my heart is full of feelings of love and respect and endearment for you, my pure-hearted friend, with hopes for your well-being and your renown, in eternal friendship.

Igrot II, Letter 355

P.S. I have now seen that volume, and that piece is indeed all pure and appropriate for the *Haivri,* and I assume that you cleansed it, in your pure disposition.

By the grace of God, the holy city of Jaffa,
may it be rebuilt and established, 29 Nisan,
5671 [1911].

To the scholarly rabbi, the distinguished researcher, Samuel Rafaeli, may
his light continue to shine, author of the precious work, "The Land Before
the Conquest of Joshua."

My apologies because, due to various impediments, I failed to
acknowledge receipt and to offer thanks for the first volume of your
important work with which you honored me some time ago. I now
present to you double thanks, both for the first and for the second volume
which, to my heart's delight, just reached me. Thank God that He inspired
our distinguished scholars to do research in the antiquities of the Holy
Land, which was heretofore, for the most part, in the hands of non-
Jews. I am most delighted by your great diligence in this important work.
We can hope that your important work will be a great stimulus to those
of special talent among us, who are equipped to investigate antiquities,
to cultivate this field which has not been worked upon properly until
now, and that they will add distinction to the study of our earliest
beginnings. There is no doubt, too, that as this spreads, the truth will
become better known and the Jewish people will be strengthened in
showing the whole world the accuracy in our Torah, which is dedicated
to truth, and all our holy traditions.

Be strong, my dear master, and bring us more of the fruit of your
harvest and your research to illumine the way in the wasteland of this
important domain of ancient history, and to inspire our children to love
the land of their fathers and its cities. "This is Zion, no one searches after"
(Jer. 30:17) — "this means that there is need to search after her" (Rosh
Hashanah 30a).

May the pleasantness of the Lord be upon you to strengthen the
work of your hands, to glorify our people and our land, and to enhance
the truth which will abide forever. With respect and sincere greeting.

Igrot II, Letter 358

By the grace of God, the holy city of Jaffa,
may it be rebuilt and established, 10 Kislev,
5672 [1912].

To my heart's beloved, the rabbi who is distinguished in Torah, and wisdom, and piety, and the pure fear of God, a man of many good deeds in Israel, Meir Berlin, may he live to a long and good life. Amen.

My beloved one, I find myself under a holy obligation to call your honor's attention to the style of the article "Judah the Watchman of the Orchard", which appeared in volume 44 of *Haivri*. It presents a mentality of hatred for the Arabs and the stirring up of the Hebrew watchman with words that are full of the revolutionary spirit. This is not in accordance with our goal and it is altogether inappropriate in the present circumstances. The slogan, "Against the Enemy", when it appears in a Hebrew periodical and is directed against the Arabs can effect incalculable damage. It offers a ready-made weapon in the hands of our many enemies who probe every word in order to find political accusation against the Jewish people. Your honor surely knows that we have Arabs who read Hebrew and also write Hebrew. Every expression of hatred for the native population or even the slightest suspicion of a revolutionary tendency is at once translated into Turkish and sent to the capital, to the most official places and to those that are most perilous to us. Apart from external enemies, we have, due to our many sins, a whole host of enemies from within, like Fresco[18] and his like, who know how to turn such words into delicacies for satan. I beg you, my friend, for the sake of the God of Israel, who chose our beloved land, who has begun to show us a glimmer of the light of His kindness and His truth, to remember His holy people, and to give them a foothold in Judah, do not allow such words in your esteemed newspaper. Their benefit is nil, and the damage they can cause is immense. On the contrary, to the extent possible, it is for us to portray the pleasant circumstances of a relationship of peace and brotherliness between the good, active people in our *yishuv* [community], and the Arabs living on the land, obviously the best among them. Preoccupation forces me to be brief when it would be appropriate to elaborate.

With respect and sincere blessing from the Holy Land, your friend who loves you truly with a full heart.

Igrot II, Letter 398

By the grace of God, the holy city of Jaffa,
may it be rebuilt and established, 18 Adar,
5672 [1912].

Peace and eternal blessings from Him who sustains all worlds to my
devoted friend, my heart's beloved, the renowned rabbi who radiates
light, who is an adornment to the Torah and to the fear of God, in whom
is every precious quality of character, our master, Rabbi Yakov Moshe
Harlap, may he live to a good and long life, the head of the *Bet Din*
of the holy city of Jerusalem, may it be rebuilt and established.

I begin by extending greetings to you who are affixed as a seal on
my heart, with much love. I enjoyed your holy words in your Open
Letter, but I was also dismayed that there were people who harassed
you with criticism, in return for your effort to do good, because of some
holy expressions you used in your important letter. My dear and beloved
friend, you must not be disturbed by such trivialities. For the most part,
it is for us to realize that those who break a relationship with a person
of pure heart because he expressed some holy thoughts from the mystical
dimension of the Torah, are the kind of people whose inner life is set
in darkness, and they cause a dimming of light in those who associate
with them. By putting oneself some distance away from them, one allows
a brighter light to shine in one's own life. One should thank Him with
joy, who is the source of light, praised be He, for such separation. God
is our Lord, and He enlightens us.

At the same time, God forbid that we reduce, even in some small
measure, the ties of love with all who fear God and revere His name.
Their omissions and their errors, and even their hatreds and their envies,
arouse in us love and inner friendship that stirs us to seek their well-
being with fullness of heart and soul.

I hope that you will strengthen yourself with the strength of God,
praised be He, and will guard your precious health. May God strengthen
you and enhance your comprehension of the light of the Torah, in the
delights of its open teachings and in the holy delights of its hidden
dimensions that embody the mysteries of God. May you be granted
wisdom and knowledge with the delights of the fear of God and an
enlightened love of Him. And be not afraid or saddened, God forbid,
in any way, and do not exert yourself beyond your spiritual or physical
strength. May you be girded with courage and firmness of spirit, rejoicing
in God and His goodness, and in the anticipation of His true deliverance
and the recognition of the sweetness of His compassion which fills the
earth, that is experienced by those who truly trust in Him.

I remain your kindred spirit linked to you in friendship, who looks forward to your well-being and your renown, to the rejoicing of all who are upright of heart.

Igrot II, Letter 418

By the grace of God, the holy city of Jaffa, may it be rebuilt and established, 25 Iyar, 5672 [1912].

To the honor of the holy, great conference of the Agudat Yisrael, peace and blessing from the Holy Land.

Your holy letter stimulated me to collect many thoughts which had long been in my mind. If I had the opportunity to come to your distinguished conference I would perhaps have discussed them. I am confident I would have received permission from your esteemed members to explain my views on your broad program of activities. However, at this time, since the date set for the opening session makes it impossible for me to consider attending, I am honored to offer by means of this letter my basic suggestions.

The call for the renewal of our people as a whole is very important. The motto of "kelal Yisrael" [the general community of Israel] which you repeat in your holy letter is an indication that the great people of our generations, the Torah scholars and the righteous men of our time, stand on the principle of the unity of our people as a whole. In this we see the hand of our God for the good of our people. After a time of splintering into separate groups, into parties and organizations, when each one was concerned only with its own power, there has come a time of awakening for general unity which gathers under its banner the nation as a whole. For a long time I was horrified with a great pain, which broke my heart each day when, in our recent past, I heard the voices of the religiously faithful. They spoke in a tone which seemed appropriate for the tiny interests of one party. This had never happened before. Thank God, my pain has been much relieved through your holy call, which goes forth with resoluteness, which does not speak in the name of, or on behalf of, one party, but in quest of the good of the people generally, in the full meaning of the term.

The consequence which follows from your broad and holy general concept is the call to give the most thorough attention to our precious possession, Eretz Yisrael, and this also in general terms, that is to say, to Eretz Yisrael as a whole, in all its sections, the old and the new, the spiritual and the material, in all its dimensions...

Let us now consider Eretz Yisrael. Here we find three primary forces, each of which is the basis for the organization of institutions of education, of charity, and of practical work. One force is established in our older holy community of early beginnings, which is wholly absorbed in its inner holiness and thrusts aside any progressive innovation in any form. It forbids in its schools every foreign language, even the language of the government and the country, and every secular subject, even the most essential for life. It trains its students in the most antiquated style of living, and is not inclined to change it in the slightest, according to the demands of the new way of life which has been introduced by the great number of our brothers who immigrated from the West, and from Europe generally. Even those among them who fear God and revere His name view these antiquated manners – which were suitable when Eretz Yisrael was an isolated corner, apart from the mainstream of life – with wonder, with shrinking pain, with feelings of embarrassment.

The second force is a recent development, which has grown stronger because of recent developments in Eretz Yisrael, and which has become better known since my youthful self has begun to be active in Eretz Yisrael, with the limited abilities with which God has endowed me. This trend maintains that our holy obligation is to strengthen the spirit of God and His people and to enhance the respect for the Torah and the commandments by acquiring all the cultural resources which are extant in the world. These give courage to those who possess them and win for them acceptance and respect among other people and, particularly, they prepare them for the battle of life with a resolute spirit. Therefore, in addition to the concern that we give primacy to the propagation of the Torah, the religious faith, the commandments, and the pure fear of God, we shall take every good element, wherever we shall find it, and crown with it our spirit and our institutions. In the second category, after the study of our holy Torah, we shall teach our children and our students the functional studies which a person needs for life. We shall accustom them to a firmness of spirit and beautiful manners; we shall train them to use the Hebrew language which, apart from the fact that it has a holy dimension and fulfills a commandment, also gives dignity and strength to the Jewish people in Eretz Yisrael. We shall establish vocational schools for the young people who are suited for it, and in those places, too, we shall infuse the creative spirit, which is sensitive to the nature of this generation, to win their love for everything holy which God loves.

The third force is the force of complete secularism, that has renounced everything holy, which has placed its focus solely on the temporal necessities of life, those of individuals and those of the community. It builds its institutions inspired by these objectives, its schools and its system of education. Obviously this retreat from everything holy does not remain a neutral activity. It is negative and destructive of our holiest landmarks, to the extent that it spreads and makes headway, and it takes away the vitality of the light of God and His holy Torah from a great part of our people who are settling in Eretz Yisrael. But there is no denying that together with this there is also some important element that sustains life: a strong love for the nation and a clear and firm goal to develop the practical aspect of the settlement in Eretz Yisrael, to strengthen the national historic spirit of this generation toward attachment to the land and the people. With all its alienation [from tradition], there remains in this group a very powerful spark of holiness that is worthy of being activated by the efforts of the faithful . . .

To begin with I think that the Agudah must communicate with all the leaders who are at the helm of these activities, and are most influential among them, in order to gain a clear perception of the phenomenon in detail. The strategy adopted should be directed to strengthening the old force, which is in decline because of its lack of adaptation to the realities of life, and to direct the recently developed second force in such a way that it should grow in strength and prove to be a factor of support for the old force, to show it love and to lend it strength, and to help it guard its distinctive qualities. It is also to try and exert an influence on the secular third force, to minimize the destructive effects which it causes with its fiercely negative disposition and without giving any thought to religion and to holiness; and to try to arouse the holy spirit of the Jewish people that is in the hearts of all the children of Jacob, in whatever way it is possible, with zeal and patience, in different forms of communication, according to the subject and the changing circumstances.

But in general the esteemed and holy Agudah needs to prepare its resources, to be able to help all, to aid anyone who would seek its help and wherever it would find that its material or spiritual assistance might bring strength and benefit. Obviously, when the Agudah would extend its help it would do so under conditions that would not be opposed to its basic general purpose which is the welfare of the people as a whole, in its holy as well as its secular dimension. Together they are the holy of holies.

I leave you at this time with the good hope that my few words will stir your holy spirit to reflect on them, and may the pleasantness of the Lord be upon you and may He establish the work of your hands to mend the fence and to establish paths to dwell in.

Be prepared, you who bear the vessels of the Lord; God is with you, men of valor.

With feelings of respect and high esteem, I extend best wishes for your efforts in the cause of Torah from the Holy Land, with hope for deliverance from Him who abides in Zion, for His people and His inheritance.

Igrot II, Letter 427

By the grace of God, 11 Menahem Av, 5672 [1912].

To my precious friend, the renowned, astute and erudite rabbi, the man of understanding and many good deeds, our master Rabbi Judah Leib Fishman, may his light continue to shine, peace and blessing.

My beloved friend,

I am guided by the statement of the holy sages that when one loves someone and does not reprimand him [when he does wrong], it is not [true] love, and I find myself obligated to come before your honor with these words of open criticism, under the mandate of our true friendship.

The news has come to me, and I cannot deny it altogether because of its wide circulation, that you honor spoke disparagingly of the holy institution *Shaare Torah* in a lecture that you delivered at the academy of R. Z. Barnet [or Brant, the original is not clear], and that you insulted the school and its teaching. I was literally appalled by such a report, and were it not for the great faith that I have in the person who brought me this information, I would not have believed this concerning an established scholar like yourself.

My friend, this is not the way, to destroy with our hands our holy institutions, our life's treasures. One can entertain the thought that the times demand of us to establish additional schools that are improved with the offering of various branches of knowledge, with programs to which our generation is drawn, provided that the spirit of the Torah and the holiness of our faith shall be alive in them. But how frightful it would be if, because of such a thought, a person should lower himself to throw stones on a treasury of holiness which is alive and functioning. More than once did I examine the students of the Talmud Torah, and I testify that it is precisely from this holy institution that we can hope to raise a generation of scholars who fear God and revere His name, committed to a love of Torah and piety, keen of mind and erudite, as in ancient times. It promises us this precisely because it adheres to our holy tradition, following the path of the truly faithful ones of the people of God, the great masters of Torah and piety of all time. And you should know, my friend, that those riches which God has inspired in their hearts will always prevail in the inner life of our people. It is precisely from this ancient *Bet Hamidrash* [academy] and from its students that Torah and light will go forth for the Jewish people, even at a time when many will turn toward new paths, to diverse ideologies. Above all, may God forbid that the *Mizrahi*,[19] a party that marches under the banner of the Torah and the fear of God, shall throw mud at what is precious to our hearts.

It seems to me that some reason which is strange to me caused your honor to stumble in his speech, and it is your obligation to mend the offense, and certainly not to continue in this perilous path any more. Your honor should be guided by this principle, that it is our duty to build and not to destroy, to add and not to diminish. Moreover, we must realize that with all the sympathy which we at times show also for the new paths, if they are not set to undermine historic traditions, we must guard the ancient fortifications against any assailing force. It would be a disaster for the Jewish people, God forbid, if religious schools like the Talmud Torahs and the Yeshiviot, with their old character, were to cease, even if they were to be replaced by schools and gymnasia adorned with the embellishments of Torah and the fear of God. We cannot be sure how those combinations will work. We cannot hope to derive from them good results unless we have Centers that remain in the splendor of their holiness and their ancient format, consecrated to God alone, marching under the pattern favored by the elders of the people of God, the sages and the righteous ones, who always serve as our source of pride. They will always be our ornament, and in their light shall we see light. "Do not touch My anointed ones" (I Chr. 16:22).

I am confident that your honor, in his uprightness of heart, will accept in love and willingly these words of mine, though they are words of reproof, for you do not desire the company of a flatterer. I express the truth which is in my heart to your honor, out of my great and faithful love. I ask you to be most careful in the future not to speak ill of this ancient and holy *Shaare Torah* which has served and will continue to serve as a tower of light and a treasure of life for Torah and the fear of God, to raise children of upright and poor parents, from whom Torah is destined to emanate. If you have any suggestions for improvement be good enough to inform me of each item in categorical order. To the extent possible, considering the programatic goals of this holy institution, we shall try, with the help of God, to mend whatever needs mending. No human endeavor can escape this. Then will good people bless you and your words will be agreeable and of benefit, with God's help.

I sign as your friend with greeting and with good wishes for your efforts in the cause of Torah, with much love.

Igrot II, Letter 570

By the grace of God, the holy city of Jaffa, may it be rebuilt and established, 19 Shevat, 5673 [1913].

To one of the elitists, the wise and renowned rabbi, a treasure of precious qualities, Dr. A. Kamika, may his light continue to shine. An abundance of peace and blessing to you.

I saw, and was illumined by the arrival of your poetic book *Zaaravim [Midday]*, with which you were willing to honor me. It was a double joy for me to infer from your statement in the *Juedische Presse* [a weekly periodical which was published in Berlin in the German language] that you found my thoughts of value. The realization that the writings by a person like myself, whose thoughts emanate only from Jewish tradition (the tents of Shem), from the well of Torah in its explicit and mystical dimensions, could win the heart of a thinker, to whom the wide world of Western culture in its many-sidedness has been opened, strengthens my spirit. It makes me more confident in my conviction that our original literature can draw to itself all the alienated that have strayed from us, through the pen that utilizes the beauty of the West, which has suddenly broken into our circles like a flood. I shall be happy if you will honor me with your other important books, especially those written in Hebrew, so that I may be able to draw from them in greater detail your principles which impress me with their riches.

Incidentally, I wish to call your honor's attention that the local Talmud Torah "*Shaare Torah*" also has a vocational department, which was established with my consent and assistance. It might be appropriate to correct this in a note in your highly esteemed essay, to help those who see your writing to know the truth.

With feelings of respect and blessing from the Holy Land.

Igrot II, Letter 493

By the grace of God, the holy city of Jaffa, may it be rebuilt and established, 28 Sivan, 5673 [1913].

To his honor, the wise and precious Rabbi Aaron Simcha Blumenthal, may the light of his life continue to shine, peace.

The pamphlet, "The Religion of Israel", which your honor has written, delighted me. Its substance and style are desirable, and are likely to win esteem for the Torah and our faith. Your honor may use it as a force to exert an inner influence, suitable for our responding to the call in the verse: "Declare His glory among the nations" (Ps. 96:3), and your essay will serve as a model for this. However, as it is, it will not meet its objective for various reasons, some of which I shall explain briefly.

1) One can only come to a distant people, in the spiritual sense, with what is written explicitly, and not with citations of homilies [*aggada*] and tradition, unless one separates the sources and makes it clear that this is written in the Torah, that the tradition of the people states thus and so. Your honor has, in many places, mixed up statements of tradition with explicit teachings in the Torah.

2) The book "Wisdom of the Soul" by Weisel, on which your honor elaborated, has nothing new for a cultured people like the Japanese, and in many basic teachings it has already become obsolete, in the light of the new science.

3) One cannot offer an advanced body of religious teaching to this people with expressions that disparage the founders of other faiths, whoever they may be. It is for us to speak only about the holy benefits of the Torah of the Lord. The negative is understood by itself.

There are other matters to call your attention to, but I cannot now elaborate.

Igrot II, Letter 557

By the grace of God, 25 Menahem Av, 5673 [1913], Rehovot, may it be built and established.

To the honored commission of the Workers' Center, and the "Maccaby", in the holy city of Jaffa, may it be rebuilt and established. Peace.

I am filled with distress and bitterness of heart because of the tragic incident involving the youth Berger who died, may his memory be for a blessing.[20] I find it difficult to believe that any Jew imbued with any sense of the Torah will not know the simple law concerning the seriousness of the duty to save a life. Even if there be a doubt, and a very remote doubt, it supersedes the law of observing the Sabbath and all other commandments of the Torah, except these three well-known cases: idolatry, incest, and murder. And whoever is more zealous to violate the restrictive rules of the Sabbath, even in the case where the peril to life is only doubtful, is praiseworthy, and whoever is negligent in doing so is guilty of murder. If a sick person was in need of one berry and ten people ran on the Sabbath, and each of them plucked a berry at the same time out of zeal to help the sick person, they all enjoy the reward of having fulfilled the commandment to save a life. It is religiously ordained to disregard the Sabbath restrictions and to perform every forbidden act on the Sabbath where there is a peril or a possible peril to life, and this is to be done by well-known religious authorities so that people see how highly esteemed is the commandment to save life, and it will be publicized to a point where it will be beyond question. For there is no need to secure a permissive ruling from a religious authority where saving life is concerned; and whoever asks is disdainful, and one who entertains such a question is guilty of bloodshed. On the verse: "And you shall keep the Sabbath, for it is holy unto you" (Ex. 31:14), when life is imperiled or possibly imperiled, the sages said: "The Sabbath is committed in your hands, you are not committed into its hands" (Yoma 85b). The general rule is: "And you shall live by them" (the commandments, Lev. 18:5) and "you shall not die through them" (ibid.). God forbid that we defer even for one moment the act of saving a sick person whose life is in danger or may be endangered, so as not to violate rules against work on the Sabbath.

In the case before us, I think it appropriate that representatives of the unfortunate father, Mr. Berger, bring charges against the physician and let him respond before the court concerning the details of this terrible case and, on the basis of the court's decision, it will be clarified how to avoid this breach of equity so that such acts not be repeated. The principle of the Torah calling for zealousness in saving life will then be established in full force, and no one will again dare to break a principle of the true teaching of the Torah which calls for safeguarding life, now and for the future.

I sign this with greetings, with feelings of respect and esteem.

Igrot II, Letter 575

> By the grace of God, the holy city of Jaffa, may it be rebuilt and established, 24 Elul, 5673 [1913].

To my precious friend abounding in understanding and in the fear of God, our master, Rabbi Levi, may his light continue to shine. May he be blessed with all good.

I received your precious letters, and I enjoyed the expressions of sound thoughts and your way of reasoning in the study of Torah, in *halakha* and *aggada*. But as to your request that I respond to your questions in detail, please believe me that this is beyond my strength, considering the many preoccupations with which I am continually burdened. I do not have sufficient time even for matters I would like to write down for myself, as you are aware to some extent. The beloved influence of conversations on holy themes at some appropriate hour — this is what is sometimes possible for me, with the help of God. At times a positive personal influence is more helpful and hallowing than volumes of writings and lectures, but it is good to embrace the one and not to neglect the other. The faithful love between friends who seek to walk in the light of God is one of the conditions of the favorable illumination which is a help toward everything worthwhile, by the help of God.

The refinement of morals — the rejection of pride and haughtiness — this is well known. However, there is need to pursue this as a new challenge constantly. One should always feel that the greatness of the divine soul abides in us, in the community of Israel, and in all worlds. It bears witness that the light of the *En Sof* [the Infinite One] hovers above everything. It summons us to cleave to all the refined character traits which are affirmed in a civilized society — with sincerity and a loving-kindness for all people. And we must not neglect even for one day some study of the works in the spiritual wisdom of the Torah, of the early and later masters who walk close to God; and the early masters come before the later ones.

One must also watch over one's physical and spiritual health, in the natural sense. It is also incumbent to awaken in ourselves holy sensibilities (even the holy imagination, which is fused with the pure intelligence) at all times, through music and a review of holy utterances with a joyous heart and breadth of mind. One is not to deviate from the holy path because of deference to any person in the world. One is to be eager to clarify the good points in everything and adapt them to one's own life. And one is to engage in the regular study of the written and the oral Torah, with concentration and innovation at fixed times.

Your friend and comrade.

Igrot II, Letter 594

[The following supplementary note is added to this letter:]

I would like to urge you and all young people who would like to be helped toward a truly significant and high level spiritual life to cultivate a disposition for literature. We must acquire for ourselves the literary talent, the vital style of writing in all its expressions, prose as well as verse. If any among us feels an inclination to write poetry or liturgical hymns, let him not neglect his talent. Let him make the effort, let him experiment to teach "the sons of Judah how to wield his weapon" (II Sam. 1:18). On final analysis, though I teach myself and others that the attribute of peace and love be the dominant disposition in our souls and in our way of acting, we must, nevertheless, be girded to battle for the Lord with the adversary [the *Amalek*] within and without, and we are under obligation to prepare for ourselves the contemporary weapon, the pen. We must translate into the contemporary idiom our entire holy treasure, the treasure of ideas and feelings of almost the entire Torah, in order to make them more accessible to our generation, as was done by Ezra who was responsible for the change of the Hebrew script (Sanhedrin 21b, 21a). One of his objectives was thereby to bring his generation closer to the study and understanding of the Torah. Obviously, this is only a metaphor. We are primarily concerned with the Oral Torah [the Talmud], and especially the *aggadic* part,[21] according to the interpretation of the holy books down to our own time. Great treasures of holy faith are hidden therein, and it is for us to draw on them each day, continually, and to express them in the literary style of the present. And "if we hear the old, we shall hear the new" (Berahot 40a).

Each day, thoughts, visions, mighty feelings will blossom for us, expressions of inner truth, capable of mastering nations, of winning over worlds with the sway of their majesty. Let us not be bewildered because of a stormy spiritual yearning that soars toward the heavens. At peace and pure-hearted, we fly on the wings of the spirit to contemplate the mystery of existence. "By His word He created the heavens, and by the breath of His mouth all their hosts." Make use of the daily *Haivri*, and the weekly, if it should be published. Do not be disdainful of any opportunity to put in printed form writings of uprightness, which are full of grace, expressing a free spirit of purity and holiness, which is the highest freedom, the highest aspiration of which the world is in need.

At all times take counsel with the person honored in holiness, Rabbi Yakov Moshe Harlap, may he live to a long and good life. Amen. Be strong and brave.

> By the grace of God, the holy city of Jaffa,
> may it be rebuilt and established, 28 Elul,
> 5673 [1913].

Peace and blessing, and a good year to my friend, the renowned rabbi, a treasure of Torah and the fear of God, a man of wisdom and a scholar, our master, Rabbi Judah Leib Seltzer, may he live to a long and good life. May he be inscribed and sealed in the book of life and may he be blessed with good.[22]

I received your honor's letter with his precious article. Your conclusion in which you express general suspicion of anyone in our time who advocates the study of the inner [the mystical] dimension of the Torah, grieved me very much. Is your honor unaware that the great masters of the Cabbala were unanimous in stressing that when we eliminate the hidden teachings of the Torah and do not explore its mystical dimension — we destroy the world? The water ceases in the ocean, and the river runs dry and is destroyed. It is a well-known statement in the Tikkune Zohar that those who remove the mystical meanings and wisdom from the Torah make the Torah arid (Tikkun 30). Rabbi Elijah Gaon, in his commentary [on Shulhan Arukh Yoreh Deah, ch. 246, section 18], disputed Rabbi Moses Iserles who followed Maimonides in the view that the esoteric teachings supportive of the divine philosophy are the natural sciences. Instead he held that this referred to the inner dimension of the Torah as embodied in the Cabbala . . .

It thus follows that there is no greater reward than in pursuing these studies, which are "a weighty matter". It is obvious then that at least the person who is ready for it through having achieved an ample foundation in the study of Talmudic texts, is summoned to study the inner dimension of the Torah, not occasionally but on a regular basis. It is also understood that this regular study must be with comprehension, in depth, with analytical acuteness, and with familiarity of the relevant material, as is customary in the serious study in the *balakha* among the renowned scholars, each one pursuing it according to his particular skill.

But we must modify the classic approach to this subject in two important aspects:

One is to moderate the prerequisites which early masters demanded before pursuing this type of study [the Cabbala]. The demand that one achieve a full mastery of Talmudic texts and codes is excessively onerous. Early masters tended to be very strict with this, but the more important Cabbalists began to be lenient on this matter even then, demanding only average mastery of Talmudic material as a prerequisite, as is well known from the statements of Rabbi Moses Cordovero in his book *Or Neerav*. In our generation the yearning for the spiritual is generally increasing to a point where we can declare that the major reason for the sickness of our generation derives from the unsatisfied thirst of this longing. Those who feel moved by their deep spiritual sensibilities to agree with those who held a lenient view on this subject, who were also world-renowned leaders of our faith, are not so mistaken. We must moderate the prerequisite at least for those who also feel in themselves a great spiritual thirst, and have come to feel that by satisfying the spiritual quest, by exposing themselves to great, holy and divinely-focused writings, they will experience liberation. They are the ones who remain zealous in affirming the primacy of the revealed Torah and the practical commandments, but they do not wish to be content with this alone, without the addition of the hidden light which gives life to everything and strengthens everything.

The second principle, on the other hand, is a demand for cultural preconditioning, that is, a broad knowledge of all branches of the spiritual disciplines which are preparatory for theological studies, and at least some knowledge of other disciplines of study. This preconditioning was not emphasized so much in early generations, as long as the Cabbala was truly a secret discipline. It was not reduced to writing, it was not interpreted, it had to be transmitted in whispers from the lips to the ear, "from the mouth of a wise Cabbalist to the ears of an understanding

Cabbalist" [Nahamanides, opening commentary on the Bible] Those who transmitted the teaching already possessed all the substantive ingredients needed for the elevation of the soul, to fill it with these basic spiritual elements, with all the lessons from all the spiritual disciplines, and a portion of the general disciplines of worldly knowledge, which were fused with it. But in our time, when the pen is so sovereign, which to a great extent has displaced oral communication, it is impossible for the heart to be conditioned for the higher meditation of the Torah of truth in the knowledge of God without the full preparatory studies in all the spiritual disciplines — of every branch of the spiritual dimension of the Torah: research, philosophy, morals, ethics, poetry, music. Many aspects in the science of the psyche are already included in this. It is thus clear that we are summoned to a great rise in our cultural development, all combined with holiness and purity.

What is the basic study of the true philosophy, if not the Cabbalistic interpretation of the faith of Israel in all its holiness and purity? As its abandonment continues, and the divine teaching is disrupted, thorns and thistles come up by themselves all about where there should be the light of faith in the God of truth. The bad plants need no cultivation. They grow through laziness. This generation that is so afflicted with the sickness of atheism, which is the weakness of religious faith — is there not reason for us to say that in order to save it we must increase the study of religion? As long as Orthodoxy maintains stubbornly, "No, only *Gemara* [Talmud] and the codes, but no *aggada*, no morals, no Cabbala, no research, no knowledge of the world, no Hasidism", it impoverishes itself; and I shall persevere in my battle against all who rise against me from all sides. All the strategies it [Orthodoxy] has adopted in self-defense, without taking the true life-giving medication, the inner dimension of the Torah, will prove of no avail. It will only become filled, as a result, with sterile anger, and with hostile thoughts and with controversy even in its own camp and its strength will continue to decline. I did not refer to its simple faith, to the holy commitment to the Torah and to religious faith generally when I said that "it contents itself with illusions and deceptive fantasies that life and reality are bringing to destruction". I referred instead to the minimal effects which it draws from its position. It stands in the midst of it all, narrow-minded and cold, thereby disallowing the expansion of light, from the deepest levels of the self to the most open expression of the active life, from the holy illumination during prayer to the illumination of wisdom emanating from the source of Torah and from the divine soul that lives in us. From this results the angry shrinking of the mind, so that every effort to improve the world, every creative force that reveals itself — it all appears as though it intends to swallow it up, to undermine its security.

It [Orthodoxy] persists in clinging to this shaky foundation, without reckoning with the thoughts of the scholars and the holy masters of the highest stature among the Jewish people and in the history of mankind throughout the generations. Thus it is obligated always to wage a war with negativism alone, focusing only on the revealed and the experienced, on the explicit teachings of the Torah and the commandments. The explicit teachings alone cannot reach the objective unless it is broadened to include its many spiritual dimensions. It is this negativism which has engendered an illusory outlook and deceptive fantasies that life and reality, the material and the spiritual, are bringing to destruction.

You continually reiterate that the basis of everything lofty must always be only the revealed and what we can experience with our senses, in accordance with the adage: "the revealed is for us and our children" (Deut. 29:28). If we follow your approach, we would suspect everyone who expresses a need for the spiritual aspect of the world and of the Torah, our chief bulwark against the idolatrous materialism in all its manifestations, as tainted with alien tendencies or with mental illness. If so, we shall be unable to find an upright person, astir with inner sensibilities, a true seeker of God, who will be able to come up with any idea for mending of our generation. For who is immune from such suspicion?

We see that in generations that were better than ours, Rabbi Hayim Vital, in his introduction to the book *Etz Havim* [a basic Cabbalistic text] sounded the great warning against the dryness of the Torah through those who confine themselves only to its external [revealed] dimension alone. With apologies he called the *Mishnah* with the names "maid-servant" and "husks" because the *Mishnah* in its obvious meaning is undoubtedly a robe, an outer shell in comparison with the hidden meanings embodied and hinted at in its inner dimension, for all its explicit teachings deal with matters of this world, with lower concerns of a material nature. However, these shells are good to eat, like the spicy husk of the balsam plant. Therefore, if they understand the *Mishnah* properly, without error, it is called "the good trees of knowledge". That introduction concludes with the observation of the renowned master Rabbi Jacob Zemah, differentiating the state of the generations: "The disclosure of this wisdom now in these inferior generations is to serve as a shield to enable us to cling with fullness of heart to our heavenly Father, for in earlier generations they were people of good deeds and zealous in their service of God, and those good deeds were their salvation." He concludes that "at this time the hidden teachings have become like the revealed,[21] for in this generation fornication, slander, gossip and hatred are dominant." We thus have the observations of the important masters of the generations, the holy people of high stature that make their claim on us even more forcefully in our generation. The urgency of the claim is all the greater because of the delay in meeting the obligations, of "the master of the debt who is pressing" (Mishnah, Avot 2:15). This is a characteristic expression in the Sefer Haidra (Zohar, Naso 127b) for the claim for spiritual illumination which is implanted in the soul of the Jewish people and in the world generally. When this is not sufficiently satisfied life does its work of begetting sterility and destruction. The healing can then come through a combination of many ingredients which might not have been necessary at all if the thirst had been satisfied in time without opposition.

I repeat once again, my friend, that it would be good to be less suspicious of those truly faithful ones of the Jewish people, scholars zealous in the study of Torah who seek only to help. Our earliest teachers have stressed that the obligation to "judge everyone by the scale of merit" (Mishnah Avot 1) applies certainly to the distinguished ones, to whatever degree they have become enlightened, but also to the lowest of our people. Instead of finding defects and seeing faults, it would be better to study and review those very subjects which are under discussion. And let no one say that one branch of the Torah is to take the place of the other, for the words of the Torah are companions one to the other, and friends one to the other, and each one enlarges the light of the other.

I close with hope for deliverance, and with good wishes for your being inscribed and sealed for a good new year.

I send greetings with much love to the beloved, renowned rabbi Yakov David ben Zeev [Ridvaz] and wish him a full recovery speedily, among all the sick in Israel, and may he be inscribed and sealed in the book of life, among all the righteous, for a long and good life, as is becoming for his noble self and as is the wish of his friend who prays for his good each day.

Igrot II, Letter 602

By the grace of God, the holy city of Jaffa,
may it be rebuilt and established, 20 Tevet,
5674 [1914].

To a precious person, a man of faith, who is loved by our entire people,
Menahem Mendel Beilis, may his light continue to shine, to him and
all that are his, peace and blessing from the Holy Land.

I extend to you from a distance, from the Holy Land, my
congratulations and my expression of joy, together with the joy of the
entire people of Israel on your liberation from jail,[23] especially on the
verdict released to the world despite the blood-thirsty and deceitful ones
who sought to destroy you, and to destroy together with you the Jewish
community in Russia. Thank God who did not deny you and us a
redeemer, and your justice and integrity have become known to the great
public, including also the good-hearted people outside the camp of Israel.

And now by beloved one – so I allow myself to call you, out of
the depths of my heart, as one of the Jewish people, all of whom feel
deep in their hearts a love for you and admire your noble spirit when
you showed strength and purity of heart during your great ordeal. You
were subjected to much suffering, and with great patience you did not
despair and you did not lose faith. In the letter which you wrote to the
author Sholom Aleichem, you expressed your hope and your faith in
the God of Israel in a dignified way with statements of truth that bring
you respect and honor. You also added, to my joy and to the joy of
all Jews, especially those who live in our Holy Land, your decision to
immigrate to the Holy Land and to establish your home and that of
your precious family in the land of our fathers in the Holy Land. My
beloved one, I greet you in love on your good plan; go and succeed.
May God grant that we merit joyously to greet you when you come
to us, and here, on the holy mountains, in the beautiful land, we look
forward to welcome you with love when you arrive, for peace and
blessing, with the help of God.

I hope, my dear,that you will not deny me your favor and will honor
me with your letter, in your own handwriting, in the language you are
accustomed to, and will notify me precisely when you expect to bring
to fruition your noble intention to come to Eretz Yisrael.

I extend to you my greeting in my own name, together with the
sentiments of respect and the greeting of all our brothers who reside in
the beloved land, especially the builders of our Holy Land, our brothers
who reside in the settlements and who labor to rebuild our nation in

the Holy Land. They all extend to you good wishes of much peace and blessing, and await your arrival with hearts abounding with good will and rejoicing. May God grant that your coming be crowned with success, and that you enjoy much good, happiness, affluence, and honor in the beloved land, and that in place of your pain and humiliation, without cause, you will enjoy much that is favorable in the land which God looks after always, the beloved land, the inheritance God bestowed on our ancestors in ancient days. And together may we merit to see the light of God's deliverance for His people and its land, and that nations recognize the justice of our cause, and kings the respect due us, speedily in our time, Amen.

With feelings of respect, and very deep love.

Igrot II, Letter 634

By the grace of God, the holy city of Jaffa, may it be rebuilt and established, Shevat 2, 5674 [1914].

To my dear beloved friend, the learned rabbi, a precious treasure, who is pure of heart, Dr. Moshe Zeidel, may he live to a good and long life, peace to you and to all that are yours.

You made me happy, my dear friend, by your precious letter, though I was somewhat astonished by your impatience, which is inappropriate for a noble spirit like you, my friend. It is not without significance that our ancestors, the world renowned sages, bequeathed to us a tradition that calls us to find strength through our joy in God. Joy in God is the basis of life, its deepest and abiding truth, the inspiration of thought and the underlying basis of all philosophy, from beginning to end.

The inclination to faith in God never ceases in the inner essence of the soul. All the expressions of life which channel this potent inclination engender every form of wisdom and talent and they inspire joy in life. Here is the most important aspect of our life as Jews, through which we assure continuity with traditional Judaism in thought and action, with all its strategies. These expressions are so noble, so loved, and pervaded with important and holy concerns. They all bear vitalizing energy which spells the joy in God in whom is our strength and through whom the modern pessimism can be transformed to a joyous affirmation of life. It assures us that "there is a reward for your efforts and there is hope

for your future" (Jer. 31:15,16), in the efforts of society and the efforts
of the individual, in the future of society and the future of the individual.
And the two are intertwined, they merge one with the other so that
every right-minded person is unable to distinguish between them or to
set one apart from the other. What justifies then this impatience of yours?

Our religious laws, the precautionary and restrictive disciplines —
we need no apologetics to justify them. They are a source of progress
and abiding joy to us. They activate and articulate our essence in all its
authenticity. Our spiritual and moral perfection, the personal and the
collective, are tied together with the ongoing flow of life of all the
generations whose very essence is formed by the commandments and
precepts, the written and the traditional, with their nobility and grandeur,
permeated with the majesty of holiness and the higher illumination.
Through them we are conditioned to live a life of timelessness, even within
the confines of time and place, even within the straight-jacket of corrupt
materiality and dimness of spirit.

If any one impeded us from expressing the full dimensions of our
being — that we shall not fashion our life according to the promptings
of our inner self, in which are rooted the detailed provisions and general
principles of the laws, the precautionary measure and the restrictive
legislation to which our whole life is attached profoundly — then we
would regard ourselves cast in darkness and misery; and most miserable
are those whose hearts are dulled that they cannot recognize this great
truth. Those who recognize it are the fortunate ones who live a life of
truth that harmonizes with the core essence of their soul and the
authenticity of their being.

You, my friend, who, thank God, have been and are within this
noble camp of the fortunate ones — shall you suffer because of impatience?
No, my precious one. It is appropriate for you to feel joy and gladness.
All of us should rejoice in the portion that has been allotted to us. "The
Lord is my portion and my cup, You support my lot" (Ps. 16:5). A people
that has been so victorious in the realm of the spiritual, that has imprinted
its spiritual and moral dimension on many nations, and that after its decline
to a condition similar to its primitive state has now begun to blossom
again on its most wondrous land, shall its distinguished sons, who know
its majesty and are the revivers of its spirit, shall they go astray and lose
patience? No, my beloved one, ten thousand times, No. "Sing joyously
to Jacob, exult at the head of the nations" (Jer. 31:7). If the distress we
feel is great because of the pain of body and soul, if the pain is great
because the world is in a state of disgrace and darkness — the light of

joy in God and the rejoicing in His anticipated deliverance continues to ascend over everything.

If in general we are grieved because of a lack of perfection, is not this an indication that we are anticipators of perfection, that we are on an ascent toward a future full of light, full of the splendor and the majesty of holiness? If the paths leading to it are hidden to us, we are summoned by the rigors of logic to trust in our faith in the Holy One, all of whose work is truth. Happy are those who trust in Him. Is there another path for the human spirit that aspires for the broad horizons of the world than that expanse which is truly without confining boundaries, the hope for the mercy of God and the power from on high? It is manifested over all existence like the grandeur that is spread across the heavens, and it has endowed special characteristics of great excellence to our people who has made God its portion, throughout the span of its history.

The ocean of beauty was not created to distress us but to refine us and to elevate us, and to be turned, with the multitude of its waves, into a channel through which to sail toward a domain of greater and more exciting, more majestic beauty. Our free soul always soars on its wings whose length and width are in proportion to our conditioning by the expanding life of laws, the restrictions, and precautionary measures, with all the vastness of thought and feeling embodied in them.

This is the way we shall prevail in our two-fold goal. The disciplines of our faith — which stem from life itself, from the higher life — they are so natural to us, to our temperament, our origins, our spirit, our past and our future. It is only because of the negative impact of exile that they have declined and been weakened. With all our energy we are called on to revitalize them through education and literature, through public and private efforts, through adopting from every side whatever is good and beautiful, true and beneficial, and plant them in our garden. Then it is for us to expand our articulation and our influence on all circles, the close and the distant, within the Jewish people and beyond it. How precious would be a life of such significance and inspiring labor; this is truly the task to which we are summoned. Blessed be all who will support those who engage in it, who will bestir themselves to enhance the vitalizing energy of their being. Through such joyous programing will the future of our labors be clarified. "And your eyes will see and you will say: 'The Lord is great beyond the borders of Israel'" (Mal. 1:15).

The suggestion to print my articles in a special collection is acceptable to me. How wonderful it would be for me if some source could be found to assume the cost of publication. And we would prepare, with some spiritual assistance, a collection of all that has been printed previously and a fair portion of notes, and writings, with supplements, amendations, clarifications, and perhaps with some expansions and introductions. Together, with this, there is need for some additional refinements in my work on the *Ayin Yakov* [the nonlegal material in the Talmud]. There are other important projects I have in mind, like a general work on doctrinal principles, a work of principles and introductions to many themes in the Torah, both practical and ideational. There are many more subjects that it would be well to articulate if I had a source of funds, so that I would be able to liberate myself from the work of the rabbinate and devote all my time to the tasks of the spiritual, to literature, in its various branches, according to my inclination. Is it possible that this hope will be realized? God knows. I pray that God bestow His mercy on me and that my prayer come to fulfillment, and that a meritorious act find its sponsor among good people, my dear friends, through our dear friend Rabbi Levenberg,[24] may he live to a long and good life, Amen. I send him greetings with true love.

I must abbreviate, and I extend to you a greeting of peace and the choicest of blessings, as befits your precious self and your faithful friend who hopes for your happiness and well- being always.

Igrot II, Letter 645

By the grace of God, the holy city of Jaffa, may it be rebuilt and established, 27 Shevat, 5674 [1914].

To the honorable Baron Edmond Rothchild, may his light continue to shine, greeting and respect, beyond measure.[25]
Our distinguished and exalted Sir:

I must turn to your honor with a request, which was sent to me from the well-known Jewish community in Kiev, via a telegram from the local Rabbi Aaronson. This is the city which suffered much from the well-known libel which the anti-Semites contrived against our people in Russia. The victim who suffered as a result of this was the well-known person by the name of Mendel Beilis, who was subjected to torture for a long time while in harsh imprisonment. After being liberated and his innocence, together with the innocence of our people, having been revealed, he is still in peril because of the members of the "Black Hundred", our mortal enemies. It was therefore necessary for him to leave Kiev where he resided, and the position from which he earned an honorable livelihood by his labor, and to come to Eretz Yisrael with limited means. The aforementioned Mr. Beilis became a scapegoat for our entire people, and it is the enemies of our people generally who embittered him and destroyed his place in life. Some important people, Rabbi Aaronson of Kiev among them, asked me to appeal to the kindness of the Baron, may he be blessed with life, in his graciousness to extend help to this unfortunate person in establishing his family when he comes to settle in Eretz Yisrael. This person is upright, and loves work and wants to work.

Let us hope that the kindness of his honor, the Baron, will move him to instruct his officials to help establish this national victim of ours, so that he will not find it necessary to leave Eretz Yisrael after coming to settle here. This, Sir Baron, is the proposal I was charged to bring to you, which I transmit to your honor in the name of those who so instructed me. I bow at a distance with gratitude for your honor's nobility and conclude with a greeting.

Igrot II, Letter 664

By the grace of God, the holy city of Jaffa, may it be rebuilt and established, 5 Adar, 5674 [1914].

To his honor, the rabbi who is distinguished in Torah and in piety, our master Rabbi Aaron Simcha Blumenthal, may the light of his life continue to shine.

I have examined your esteemed pamphlet, which bears the name "The Religion of Israel and Its Mission", and I found it a source of delight. I will not discourage the thought which your honor entertains to translate it into English in order to spread its ideas in Japan. This enlightened and free people, which is now awakening with renewed vitality from its long slumber, is indeed suited to confront the illumination of Judaism with a clearer perspective than other nations whose spiritual life has been poisoned by superstition and hatred for the Jewish people. But I must explicitly caution you about the introduction, which downgrades the certainty of religion to an assumption. This concept is prevalent in European thought, but it is not the living conviction that should be conveyed by the Jewish people to a nation that is being stirred to revival.

"Praise the Lord, all you nations, extol Him all you people, for mighty has been His mercy toward us. His faith will endure forever. Praise the Lord" (Ps. 117).

May God be with you, and may your hands be strengthened to hallow the name of the God of Israel and the name of His people that is dedicated to Him.

Your firmly committed friend.

Igrot II, Letter 669

By the grace of God, the holy city of Jaffa, may it be rebuilt and established, 14 Sivan, 5674 [1914].

My precious one,[26] a multitude of preoccupations surround me, including the pleasant duty of responding to your letter. For moments I escape from the choking folly of petty problems with which people are pressured, and I turn to communicate with you a little, my dear, from a distance.

But are the small matters really small? Is there a yardstick by which to measure the spirit, and all these claims, varied with deep feelings of the heart, through which each person expresses the justice of his cause — can we not hear the overtones of a holy discourse in them? Do they not embody the elements of the mysterious workings of Him who in His mercy guides every generation? Is there not hidden in this darkness a shining light? Like oil that floats on the water, the holy dimension of the living world hovers over every gesture, every quiver, on every utterance of speech and on every feeling of the heart. That illumination which releases eternal life on all sides shines in a perceptible manifestation, and lights up for us every dark area. "And the eyes of the blind shall see out of obscurity and darkness" (Is. 29:18).

You made me happy with your precious letter. Ascend and be successful, and always apply the holy light emanating from the torch of knowledge to the emotions which sensitize the heart and refine it. Together they will enlighten our world, and our world will be filled with knowledge and adorned with the joy of the upright.

Concerning the trip to the conference of the Agudat Yisrael, it is very difficult for me to decide to leave for days, above all for weeks, the beloved land which fortifies my spirit with the mercy the Rock of

Israel releases upon us all the time. We shall think it over and however it will be decided, we offer a prayer: May it please the Lord to bestow His blessing on us, to establish the work of our hands for good and for blessing, to enhance the people of God, all of it, with knowledge and understanding, with courage and uprightness of heart full of purity and the holiness of truth and justice, with peace and love without limit. Would that the Torah scholars be inspired with a love for the entire people, for the great and beloved family that is worthy of a noble compassion and unlimited love for all her children, those close and those distant. And may the holy discussions inspired by a love for truth find their application in life, and then the light of God will fill every spirit and soul.

Igrot II, Letter 691

By the grace of God, St. Galen [Switzerland], 16 Kislev, 5677 [1916].

To the esteemed Rabbi Dr. Wolf, may the light of his life continue to shine, rabbi in the city Shadefan, may God watch over him.

Great peace to you. I depend on your generous spirit to propose to you that in your goodness you lend support to the cause of saving lives among many of our brethren in the holy city of Jerusalem. I received a telegram from the Board of the general hospital there which, in addition, is also signed by a number of important and dependable people, that if they do not receive speedy help the institution will close. I know how great will be the tragedy if, God forbid, this great institution should close. Hundreds of sick persons among our brothers, who are poor and depressed, find there healing and rescue.

I issued a call for help in the weekly periodical published under the auspices of Rabbi Dr. Litman in Zurich, and some noble and good-hearted people responded. Letters that I have written to rabbis in neighboring communities have brought some results. They have all recognized the great obligation and the moral imperative which confronts us at this time to extend help to our brothers now in distress in the holy city.

I hope that you, too, who are well known for your good works and are glad to perform acts of justice, will at the earliest possible time lend your full support to this great cause and will initiate in your community and in your circle of acquaintances and friends a serious effort for the benefit and the rescue that is urgently needed. I also hope that you will appoint a respected person in your city to assume responsibility for this important effort, and advise me of his name. Perhaps you yourself will attend to this duty of saving life, as would be appropriate for a sensitive spirit who is accustomed to do charitable acts for the benefit of our Holy Land, and that the love for the Holy Land runs deep in your noble soul.

I look forward to receiving your esteemed reply and to your good work, and your heavenly reward will be double.

Igrot III, Letter 749

By the grace of God, 21 Mar-Heshvan, 5673 [1913].

To my dear and precious son, may he live to a long and good life, Amen.

Thank God for our well-being. We hope to hear good news, rejoicing the heart, from you and from all our dear ones, until the Rock of Israel, praised be He, will show His graciousness, and peace will come to the world, bringing deliverance to His people and enabling each of our stranded ones to return to His own home.

I have been very busy these days with various matters. Though most of them are spiritual, they take up my time, and impede me from attending to other matters more responsive to the deeper claims of the soul, and they turn the mind in various directions, and to focus on all kinds of particularities. You have undoubtedly received our previous letter, and I am eagerly expecting to hear from you, that you inform me concerning all the circumstances of your present situation in matters of the holy and the secular, and what are the new developments that you wrote have happened, of what category are they.

Has your article been published in any periodical? If so, you will surely send it to us, and I express to you my thanks for this. I would like to know in detail about your studies in the past, and what they are in the present.

The letter from David Cohen brought me to a predicament. I find it difficult to advise him to come here. For one thing, he may be called to military service, for all the documents of exemption cannot be entirely depended on. Secondly, the conditions for earning a livelihood are very difficult here. The costs of rent and the necessities of sustenance for a single person are very high, and I think they will be double what they are in the place of his present residence. Moreover, as to his desire to be together with me, if not for the fact that I am unworthy of this, I would hint to him what Maimonides wrote to Joseph ibn Aknin, when he was overcome by a longing to travel to him. He cited to him his many preoccupations which would make it difficult for any person to isolate himself with him for discussions of an esoteric nature. The freedom to explore mystical themes which I might have pursued with him when I was in St. Galen, liberated from the public responsibilities, I cannot allow myself here. If at times I am left with a free hour, I must seize it for myself, and to the more pressing obligations. Nevertheless, it is difficult for me to tell him not to come, for I do not wish to deny nourishment to a person so upright of heart as he is, even if under the circumstances the benefit to him would be minimal. May the Lord, praised be He, in His mercy, help us.

I will abbreviate and extend greetings of peace. Strengthen yourself, my son, and be firm, with largeness of vision and an illumination of spirit in the light of the Torah, with the splendor of holiness and the joy of knowledge and understanding, as befits your precious self and your father who looks forward to your happiness.

Igrot III, Letter 791

By the grace of God, 6 Shevat, 5677 [1917].

To my precious son, may he live to a long and good life, Amen.

The publication of *Rosh Milin* [a tract on the mystical allusions in the Hebrew alphabet and punctuation marks] took longer than it should have, for so small a pamphlet. This came about as a result of dislocation in the publishing establishment of Dr. Zelkind, and the discontinuance of his newspapers. I am now hopeful that, with the help of God, it will be completed this week. With it all, it will not appear in as attractive a form as I should have liked. However, it is my hope that, with the help of God, it will be of help to a chosen few, and automatically it will also benefit the community as a whole, which is dependent on the progress of individuals. Who can assess the value of any gesture that stimulates an ascent of thought and aspiration? May it be God's will that this spark be joined to the great lights which God will soon release, in His great mercies, on His world sunk in darkness, and the dark places will be transformed to light, and from narrow places He will bring us to broad horizons.

I have already written you in my previous letter my thought of establishing an organization to redress the plight of the *agunot* [an *agunah* is a deserted woman whose husband will not consent to divorce her, or whose husband has disappeared, as in time of war and there is no evidence of his death]. May God deem us worthy to be a helper and protector of our troubled sisters, to speed for them help in their affliction. Though I have often been held back by misgivings whether I, with my limitations, am worthy to undertake such actions, I strengthen myself, however, in God's name. At a troublesome time like this, a weakling must say: I am a strong man; Whoever comes with any program of rescue, and he intends it for the sake of God, then he is doing good for the people of God. May the pleasantness of the Lord in His mercy be upon us, to establish the work of our hands. I have in mind soon to publish a proclamation to establish an organization to redress the plight of the *agunot* in the name of the Board of the rabbis of the Jewish community, about whose beginnings and formation I have written to you several times.

All these preoccupations, and add to them problems brought to me of a private and public nature — these impede me to attend with any length of time to matters of my own interest, as I would like to. I hope that, with God's help, when He grants us some liberation, I will be able to take time to focus again on the sources of enlightenment which emanate from the realm of the holy, by the grace of the Rock of our deliverance, praised be He. There is our heart's delight.

Extend our regards to our friends, the great and learned rabbis, may they be blessed with life, and all that are theirs.
P.S. We have now received your precious letter. Congratulations. The time now does not permit me to elaborate. May God grant that we merit to enjoy the light of the Torah and the illumination of knowledge in the Holy Land, when the Lord in His mercy and great compassion will soon return us from exile.

Igrot III, Letter 804

The day before Shavuot, 5677 [1917].

Eternal blessings to his honor, my close friend, the great rabbi who releases illumination, who charts a path to study the history of a holy people, our master, Rabbi Zeev Yavitz, may he live to a long and good life. Amen.

I wish you great peace, and holiday greetings, and the joy of illumination in the Torah.

My beloved, renowned rabbi, your precious letter reached me all abounding with wisdom and with excessive humility. I thank God that in my lowly state and while I am in exile, He has bestowed on me grace and kindness in the eyes of the noble and devout members of our people, the small group of very special individuals. I suffer endless embarrassment, however, over the unduly high esteem from the renowned leaders of Israel, like your honor. It is a result of exaggeration, inspired by their generous and gentle spirit.

As to the concern over my health, I find that maintaining a discipline which is hygienically viable is for me one of the most difficult labors. It is due not only to outside distractions, but more so because of inner burdens, out of the necessity of rushing from one subject of study to another, from the various idealistic claims, each of which requires special spiritual, intellectual and emotional labors, and an adjustment in the feelings of the heart and in the way of life. Certainly the pressure resulting from being in the condition of exile,[27] and the subservience to petty tasks, which hold no appeal for a more refined way of life, add a feeling of depression and they also cause physical weariness.

What my spirit craves is basically to find some possibility for literary efforts in some measure and form. Most of my scattered notes are in my home in Jaffa, and a few are in Switzerland, with my son, may he live to a long and good life, Amen. If my circumstances while in exile were free of petty obligations, I would long to pursue a fixed regimen of work in the realm of ideas in their diverse aspects. This could be done in the form of essays which I began to work on in Eretz Yisrael, with the help of aides who audited my teachings, and through lectures and general and specialized discourses. I might be able to add to this some writing of my own which I might be able to do, without aides, despite my physical and mental weakness, when the external conditions are favorable. But I see that the life of holiness and strength, invested with idealistic delights, the mighty will and the clear understanding linked with holy songs and the pleasantness of the light divine, which fortified me at least occasionally in the precious land [Eretz Yisrael] — this light has receded from me in this spiritually uninspiring land. This is the reason that I am so eagerly awaiting deliverance, when God in His mercy will enable me to return to His beloved land, on which He has bestowed His heavenly blessing.

In practice I shall try, with God's help, but without a formal promise, to meet the wishes of my true friends, to the extent possible, in taking periods of rest and going on walks, so as to regain my strength. And may He who restores strength to the weary, praised be He, restore my strength, exemplifying in me the statement in the verse: "They who revere You will see me and be glad" (Ps. 119:74).

As to some rearrangement in the pattern of my duties with the congregation Mahzike Hadat, because of whose invitation I came here, your esteemed and distinguished self, may you live to a long and good life, and those associated with you in the concern for peace and the love of Torah and the fear of God, surely have my consent to act in accordance with your good intentions.

I sign this with a blessing, a blessing of life and peace and all good, and greetings on the occasion of this great day,[28] the day of supreme illumination for heaven and earth, and for all the nations, the day commemorating the giving of the Torah, the anchor of our deliverance forever. It is this day which has endowed us with eternal life and splendor, that will break through all the dark places and be manifest for all to see in all the places of the earth, in accordance with God's faithful promise. I extend these greetings as is appropriate for your noble and distinguished self and your friend, tied to you with ties of true friendship, with feelings of respect and endearment.

Igrot III, Letter 829

By the grace of God, 5 Menahem Av, 5677 [1917].

To my dear and precious son, may he live to a long and good life, Amen.

We have already grown thirsty for a communication from you, of some length at least. You will surely soon satisfy our quest. I hope that you have already received the letter we have written to you from here.

Thank God for our well-being. Our recovery proceeds slowly. May God grant that the results will prove beneficial in the forthcoming days. I suffer much harassment and distraction from many sources. May God help us and strengthen us with courage and firmness to attend without ambivalence to the work of service to Him and of service to His people.

Today I enjoyed the visit of our friend Zeev Yavitz, who came here also for the purpose of health and it was delightful for me to find a listening ear like his, who is responsive with due thoughtfulness to our ideas. He also has a circle of influential people; they are important individuals before whom he sometimes lectures on historical subjects.

I spoke about the domain of the holy and its impact on the secular order and its constituent divisions. The holy sometimes conceals itself and ascends in its manifestations to a higher realm, revealing itself only to some individuals, but releases practical effects which have a strong impact on the forces of secular life. Through its preliminary manifestations, the domain of the holy prepares the world for its moral values. But the foundation of the world is shaky, it cannot stand on one base. The secular order, with all its creation, totters until the light emerges from its concealment, and the holy becomes manifest in all its purity as the basic source and the substantive inspiration for all that is equitable. It lights up the way for the life of the individual and society, for eternal as well as temporary existence. And the world draws closer to perfection through a multitude of refinements and troubles, and it emerges out of darkness to a great light, and all the reforms which were robed in secular garments will become adorned through the light of the holy which will be revealed in them. They will then be remembered in their brighter forms and become the foundation for a joyous and pure life.

May God grant that out of darkness His light to shine on us and strengthen us with His help, and bring us out from narrow places to broad daylight, speedily, in our own time, Amen.

What news is there about Dr. Hertz, may the light of his life continue to shine? And what is the program of the trip of Dr. A, may the light of his life continue to shine, and how could we secure through him regards from those that are dear to us, may they be granted life?

Strengthen yourself my son in all good qualities, ascend and succeed, and the strength and the blessing of the Lord will hover over you always, as befits your precious self and your father, who hopes for your happiness always.

Igrot III, Letter 837

By the grace of God, the eve of Rosh Hodesh Menahem Av, 5679 [1919].

May He who builds Jerusalem and establishes Zion release a sevenfold light, like streams of water, in Zion. To my life's beloved and my dear friend, the great luminary who enlightens the eyes of scholars, a pioneer in historical research, our master Rabbi Zev Yavitz, may he live to a long and good life, Amen. Peace and eternal blessing to you and all that are yours.

I begin after wishing you well, with great love. There has been a delay in my reply to your highly esteemed letter, for various reasons. I hope that in your goodness, my dear friend, you will forgive me.

I have as yet not made any clear decision as to where we will live when, with God's help, we return to the Holy Land, but circumstances point to our making our fixed residence in Jerusalem, may it be rebuilt and established. May God in His goodness be gracious to us and help all right-minded people who desire to advance the restoration of the people of God on its beloved land, in a way of peace and equity.

I hope that the inclination to controversy and hostility which has been intensified in some circles will be like a passing shadow. Ill-will will eventually give way and the righteous path which is the way of peace that proclaims God's name, to which we are attached for all time with living ties in the depths of our soul, will assert itself with ever with ever greater force. All acrimony will then recede, and in place of hostility and competitiveness there will emerge a flowering of brotherly love and true friendship and mutual helpfulness. A fountain of light will go forth from the divine source to show the whole world, those who view the outer things and those who focus on the inner essence, that our ties of unity inspired by the benign light of Him who is the Rock of Israel lives, and overcomes with its triumphant peace all the tendencies to fragmentation and separatism that can arise in any individual or group.

I hope to write you again, my dear friend, before we set out on our travel, with the help of God. But now I must abbreviate, because of my preoccupation. My greeting of peace and blessing, and best wishes for a long and good life, a good old age, and fruitful labors, and joy in God's help and consolation for His people, as befits your noble self and your friend tied to you in love with heart and soul.

Igrot III, Letter 966

NOTES

1. The so-called "scientific study of Judaism" was a product of the Jewish Enlightenment in Germany which was pursued in a detailed scholarly fashion, often with an antireligious bias.

2. These texts were all incorporated in the liturgy. In the first citation from Isa. 60:1, he changed the past tense of the verb *Zaruh*, "has shone", to the future *yizrah*, "will shine", giving the promise of a more relevant reference to his own time.

3. Rabbi Kook's meaning here is not very clear. He seems to parallel the Platonic doctrine of ideas, as the eternally existing archetypes, that are laid up "in the mind of

God", of which the finite ideas of man are only the imperfect efforts to interpret them and to express them.

4. This is an abbreviation for Rabbi Aaron Mendel.

5. Rabbi Moshe Seidel, to whom this letter is directed, had apparently expressed his disillusionment over moral deficiencies in the Jewish people, and Rabbi Kook's reply tries to answer this.

6. The original is in the past tense but Rabbi Kook, to fit it into his homily, gives it a future meaning.

7. Rabbi Samuel Alexandrov had written many letters to Rabbi Kook on some of the basic issues in theology, projecting controversial positions on which he wanted Rabbi Kook to react. He apparently released this correspondence, creating the impression that in some sense Rabbi Kook was sympathetic with his views.

8. The expression used by Rabbi Kook is "The twenty-two letters in the Hebrew alphabet unfolding in the Torah of truth testify..."

9. Rabbi Kook was a *koben*, of a priestly family, that descended from Aaron the High Priest, who is pictured in Jewish tradition as having been especially concerned with conciliation and peace.

10. Shmuel Alexandrov, to whom this letter is directed, had described the intellectual climate among the enlightened elements of the Jewish population during that period. They had come to question the basic norms of Jewish tradition in the name of the new ideas which were making headway in the general culture, and among Jews as well. One of these ideas was anarchism, which saw the individual as a self-sufficient embodiment of all values, who could live in free interaction with other individuals in an idyllic society, if only the coercion of the state and the externally imposed disciplines of religion were withdrawn.

Alexandrov undoubtedly felt that he had support for this view in a Talmudic text which discloses that the commandments would become obsolete in the hereafter (Nidda 61b). This seems to imply the belief in a utopian future when men live in freedom, without the external restraints of law.

We do not have his original letter to Rabbi Kook, but from Rabbi Kook's reply it is apparent that he expounded those views and wanted Kook to react to them. We have translated only part of the letter, in which Kook defends the continuing need of religious disciplines and in which he reacts to the philosophy of anarchism generally. As is customary with Kook's thinking, he does not dismiss the views of his challenger altogether, but finds a measure of validity in them, rejecting only the dimension which he thinks erroneous.

11. This is apparently an allusion to Nadab and Avihu who offered "alien fire" on the altar, and they died as a result (Lev. 10:1,2). The offense is explained in Sifra, *ad locum*, as a repudiation of the instructions Moses had given them.

12. The Alexandrians seems to be an allusion to the Hellenistic Christians who regarded the law as obsolete; the Judeo-Christians kept the law.

13. Rabbi Kook does not specify the particular expression about which his correspondent had questioned him. The editor suggests that it was an expression in his controversial essay "The Road to Renewal" which had appeared in the journal *Hanir* (1904).

14. The allusion is to an article signed by seven rabbis which appeared in the journal *Haor* defending his ruling allowing agricultural labor during the Sabbatical year and denouncing his adversaries.

15. *Shemitah* refers to the Biblical law forbidding agricultural labor during the Sabbatical year. Rabbi Kook, through a legal fiction, suspended this prohibition.

16. Rabbi Berlin had assumed the editorship of the periodical *Haivri.*
17. *Yishuv* means settlement. The old *yishuv* refers to the Jewish community which existed in Palestine before the beginning of the Zionist inspired colonization; the new *yishuv* refers to the community established by the Zionist pioneers who came under the inspiration of the Zionist movement.
18. Fresco, a Jew, lived in Istanbul, and was active in spreading hostility toward Zionism among the Turks and the Arabs.
19. Rabbi Fishman was a leader of the *Mizrahi* organization.
20. This youth had been ill and was brought on the Sabbath from Jaffa to a hospital in Jerusalem. He was not accepted, apparently because there were no admissions on that day, and he died.
20. *Aggada* refers to the nonlegalpart of the Talmud, primarily the moralistic and the spiritual.
21. This letter is a follow-up to a letter which Rabbi Kook had written previously to Rabbi Seltzer. It is included in *Abraham Isaac Kook* (Paulist Press, 1978), pp. 354-358).
22. What he means is that because of the evil state of his generation the mystical teachings can no longer be left to be pursued by an elitist group, but they must be communicated to the general public to help them overcome the current moral decline. The focus on spirituality serves as a buttress to religious faith and to a strengthening of moral values.
23. Mendel Beilis was involved in a ritual murder libel in Kiev, Czarist Russia, being charged with the crime of killing a Christian child for Jewish ritual purposes. The trial (1911-1913) became a crusade against Jews generally, but in the end Beilis was acquitted.
24. Rabbi Joshua Heschel Levenberg was a rabbi in the United States who served as the head of a Yeshivah in New Haven. He had apparently expected to raise some funds to enable Rabbi Kook to devote himself wholly to his literary labors, but nothing came of it.
25. Baron Edmond Rothchild was the great patron of the Zionist effort to bring settlers to the Holy Land, and this was one of the main objectives of his beneficence.
26. There is no indication to whom this letter was directed, but the context suggests that it was to his son. The conflicting claims which come to him and about which he complains reflect on the role of the rabbi at the time. He served as a judge to adjudicate cases on the basis of rabbinic law.
27. Rabbi Kook was then in Switzerland stranded by the first World War.
28. This letter was written the day before Shavuot, the festival which celebrates the revelations at Sinai.

IV.

Meditations

The Harmony of Ideas

There is no perception or knowledge in the world that a person, or any creature, can gain that does not tend to bring in its wake some obscurity or error. The degree of error and obscurity, which may emerge while we seek knowledge, varies. In the clarified particulars themselves the deceptive shadows will be at a minimum, but they will increase in other areas. The more remote the subject clarified is from other subjects of study, the greater will be the obscuring shadow.

If the subjects explored should seem opposed to each other in their inner nature, in the substantive ideas which lend them their validity, and which draw to them the investigators and researchers, the shadows will be thicker and darker at times, even effecting distortions. They will engender very frightening opposition and contradiction. This will certainly be true in the confrontation between those ideas which are based on a probing of the external world, through observation or experience on the one hand, and those ideas which emanate from the inner fountain of the heart's intuition and the original workings of the spirit. By their nature these two conceptual realms tend to negate one another, and each one sets a stumbling block on the path of the other.

It is only in the treasury of the supreme intelligence, in the source whence emanates the light of the soul, that there appears a light that vanquishes these shadows. It will be efficacious as far as possible considering the level of a person's state of holiness and purity. Thereby a healing is effected for the defects which one perception engenders in the other. There is no harmonization in the content of ideas except in Him, who is the source of wisdom, perfect in knowledge, praised be He.

The inner cleaving to God, which is the source of all knowledge, heals those wounds and blows that were inflicted in the house of our beloved. God Himself is called by the name, Peace. The initial impediment to our quest for comprehension turns out in the end to lead to a wider comprehension, and its wounds are therefore the wounds inflicted by our beloved, in the world of God's creation.

Just as perceptions in the realm of ideas release shadows on each other and need help for harmonization from the divine source whence they emanate before they are concretized in specific conceptual form, so do moral principles. Initially they contradict each other. Each one fashions his world on a broad, radical basis and is unconcerned with the world-view and the moral claims of the others. It is only from the supreme, universal fountain, the source where the Righteous One of the universe abides, from the supreme *Zaddik*, that blessings emanate, and the blessing which embraces all is peace. It is the unification of all moral claims which enter the heart of every creature, which embrace all human communities and unite all worlds.

The greater the contradiction between one perception and another, between one system of moral principles and another, so will grow the yearning for peace between them, and the more they will be prepared to turn back to their higher source, and to drink the waters of deliverance with great thirst. "Like cold water for a weary person is the good news from a distant realm" [the allusion here is to God, Prov. 25:25], and "He is called Wonderful in Counsel, the everlasting Father, the Prince of Peace" (Isa. 9:5).

Orot Hakodesh I, pp. 11-12

The Basis of All Thought

All thoughts are rooted in logic and are systematically linked to each other. Even those in which we recognize only a minimal aspect of rationality, if we probe deeply into their beginnings, we shall find that they originated from a source in logic. Such is the nature of thought.

We, therefore, know automatically that there is no thought which is wholly devoid of significance. There is nothing that is without its place, for everything emanates from the realm of wisdom.[1] If we encounter thoughts which seem to us defective or empty, their defect or emptiness is only in their outer expression. If we reach deeper, into their inner essence, we shall find the elements that sustain life, for wisdom is the source of life.

In every person there are treasures of thought which embody higher life, and which are destined to be refined and to take their place in exalted splendor when the world reaches its perfection.

The more a person progresses and the closer he is related to the inner content of existence and life, the more he draws from every thought its eternal, logical, good core which stems from the source of wisdom, whether this be his own or that of others. He grows through them, and they develop through him. "Who is wise? He who learns from all men" (Avot 4:1) — without any exception.

No wonder then that for those zealous for the spiritual life, those who are upright of heart, there is no darkness or distress. From every subject, whether close or remote they draw the element of the good, the fruitful, the holy, and bring them closer to the realm of the holy, as indeed they are part of it. All things find their unity in the source of the holy.

We therefore realize that the difficulty we have in assimilating any thought and in developing it in proper exposition is because its creative potentialities have not been disclosed. This applies to our own thoughts as well as to those of others which reached us by hearsay or by some other means.

This sustaining principle hinged on the recognition of the source whence all thoughts are generated. Its source is wisdom, the work of logic in all its creative potentiality.

This is the mission of every upright person, to bring to every thought its original thread of logic, which gives direction to its life, the identifying sign of its truth. Then it [thought] will return to its source [wisdom] and "will endow life to him who has embraced it" (Ecc. 7:12).[2]

Orot Hakodesh I, pp. 17-18

The Hidden Spring

Higher thoughts emanate from a distant realm; they are presented to us in an inchoate state, without defined form, with no conceptual structure. Our inner longing is directed only towards them. It is by a link with their riches that a blessing is bestowed on the structured thoughts, through which wisdom and knowledge go out into the world in all the expanding flow of their currents.

And when a person experiences a lack of understanding, and a decline in spiritual creativity, let him at once run to the hidden spring. Let him take shelter in the shadow of the Almighty, let him satisfy his thirst from the deep wells of the great masters who are wise of heart; let him study even if he does not fully comprehend what they say. Refreshed by the higher waters he will blossom and his spiritual vitality will be restored. Let him reflect on his experience after returning from his intellectual adventure in the distant realm to the home ground of structured ideas, to the sphere of customary mental activity. He will then see, and behold, that the Lord's blessing has returned to him, and he has become like a spring that flows with increasing strength and a river that does not cease.

For the source of blessing is in the place of mystery, in the hidden place where the highest secrets abide. The source of blessing is in a realm that is closed to the eye, as it is written: "The Lord will ordain blessing for you in your hidden places" (Deut. 28:18).[3]

Orot Hakodesh I, p. 100.

Silence and Attention

The whole rational world, with all its branches, to its lowest levels, fluctuates between periods of silence and periods of speech. When one is in a state of readiness to receive the higher influence, then all is quiet and silent. But when a state is reached that the recipients are to release an influence on what is below it, then communication begins.

The same fluctuation is also operative among people. When the rational state is prepared to clarify concepts that are below one's level of understanding, then the limited form of reason operates, and the activated force does its work. But when the higher attentiveness asserts itself, then the particularized mentality cannot perform its work and silence begins to hold sway.

When a person reaches this state, then the customary operation of the mind, whether in the realm of the secular or the holy, is below his level and he will always find within himself fierce opposition toward any rational endeavor which follows a structured logical course. It becomes necessary for him to prepare himself for the state of silence, to listen to the voice from on high coming to him with blessing, with an offering of the will and with generosity. The word of God will come to him, and "day by day He will communicate His utterance" (Ps. 19:3).[4]

Orot Hakodesh I, p. 116.

The Goal of Unification

All the deficiencies in the world, both the physical and the spiritual, derive from the fact that every individual comprehends only one aspect of existence which appeals to him, and all other aspects which are outside his comprehension, as far as he is concerned, might as well disappear. And the notion registers its impact on individuals and societies, on generations and epochs, that whatever is outside one's sphere of interest is disturbing and destructive. As a result of this, controversies grow in the realm of opinions and beliefs, in cultures and social systems. The individual, too, suffers from inner tensions, for feelings do not meet one another with appropriate sympathy. Thoughts repel one another in a spirit of disdain and hostility. The interchange of views in friendship becomes an impossibility and the feeling of general harmony, to delight the spirit, continues to decline.

To cope with these deficiencies, of which the the whole world suffers, and we especially, is the mission of the *zaddikim* [the righteous] who, by reason and will, strive for unification. It is their vocation to mend, to integrate, and to extend peace in the world by effecting peace in the inner realm of their own soul, by exemplifying an outlook which is comprehensive and universal, which always releases light and life in all directions.

This is the goal of the faithful servants of God, in whom, and through whom, the hidden dimensions of existence are revealed. They manifest a great concern for the particularities of existence, a love and attachment to life's experiences, in all their proper claims, a high level act of will and thought to embrace all manifestations of life, all theories of politics, all patterns of personal behavior, all the diverse values of religion and art, all systems of ethics and economics, all standards of aesthetics, all the paths through which truth, justice, beauty, courage, and all that invests life and existence with the potency of their being.

This is the goal we proclaim when we invoke God's name at all times.

Orot Hakodesh I, pp. 120-121

The Creative Flow of the Soul

Great souls live especially in the wellsprings of their creativity. The masters of creativity, for whom bringing forth the new is of the very essence of their life, will always recognize their spiritual progress in the stream of new ideas that flow continually before the eyes of their spirit. They recognize the soul in the deepest aspect of its essence, how it constantly pours forth the flow of its creations.

As the body releases a flow of light from within itself ceaselessly, so does the soul, the source of perception and aspiration, feeling and vision, release its vital spiritual illumination. And the stream flows on, the visions continue. It would be impossible to record the significance of the vision conveyed during any span of time in the soul's radiance. This is true even of the most humble of people. In the case of the great masters of thought, the great men of vision, this process of enrichment reaches a level so wonderful that many are surprised at the enlightenment that becomes manifest in the fruit of their visions.

What is disclosed in the vision is necessarily the least significant in the creative process. The act of creation itself, in its mystical character, its wondrous effects, the speed with which the streams of ideas flow does not permit us to comprehend the inner essence and character of the particular components of these flowing streams.

The most significant talent is the ability to penetrate to the depths of our own being. But to effect this penetration it is important to know that it is a easy endeavor, that labor and exertion only impairs this august domain, that it is necessary to heed the claim for the delight of inner tranquility. Thus will be enhanced the substantive significance in the fruits of creation, and the sparks of holy light will begin to flash on all life and its spiritual concerns.

Every fleeting moment we create, consciously and unconsciously, multitudes of creation beyond measure. If we would only condition ourselves to feel them, to bring them within the zone of clear comprehension, to introduce them within the framework of appropriate articulation, there would be revealed their glory and their splendor. Their effect would then become visible on all of life.

And eternal truths will be released to us from the fountain of life, the source of the soul, which knows no falsehood or deceptive speech. It is hewn from the torch of truth. What flows from its light is only truth and justice which will abide forever.

Orot Hakodesh I, pp. 172-173.

Attentiveness to the Vision

We listen to the holy voice that speaks to us from on high. We absorb the impressions registered, that sparkle like the lightning from the higher domain of the soul and the source of its being.

Every vision that is revealed is a voice from on high that is calling to us. It comes from the source of knowledge, form the treasury of life that abides in the soul of Him who is the life of the universe. It reveals itself to each person, according to the levels of his self-refinement. As the sins which alienate the person from his Creator, the Creator of all existence, are removed, the voice from the realm where all is embraced in a higher unity reaches us with a greater disclosure of truth.

When all the physical and spiritual instincts of a person are in a state of readiness and purity, and the holy aspirations for the majesty of God in all its glory, adorned with all the moral norms affecting all aspects of life, is fully assertive, the obstructions disappear. And a clear light and a clear voice, permeated with the treasure of life and the wisdom of truth, reach us. "The ear listens, and the eye sees, for God has made them both." (Prov. 20:12).

Orot Hakodesh I, p. 176.

The Revelation of the Soul

It is possible to feel the stirrings of the soul in the zone of its concealment, its link with those exalted realms, from which it derives the secret of its life, its light and its splendor.

And the more a person is hallowed, the more distant he is from sin and is inclined toward holiness and the divine, will the soul reveal itself to him, its light will pervade his entire being, and his whole self will summon him to identify with the source of his life.

The body will all its inclinations will move close to holiness, it will be drawn to the essence of the soul, its instincts will become more clearly defined, and thereby they will rise higher, they will be hallowed and refined. The sense of smell, of attentiveness, of sight — all will be raised, all will be illumined.

The soul draws its light from its sources in the higher realm, and from this original illumination it releases an influence on the living self, on the powers of the body, the spiritual and the physical. There is a growth in strength. Confidence, firmness of heart, tranquility of spirit spreads. And the yearning for greatness, for uprightness and equity, for life and light, for knowledge and beauty increases.

And man continues to be victorious over worldly existence. Envy, lust, honor, wealth, which are so precious to most people, become for him repulsive and cheap, and his spirit yearns for purity, for the absolute good, for the luminous truth, for the enduring, in all its majesty, for the light of God, the God of eternity.

Orot Hakodesh I, p. 184

The Meeting of the Streams

At times the holy spirit does its work quietly within the body and soul. It links all the concerns hidden in them with all the higher realms beyond them. Thereby the person is elevated, hallowed. He is lifted toward all the higher realms. He experiences within himself every influence coming from above. And paralleling it, from within himself, from the depths of his being, forces stream forth and rise upward. The lights meet and reveal to each other the majesty of their self- revelation.

And everything holy and exalted is directed to and rooted in the deep sources of its origin. Every good inclination, every virtue, every act of service, every holy thought, every divine commandment, every impulse to equity is experienced as having reached us from a mighty world beyond, from a world ancient and new. It streams toward us from realms distant and near, from the souls of ancestors, from a chain of many generations. It is precious and beloved, full of life and shining beauty.

The living word kisses us with abounding love, and we kiss it with profuse endearment. "I am for my beloved, and my beloved is for me" (Song of Songs 2:16).

Orot Hakodesh I, p. 190.

From Pain to Delight

Great is the suffering of creativity which draws a person away from the coarse world, where all the forces of material existence are rooted, toward the world of the spiritual and purity, where the soul is at home and acts in a free expression of its powers. And how great also is the joy of creation, in that here the soul finds its rest, the play of its independent life.

And every creator must take stock of this fact of life, that he should not be disdainful of the sufferings of the love involved in creation. It is only thereby that he will merit to attain those great and wonderful delights. Let him not be troubled even if his pains of creativity be many , for it is commensurate with them that the delight and the blessing will increase.

He must never seek the pleasures by themselves without their accompanying sufferings, for then they will lose their precious worth. The living light from the heavenly splendor reveals itself only through a refinement of the will that rejoices in the sufferings which are the source of the delights.

Orot Hakodesh I, p. 197

The Grief of the Soul's Redemption

A person must seek a clarification as to the nature of the spiritual problem which presses on his heart, which troubles him and embitters his life, when he is unaware of any reason for this grief and bitterness. For the most part when one seeks and finds a cause for this condition, it is only a superficial one. The truth is deeper than anything that can be envisioned and recorded concerning this state, in any clear explanation.

This spiritual grief is the theme of the soul's song, the claim made by the soul in search of its freedom. It battles against all the confinements that hem it in. It wants a life of freedom, a higher life of nobility, clear and luminous, and it does not find it because of the material constraints in which it is imprisoned. This is the secret of its grief.

It is therefore in order to confront this condition, as far as possible, and draw from this abyss of darkness many jewels and noble feelings. In the final analysis, the soul's challenge to a person is itself an intimation of redemption. The light of deliverance is about to manifest itself, after this period of discouragement.

The experiences we have mentioned are prevalent in the life of the individual, and also in the general life of a people, in various forms. At times, particularly in the life of society, these conditions are manifested through thinkers of distinction who hear the echo of the world's voice. At times this voice, in its troubled state, is conveyed through society as a whole. But this grief is an announcement of redemption, and it comes gradually; it comes and it shines.

Orot Hakodesh I, p. 199

The Questions About the Origin of Certainty

Sometimes a person is troubled because of his riches. What do we mean by this?

Many illuminations come upon us. Vision after vision appears before our spirit. We look at books, the most holy books, the most profound, and their treasures of thought become alive and radiate their influence. With the strength of their originality they lift many wellsprings of thought in us. And with every vision an inner voice is born in us. Where does all this come from? Where does the initial vision and its certainty come from?

And the soul is troubled because of the joy of its riches, and this delights the spirit, sharpens the mind, and nourishes the spiritual life. And original perceptions and sensitivities of profound significance, of great and wide scope, are born and they come with proof of their certainty, and they raise the soul to a lofty realm.

And in the lofty place the question arises again concerning the new certainties, the highest kind of riches, which make their appearance in all their splendor and joyous delight: Whose child is this youth? Is he worthy of being admitted to the community?

And the probing thought returns and is awakened, and seeks a path for itself. It seeks and finds, and the new certainty becomes rooted deeply in the soul. It becomes active, it presses deeply to exert an influence, to shape life in a wide area. It comes and stirs until a new ascent is reached, through which all the old is forgotten. All the past riches recede and withdraw, and images from a higher realm come from a turbulent atmosphere, pure and fructifying. Lights shine in a form never imagined before. There is no mention of the past. The present and the future stimulate and bring delight. The process of creation continues, and the certainty reaches its climax.

And now the spirit of inquiry comes and releases a new anxiety in order to bring into birth a higher joy and the revelation of a more perfect world. "What they have not been told, they saw, and what they have not heard, they understand"[5] (Isa. 52:15).

Orot Hakodesh I, pp. 205-206

The Concepts That Transcend Science

Our love for clearly established knowledge must be within limits so as no to impede us from aspiring after the transcendent, for that can only be reached through legitimate conjectures, inchoate feelings and at times through intuition and the imagination.

These resemble dreams and visions while awake. They cause great injury if they are pursued out of laziness, in areas where science could establish its authentic data. But they are an adornment to us, and also lend support to the clearly established aspect of knowledge, and uplift our whole being if they focus on subjects of a transcendent nature that are beyond our scientific reach.

Out of our desire, our soul's deep yearning for spiritual illumination, we are under pressure to probe what is concealed from our clearly defined comprehension. We are drawn to judge on the basis of conjecture, and to enjoy spiritual delights in precious aspirations on the basis of inner meditation, with the help of the imagination. This, too, is hallowed and joins the good in the domain of science when it functions within the limits appropriate to it. Concerning this it has been said: "Within the realm allowed to you, seek to understand".

But one must beware not to mix up the two domains, to regard the concept based on conjecture as though it were a scientific concept, and the concept based on imagination as though it were a conjecture based on reason. One may then be trapped in the web of deception. One must guard the boundaries of his perceptions and know how to ascend from the realm of the known to the realm of the mystical, where the subject is so transcendent that we can proceed only by conjecture and imagination. Then the person will find within himself heavenly might, and light from on high will shine in him, for God will establish his path.

In the course of time, many imaginative elements will change to the status of conjectures and elements of conjecture will be authenticated by knowledge and clear discernment. The imagination and the conjecture will then shift to more esoteric subjects, of more delicacy and transcendence. The person will then go from strength to strength.

In terms of God's existence, linking our life with the divine is rational and is explicated by science. But it is the stirring in the person's heart of spiritual sensibilities emanating from the divine realm, the inflow of visions that partake of prophetic illumination, the luminous life of the soul, and the radiance of the divine in its glory — these bring a person to great bliss. The particularizations in this process rest on the potency of conjecture and the higher imagination, which are more precious than all rationality and logic.

Through the power of conjecture and the higher imagination we are raised to the source of wisdom and the place of understanding. These are the stepping stones released by wisdom and understanding themselves. "Where is wisdom to be found, and which is the place of understanding? God prepared its path and He knows its place" (Job 28:12,23).

Orot Hakodesh I, pp. 220-223

The Unity of Mind and Will

The perfection of the mind does not depend on the number of concepts, but on the harmony which prevails among them. Obviously, the more numerous the concepts, the greater the potency which is manifested by that unity and the more profound is its being.

This objective of the unity of thought cannot be gained through out—side directives. This higher virtue reposes in our souls, and we must learn to know it, so that we might be sustained by this exalted blessing of the unity of the mind.

The more the mental powers act in us as an inner disposition, the stronger will be the unity in our mind, and the more the concepts will shed their solitary, fragmented, diffused form and become the lights of life, a life of mighty harmony.

As this applies to the mind, it also applies to the will. The separate wills become one entity, one mighty and firm will. The more numerous and the nobler the objects willed, and the more significant they are, to that extent will these acts of will shed their separatist forms and they will become united, embraced in one mighty, living exalted and holy will.

In the perfected form of the enlightened unity of the soul there is revealed the unitary light of the mind and the will, together, and all the expressions of the will join with the expressions of the mind, and the comprehensive functioning of the mind is united with the comprehensive functioning of the will. Both shine with one distinctive light, full of might, full of holiness and majesty, full of beauty and authority.

And this edifice we are building in our souls does not remain a private edifice, one limited edifice, but becomes a universal edifice. The whole world is [inherently] united, and as one part of existence is illumined and alive, exalted and elevated, all of it becomes alive, all of it is hallowed, exalted and elevated.

It turns out that the unity achieved in our souls serves to unite the world as a whole. And all those noble effects of the riches of the soul which everyone who is wise of heart, of a sensitive and holy spirit, can feel within himself through his own ascent because of the manifestation of the mystical discovery of inner unity — these spread and release light and vitality and become a source of blessing and an ornament of peace to the world and its fullness. "May the glory of the Lord abide forever, may the Lord rejoice in His creation" (Ps. 104:31).

Orot Hakodesh I, pp. 259-260

The Life That Transcends Life

When we soar on high as on eagles' wings in the spiritual world, our soul stirs us to speak and to think about the most universal themes. All the values in the diverse aspects of our life present themselves to us all in one embrace, which divides itself into a multitude of groupings, and every group is also divided into endless parts. But all are held together and are woven to each other, and they are organically attached to each other. A great mighty life force pervades, moving forward and backward, like flashes of lightning.

And all things are joined in a more comprehensive whole, different worlds are united. They flash to each other their sparks of light, and all are joyous, full of delight. The holy and the mundane stand facing each other. Their destination is clearly discernible, but despite this we note among them love and brotherliness, peace and friendship. The holy ascends and is exalted in its splendor. It releases an influence which descends and reaches down ever lower in its great humbleness. The mundane is filled with joy and delight, and it rejoices to serve as an aid to the holy. It is filled with its majesty [that of the holy], and is adorned with its splendor.

And the exalted domains where abides the spirit that endows life to the living is disclosed to us. The worlds are perfected, the souls are mended and cleansed of their deficiencies, and the blessing of God is spread over all life.

And from the depths of the dark they rise to be sated in the delightful abode, full of great beauty, proclaiming the majesty and praise for God who is the life of the universe, who sustains life, and rejoices in His works and brings joy to all His creatures, releasing His mercies with their majestic potency robed in the holy of holies.

Happy is the people who experience this, happy is the soul that is sheltered in His light, that abides in the place of His adornment, that is illumined by the light of His enduring mercies forever and ever.

Orot Hakodesh II, pp. 366-367

The Life of Holiness

How does holiness affect a person's consciousness? His mind is illumined with the purest and noblest perceptions. The profusion of the perceptive light stimulates a constant desire to live within the realm where the higher life is dominant. Through the growth in perception which has its impact in the domain of the will there develop sensibilities of a higher life. One's attachment to a lofty way of life grows ever stronger until the very center of one's life is increasingly fixed on those exalted heights.

The bodily feelings become sensitized, and all its values are fused with a thrust toward holiness. The whole passion of one's life becomes holy and exalted. But the regular pattern of life does not lose its character. The customary movements and conversations, the physical life of the individual and of society, the standards of good manners and respect are not blurred. But they rise to a more ideal level.

The essence of life is elevated, its goals are hallowed. The desire for a higher good, universal and all-embracing, at the same time also personal and penetrating, comes to increasing expression in practical form. The grandeur of a life dedicated to God grows in perfection. This is the life that reflects the holiness of existence, the life of souls, of angels, the life in which the splendor of equity, the beauty of courage set in justice and truth, are all interwoven. The person himself — in all his feelings, thoughts, desires, norms of behavior, his passions, meditations, imaginations — is firmly set. His roots draw their strength from the whole of nature and from what is beyond nature, harmonizing his life of confinement with the life that transcends all confinement. The individual person is thus turned into a force that integrates everything into a fixed ideal of endless nobility, embracing all being, without losing even the slightest spark.

Divine equity, heavenly, eternal truth, norms of human morality, ways of peace and pleasantness merge together; stage after stage comes the recognition of what God wants in His world, of the ideal underlying all creation. Once we reach this state of freedom, there is revealed to us the source of that goal which, in its grandeur, may properly be looked upon as expressing the will of God, the Creator of all things, whose greatness is beyond our understanding.

The vision of grandeur is completed with the removal of its defects. Increasingly it brings delight to man whose life is filled with divine happiness, and to all existence which is established in the spirit of the wisdom of the living God.

Orot Hakodesh II, pp. 302-303

The Delight of Holiness

The higher thoughts of holiness that flow from the source of the holy, from the light of Torah and wisdom, bring delight to a person's life. They endow him with the light of true life. The few wise men rise to this higher delight because their souls are linked with this divine wisdom. By their connection with the general populace they also bring delight to their souls as well. This is especially true among the Jewish people, because of the unity that prevails among this wondrous people, this one people.

As this concept is clarified to the remnant called by God, they strengthen themselves in holding on to the higher Torah. Even if it should happen, because of impediments due to circumstances, physical or otherwise, they do not experience this delight, and wisdom and holiness are revealed to them without the accompanying full joy and splendor, they will still persevere in their service, and they will not abandon their position. They will trust in the help of the Lord, that He will still cause His light to shine on them.

In any case they know fully well that the more they rise to the higher conceptions of holiness, the more they contribute significantly to elevate many souls from the depths in which they are sunk, to raise precious jewels from the lowly state to which they were brought by a host of physical and spiritual afflictions. Through the unnoticed fusion of the lights of these holy people with the desires and inclinations of the general populace, the essence of life becomes refined, the joy of the inner life is elevated. The feeling of the good and of the equitable, and the hidden light of the holy begin to break through their concealment. The whole world assumes much more worth.

The fruit of this service shows itself in places where no one would surmise who bestowed this blessing, who released the pleasant influence, who introduced the feelings of peace and friendship, who caused the equitable working of the mind, the assertion of vitality, the refinement of spirit, the increase in hope. All these are contributions from the world of light that lives in the souls of these people of uprightness.

These are the nobles of the world, the princes of holiness, the great lovers of the works of service, in whose souls abides the spirit of mercy and love of the Master of all worlds. They are the masters of the mighty will to illumine and to improve, to glorify, and to spread happiness, to respect and to beautify everything. These are the honored holy men of God. Honor abides with them, it pervades their souls. It does not leave them even when the whole world looks at them disdainfully. They are the great thinkers, the people of great humility, who are filled with the pride of God. They are weaklings in their outer appearance but they all are full of strength and inner courage without end. They are "the mighty ones who do His bidding" (Ps. 103:20).

Orot Hakodesh II, pp. 305-306

The Holy Edifice

What is it that takes away the sense of satisfaction from higher contemplation? What is it that poisons people not to feel the delight of the holy, the light of God, and thus they fail to base their actions and aspirations in conformity to His will? It is only this deceptive notion that shows the spiritual as sterile, while all the tumultuous life is seen as settled and stable. This is the most despicable falsehood in the world.

This is the holy task of good-hearted people: to seek unceasingly the wellspring of spiritual life, to feel in their own hearts and to reveal to others the majesty and the beauty, the firmness and the stability of the spiritual life, which has its roots in the light of holiness. It is supported by the higher love, the love of God, in its purity and its substantive radiance. This perception will release illumination, life will be purified, and the nation as a whole will recognize its purpose, the secret of the battles that it waged in its long and entangled history.

Then it will know that it will find the source of its happiness only within the teaching of prophecy, in the values revealed by the holy spirit, in the way of life proclaimed by the Torah of the living God, in all its norms and directives for the individual and society, in all the aspects of its outlook on life. Only in them will it find its happiness, and through them will it establish the basis of its revival, and the sure foundations of its return to its land and the perfection of its national life.

Orot Hakodesh II, p. 320

The Building of the Secular for the Sake of the Holy

One cannot say that the soul is disdainful of the body, though the concerns toward which they each aspire, and on which they act and direct their creative labors, are so divergent from each other. It is similarly inconceivable that the *soul* of all souls, the higher spiritual essence which sustains the soul, can be disdainful of the soul, though the latter is, in comparison with it, confined and lowly, as the body is confined and lowly in relation to the soul. So it is with all existence, with the pattern of behavior, the general and the particular, the personal and the social. This is the way of life.

We see people trying to embrace objectives which focus on the physical or the secular life, endeavoring to upbuild the nation or the world. We, on the other hand, feel that the basis of life and the source of fulfillment lies in higher objectives, not in building the material but the spiritual dimension of life, and not the spiritual which is seeking to shape the secular, but that higher aspect which is hallowed in the holy of the holies. Let us not be troubled by all these activities. Let us not forget that the *soul* of all souls, for its functioning, needs the soul and the body, and their proper integration. In other words, that the higher holiness, the ideal which emanates from the divine source, must be centered on a spirituality that acts in the secular plane, and that the latter must be centered on the physical in all its aspects. When these forces are united, then is the edifice complete.

Orot Hakodesh II, p. 323

The Divine Emanation

How beautiful is the mystical conception of the divine emanation as the source of all existence, all life, all beauty, all power, all justice, all good, all order, all progress. How great is the influence of this true conception on all the ways of life, how profound is its logic, what a noble basis for morality. The basis for the formation of higher, holy, mighty, and pure souls is embodied in it.

The divine emanation, by its being, engenders everything. It is unlimited in its freedom, there is no end to its unity, to its riches, to its perfection, to its splendor, and the influence of its potency and its diverse manifestations. All the oceans of song, all the diverse torrents of perception, all the force of life, all the laughter, the joyous delights — everything flows from it. Into everything it releases the influence of its soul force. Its influence, its honor, its deliverance reaches to the lowest depths.

The innocent and luminous will of man has already embraced some of its splendor. He continues to ascend, and he elevates everything with him. Everything proclaims God's glory. "The grandeur of Your holiness fills Your creation, You are forever more, O Lord" (Ps. 93:5).

Orot Hakodesh I, p. 361q

Everything Moves and Aspires

Everyone of the sparks of life that we behold from the distant heights is richer and mightier and full of purpose and energy and design for living.

We cannot define the treasures of life in living beings, the small and the great alike, not even the treasure of life enclosed and hidden in the vitality of plants and inanimate objects. Everything continues to flow, to stir and to aspire.

Nor can we assess our own inner riches. Our inner world is also hidden and sealed for us. It is linked to purposes hidden from us, with a world that is not our world, to come within our perception, our knowledge, our probing.

Everything is full of riches and greatness, everything aspires to ascend, to be purified and to be elevated. Everything recites a song, offers praise, magnifies, exalts; everything builds, serves, perfects, elevates, aspires to unite and to be integrated.

Life abounds with beauty and wisdom, courage and influence. It begins not from the place where there is already an utterance, a spoken word, an articulated thought, but in the palace of thick darkness [mystery]. "I was made in secret, I was designed in the lower parts of the earth" (Ps. 139:15). And our mind that contemplates the unity of all creation finds the distinction of man in every corner, in the heights of the heavens and the depths of the earth. "God decrees death and restores to life . . . He lowers and He raises up" (I Samuel 2:6-7).

Orot Hakodesh II, p. 386

The General Trend and Divine Providence

When one looks at the world from an ideal perspective, which has been illumined by the light of the holy, one does not see particular beings in the aspect of their particularity. In every phenomenon, in every grouping, even the most minute into which beings and functions are differentiated, one sees the result of the unfolding of the whole.

This lesson is increasingly being established on the basis of the newly promulgated science, which moves closer, through the methods of the secular, to the central teaching of the holy. It goes beyond the analysis of the atom to the recognition of motion and force. While each atom can be seen as an independent entity, a separate substance, motion is looked upon as effected by the interaction of all: it is acted on by all and it acts on all.

Thus all existence rises above its unfortunate fragmentation and its disjoined particulars are rebuilt into a complete edifice, fashioned by the Creator of all with wisdom and dependable mercies. The knowledge of the nature of matter brings us closer to the higher spiritual perception through which is established the basis of the holy that sustains everything, including the systems of morals, both personal and social. Philosophy, in its basic teaching, is now liberated from the dark constraint that hemmed it in, which created a wall of separation between the world and man, and their heavenly Father.

Logical reasoning no longer needs to force itself to embrace the higher concepts of religious faith which relate the soul to the source of its being and acknowledge its nature in all its fullness. Consider the concept of individual providence, not in its minimal aspect, which separates the particulars from the universal and thus diminishes their significance, nor in the form in which the particulars are swallowed up so that they seem to the analyst as having been eliminated. Philosophy demands that knowledge of God be seen in its aspect of universality, while religion and morality demand that it extend to the element of particularity. This concept of divine providence is all being clarified through that analysis which is being increasingly validated, and which encompasses experimental and inferential teachings of science, the most profound intuitions and the most penetrating reflections. Logical reason can now proceed on its course, supported by established truth and based on the full claims of holiness and religious faith which are affirmed by the integrity of the upright.

All existence is elevated when perceived in its true nature. Particularity develops to a form of the more general; it is robed in great, limitless universality. It is there that the particular finds its authenticity. The knowledge of God, in its august truth, in its universality, also includes the most specific particularity which abounds in truth and is related to a larger category of being. Not even a pebble is lost to His attention. The divine understanding, which embraces all worlds and the Creator's architectural wisdom, which is concerned with each distinctive world and each creature, is united in one comprehensive whole. The branches join at their roots, nourishing themselves from their vitalizing substance. This harmony resounds in the spirit of every upright person, in every righteous person who loves righteousness. And the Holy spirit, the most Holy spirit, continues to grow in potency, to give life to eternal worlds and all the beings that inhabit them.

Orot Hakodesh II, pp. 426-427

The Unity of the Human Family

When we contemplate the physical creation as a whole, we realize that it is all as one organism, that the parts are linked in varying gradations to each other. We see this in every plant, in every living being. We see this in man, how his higher organs which bear an important and ideal function are dependent, in their formation, in their being and continued existence, and on lower organs, on which we sometimes look disdainfully. The same is true when we assess the parts in their integrated state. To whatever extent we pursue our general analysis, the more clearly we understand the nature of the particulars. Even where the eye cannot penetrate we discern with clear perception and a profound spiritual conjecture to what extent the differentiated parts in existence are dependent on each other. The depths below and the heights above are linked to each other. The realization dawns on us that were it not for the lower beings, the uncouth and the unseemly, the higher beings could not have emerged in their splendor, their esteem and their luminous quality. We continually become more conscious of the integration and unity of existence.

From the material world we move to the spiritual world, to the thoughts and designs of man, to the different cultures, religions, ideologies. We are appalled when we see the evil and the folly which have dominated and still continue to dominate the hearts of people, in their norms of behavior, their opinions, their beliefs, their individual and collective lifestyles. We see all the abominations that were perpetrated in the name of religion, the human sacrifices offered up to idols, victims of its despicable moral norms. We see all the evil, the vulgarity, the weakness and the ignorance to which it gave its approval. On the other hand, we see the flashes of light, the glory in human reason, and its uprightness. We see the wisdom of scholars, the courage of the brave, the torch of the holy light of faith in its purity and exaltation, the aspirations and hopes for the great future, and the torches of light shining in the present. At once we conclude: The entire phenomenon of the spiritual is one world. This, too, has an organic character. This, too, with all the splendor of the soul, with the sparkling light of the holy spirit and the might of God which pervades it, is dependent on everything below it. Were it not for the dregs and the dirt in man's spirit, he could not have produced the fruit of his harvest that brings joy to God and man.

At once we are consoled on being lowly creatures,[6] and accept in love the profound design of the architect of the world, the Creator of all events, the God of all beings, the Lord of all souls, who endows souls to the people of the earth, and spirit to all who walk on it, and from whose goodness all derive good. Increasingly we are girded with holiness and might, and we begin to understand our lowly state as well as our greatness. We cherish the flowers of grace and beauty that grew in the garden of human development. We then recognize what transcends this in nobility, what stands far higher in significance. We all feel a great yearning to sing in celebration, and we are imbued with strength to walk proudly toward the light, to know the harvest of ideals brought forth by the spirit, which nurtures all good and uprightness, all enlightenment and freedom. We embrace the fruit of religion in its pure and developed state, to the extent that our understanding can reach it. And we accept the stirrings within us which exceed our understanding, confident that One higher than the high is watching over us. We are fortified by our sound counsel, and are strengthened by the grandeur of God, which we know as our inheritance from the teachings of the holy ones in early generations. "Who is mighty like You, O Lord, and Your faithfulness is round about You" (Ps. 89:9).

Orot Hakodesh II, pp. 431-432

The Basic Changes in the New Thought

Recent developments popularized new ideas which resulted in the rejection of convictions which were inherently not opposed to the new ideas. It is only because of habit that our ideas are grouped together. Man links all his ideas to each other, and since some of them undergo change, the change is extended to the entire domain of thought. It is only through critical knowledge and evaluation that one can define the boundaries, to discern how far the change effected by the new ideas is to be extended, and where their legitimate sway comes to an end. But the fact that it is in the nature of the mental and spiritual outlook to feel the impact of change in any of their elements makes for greater perfection and advancement.

Three basic changes have occurred in man's outlook in the new period, which stimulated many additional changes. but there was no attempt to determine the valid core of thought represented by these changes, in order to know how far they were to reach out, and to influence additional changes in thought and action. Thus these new developments, though in themselves beneficial, also brought about confusion and disorder. They will regain their beneficial effect through a clarification of outlook, resulting from a study of the spiritual life, focusing on the nature of the person and the body of beliefs which it is appropriate for him to entertain.

The three basic changes which have occurred are: 1) the change in the social outlook; 2) the change in the cosmological outlook; and 3) the change in the development of the concept of evolution.

The understanding of human society, and of societal existence generally, was a closed secret to the masses in former generations, like all the secrets of existential and speculative thought. Every community and group was enclosed in its domain. Every individual seemed affected by developments only in his own environment. In their naïveté every individual and every society thought that their own spiritual and physical environment comprised the wider world. The children of Israel, who are unique among the nations, were also enclosed in their own sphere, and even to a greater degree, for two important reasons. There was the factor of the many persecutions which they had always encountered from the people of the wider world, as far back in the past as they could recall, and there was the basic differences in the spiritual and practical lifestyle between us and many other nations from the very beginning of our history.

Special individuals, the sages of great understanding, always knew the secret of spiritual unity. They knew that the human spirit is a universal spirit, that although many divergences, spiritual and material, tend to separate person from person and society from society, greater than all the differences is the essential unity among them; that the processes of thought are constantly interacting, and ways of life tend to be harmonized. The objective of harmonization is surely to embrace the best, the healthiest and most sensitive in every society and to plant it on the soil of the larger human family. But the masses never looked out beyond their own circle, and they assumed that there was no intereaction between their own circle and an alien environment, certainly if it was remote from them. In the sphere of this limited outlook was registered the typical image of our most inner spiritual world. From this perspective one defined his idealistic love for everything holy, his attitude to his own people, and everything that pertains to it: his hopes for the future, his vision of the transcendent realms beyond the senses, his outlook on life and death, on freedom and bondage, on independence and discipline. Everything was woven in this limited weaving. The conception of an isolated environment was seen as the sum total of existence.

The times have wrought an absolute change in this outlook, not only among the elitist elements but among the masses as a whole, the small and the great alike. The social outlook has matured and widened. Every individual feels that he is not alone, that he is not enclosed altogether in an isolated zone, that he acts and is acted on by many circles, from different and even strange environments, and that one cannot dismiss any expression of the spirit and say that one need not take account of it, no matter how remote it appears to be. But here the process of evaluations becomes formidable, the possible confusion increases. The need to learn how to structure a multi-colored thought pattern within the narrow sphere of the customary ideas of the general populace, how to leave unaffected all the good in the spiritual world after the revolution wrought by the alien influences, and how one draws from everything only the good and the true, the equitable and the worthy — this has become more urgent. It will be impossible to do this satisfactorily except through the impact of good explanatory interpretations, focusing on the inner spiritual life. It will be impossible to realize this objective unless we invoke the help of many sensitive spiritual persons who abound in understanding and feeling, so that they will be able to influence the general public in a most desirable manner.

The cosmological outlook also led to a great change in the development of the spiritual life. The thoughts which were based on the miniature version of the world as a whole, in accordance with the old astronomical doctrine of a limited universe,[7] corresponded to the conceptions of a limited environment. The general new spirit which resulted from the expansion of our perception of reality, when it becomes widely known, must necessarily stimulate among the masses a new perception of the spiritual world, with all the ideas associated with it. There will be need to reflect on how to reinterpret everything in a new form with the utmost care, so as to assure the most effective continuity of all the basic good of the old in the new. This can only be accomplished through a regular study of the deeper dimensions of the spiritual life, which will yield us many clarifications, which will establish the spiritual stratum of our outlook on an enlightened basis. It will even add new light through the good that will be derived from the breadth of all the new conceptions, after they have been harmonized with all the good embodied in all the old, according to its purified version.

The concept of evolution, which has become widespread in all circles as a result of the new studies of nature, wrought a major revolution in the circle of those accustomed to conventional thinking. This was not the case with the enlightened individuals, the masters of thought and reflection who always envisioned gradual development — even in the realm of the spiritual, which they viewed with profound mystical probing. For them it was not strange to understand in a parallel fashion the development of the material world. It is indeed appropriate to envision its emergence as similar to the unfolding of the spiritual dimension of existence, which does not show a hiatus of a single wasted step. But the multitude was not accustomed to understand the principle of development in an all-embracing concept, and was unable to comprehend on that basis its spiritual world. It is not the difficulty of harmonizing some verses in the Torah or other statements in tradition with the view of evolution that made it difficult for the multitude to accommodate its thinking. This task is simple enough. All know that the parable, the allegory, the intimation is common is such matters, that this is a basic principle in interpretation everywhere. Even the ear of the multitude is accustomed to listening to brief pronouncements that this verse or this statement belongs to the realm of the hidden teachings of the Torah, that its direct meaning is elusive, and they are satisfied. The people adjust to the probing thinker who seeks to discern the mystical higher song which is to be found in the expositions of the allegories of ancient days. But how is one to reconcile the spiritual implications in an outlook which found its unity in the concept of [the world's creation] with suddenness and leaps,[8] which spares the mind from probing into realms distant from its own circle, with the new, increasingly more popular concept of evolution? For this there is need of great illumination, which is to penetrate all strata of society, until it reaches with its agreeable harmonization even the simplest circles of the masses.

The times force us to spread the knowledge, the most exalted, the broadest and most idealistic knowledge. The crude form of religious faith cannot maintain its position after it has suffered many declines and has sought to shut out the world by covering itself with thick sackcloth. Who will robe the pure religious faith with the garments appropriate to it, who will place on its head the pure turban suited for the splendor of its majesty, if not the great people of talent, the wise of heart, the people of holy feeling and purity of soul who are planted in the courts of the Lord, the sages who are dedicated to thinking and working in the cause of the Torah?

Orot Hakodesh II, pp. 556-560

The Ascent of the Human Will and Reason

There is in the world a substantive good which is continually progressing, and this substance is also revealed in the will and the nature of man. In the past man's nature and will were more savage than at present, and in the days to come they will be gentler and better than at present. In the past the thrust of the Torah and of morality was to overcome the natural will because evil was abounding in it. In the future this will take on a new form, to a point where the demand for the will's freedom of expression will become a moral claim to allow its sought-after unfolding, so that it may then show how much good is embodied in it as well.

But in the present state the will still has many base elements. Benefitting from the good elements of the will which have been liberated, these base elements also seek freedom, and their freedom will contaminate the world and destroy it. This engenders a fierce war, and each camp defends [its cause] with justice, and fights with justice. The libertarians fight for the good elements of the will, that they not suffer needless confinement, which is detrimental. The conservatives, who know the past and know the good achieved, defend the confinement, that the corrupt elements of the will shall not destroy the noble edifice of the world. The great spirits must be mediators of peace between these warriors, to show each of them the proper boundary within which he is truly summoned to act.

Orot Hakodesh II, p. 562

The Doctrine of Evolution and Divine Providence

Wherever the heretics find the basis of their disavowal of religious belief, there one can also find an appropriate response to their views. As this is demonstrated in the interpretation of texts in the Torah, so it is demonstrated in the basic tendencies of the person's life and intellect. All those arguments that are cited as leading to heresy, when one probes their basic assumptions, are themselves supportive of a deeper religious faith, more luminous and vital than was conveyed in the simple conception that prevailed before the confrontation of the challenge.

Creative evolution, which tends to be embraced by all who follow the lessons of rationality based on sense perception, at first poses a challenge to religion which stresses the all- pervading power of God. In truth one cannot overemphasize the importance of the concept [of evolution] which eliminates all deficiency in the emergence of existence. Every creature is under a sufficient providential directive from God, and the infinite power of God is sufficient to guide the destiny of all things. When this concept emerged, though its initial direction was uncertain and, when viewed on a superficial level, it seemed to remove the light of God as a factor in our thinking, in its deeper implications it was the most significant source for establishing the belief in divine providence.

The development which proceeds with such resoluteness, from below to above, from the lower creatures to the highest, without deviating from its path, points to a goal envisioned in the distant beginnings, beyond precise calculation, and it indicates an appointed goal for all existence. Thereby the greatness of God is enhanced and all the objectives of religion are more authenticated. The place of faith, of trust, of the service of God is broadened. Since everything moves toward a goal, there must be an eye that watches over everything, and since everything evolves, and there is room in man's self-perfection and his perfection of the world for ascending in stages, he fulfills in such acts the will of his Creator. The highest level of man's spiritual development thus reveals itself as more basic in the rhythm of existence, and man's ascent to higher levels thus appears preplanned. Moreover, the end of the design, and its anticipation, reveals the ultimate objective which was there from the inception, and the occasional leaps as well as the unbroken path on which it proceeded are all accounted for. "The Lord is good and upright, therefore, does He direct sinners on the way. He leads the humble with justice and reveals to the meek His way" (Ps. 25:8).

Our thinking necessarily reaches the position that the creation of this world and of the world to come, of the future of the individual and the general future of the world, were all envisioned in one perspective and all are interrelated. The belief is strengthened that this world is only an anteroom leading to the world to come, which enables us to understand a basic position of religious faith. All the moral values rise, invested with the divine significance. Moreover, we are given a basis for our hopes and an assurance that our hope will be fulfilled. The potency of anticipation is matched by the potency in the process of realization.

It thus turns out that the possibility of progress beyond the limits of natural law becomes conceivable, and it is compatible with all the elements of accepted teachings.

Orot Hakodesh II, pp. 565-566

General and Individual Providence

Philosophy was always inclined to acknowledge divine providence for life in its collective, but it is disinclined to acknowledge providence over individuals, which is especially emphasized by religion. But when traced to their sources, the two positions which seem opposed to each other tend to fuse into one central theme.

The concept based on a critical assessment will indicate that the entire notion of a detached individual cannot be truly established. The higher truth portrays the all as one entity. Whatever presents itself to us, a particular individual is, in truth, only one manifestation of the collective in its integration. And this is clear that the divine providence is focused on the higher reality, and in its essence there is no room for a concept of particularity. The general providence reaches all the particulars which we, in our dimmed vision, see as particulars and it reaches them with a more profound providential direction that we can envision [in the conventional notion of] individualized providence.

The weakness which developed in the philosophic explanation of the concept of providence was due to its assumption that in considering general providence there was also a category of particulars which were outside its concept of providence. This is invalidated and denied by the essence of a deeper, purer kind of philosophy.

This position, in its true depth, was maintained by Rabbi Levi ben Gerson [1288-1344], who tended to explain God's providence in terms of the collective, and that righteous man was spared from the sin of denying providence to particular individuals.[9]

The explanation of general providence and the knowledge of the universal in philosophy, in relation to the divine realm, is based on the profound truth that the very fragmentation into particulars is a mistaken notion, because creatures, even the highest among them, can see but dimly. The truth, however, is that all existence is one universal whole. In the divine order, where the truth is clearly known, providence and knowledge are truly universal.

Orot Hakodesh II, pp. 567-568

Progress and All-Embracing Unity

The mystical conception that each person is called on to bring up the holy sparks [the divine elements diffused in the dross of existence] goes together with the idea of the unity of existence which is increasingly winning recognition. It thus becomes the basis for defining man's moral responsibility. It becomes clear that whatever involves man, directly or indirectly, is part of his own destiny, and that everything ascends or descends with him.

On the basis of the great conception of the unity of existence there is eliminated the problem of self-love, which for some is the chief sin and for others the basis of morality. There is only the love of everything, which is in truth the higher, enlightened self-love. The fraudulent self-love, which focuses its love only on the tiny spark seen by bleary eyes and hates the more authenticated self — this is only a blindness, which is no less foolish than it is wicked.

There are many levels of bringing up sparks, and each one defines it great influence, and its cultural significance in the world. In general, every faculty that is developed and every talent that is elevated adds to the progress of existence. We live at a time when doubt and pessimism are prone to invade the heart with the suggestion that whatever man does is all vanity. We will safeguard the dignity of life generally when we make it clear that the truth about the self is its love, and that the force which presses us to life and to action and to the expression of talent is inherent in all beings, and that the all is only a more clarified version of the particular individual. All the efforts of science and morality only seek to clarify this simple proposition, which is understood by the righteous and the upright of heart, but is hidden from the eyes of the perverse and the wicked, to the degree that they are trapped by evil and folly.

It is obvious that every idealistic thought which is an improvement over the vulgarity of materialism already represents some enhancement of the light of life, and the force that serves to develop the world, to establish it and to strengthen it. All the subsidiaries to this force rise with it, and they are embarked on the path of progress, participating in the movement of all existence. Obviously every limited ideal in man's mind is only one unit in the world's stellar ensemble, and joins in constellations with other stars.

There is no doubt to the cultivated person that the higher ideal, which transcends our ideals, which is concealed and secret, is more exalted than its fractional manifestations. Its light which flashes out of the dark illumines life more than the visible minimal light which is seen in the partial ideal, whose banner people can carry with shouts of acclaim. For this reason it is incumbent on people to remain attached to the highest ideal, the source of everything, to remain linked to the holy King. "My soul said to me, The Lord is my portion, therefore will I trust in Him" (Lam. 3:24).

Faith in God, in its might and greatness, will always be the soul of all development, human and worldly. The creative speculations of all existence are songs to the King of glory. Whoever heeds their mystical discourse sings with them their song which is His song. Thus there is at work a general elevation. The ideal aspiration which is consecrated to its mission draws with it every spark, every drop that is fused with it, toward the heights. Even one who comes in touch with it only marginally, according to the measure his particular will has imbibed from the community of the upright – every such spiritual person will come to direct his feelings, his nature, his inclinations, everything, toward the divine elevation. This is the holy thought of those who come close to God, who are endowed with noble souls.

Orot Hakodesh II, pp. 586-587

The Higher Perfection

A chaotic world stands before us, as long as we have not reached the state of higher perfection of uniting all life forces and all their diverse tendencies. So long as each one exalts himself, saying, I will be sovereign, I and none other, there cannot be peace in our midst and God's name is not associated with us. God Himself is designated by the name, Peace. It is only from Him and through Him that the light of truth becomes manifest.

All life's endeavors, especially the spiritual endeavors of all thought, must be directed above all to disclose the light of the higher general harmony. This is effected not by rejecting any force, any thought, any movement, any tendency, but by including each within the vast ocean of infinite light. There all is united, all is elevated, all is exalted, all is hallowed.

Beloved are the spiritual sufferings of every one who serves the God of truth with full love, borne by his dedication to this holy, pure and noble ideal. These sufferings refine the soul, and bring it, and through it, the world as a whole, to the highest bliss, to the embrace of the holy spirit, the revelation of the highest presence of God, and to the true attachment to the light of all life. "And you who are attached to the Lord your God, all of you are alive this day" (Deut. 4:4).

Orot Hakodesh II, p. 588

The Elevation of Everything

We seek to raise everything, the whole world, all creatures, all living beings. We are under obligation to raise and refine the root of everything. We aspire to uplift, to attach [it] to the source whence the light of life emanates, the foundation of the life of all worlds.

From the permanent yearning written visibly in the depth of our souls, in the nature of our origin, in all the circumstances that pass over us, society and the individual, we draw every thought, every desire, every feeling of hope and every deeper understanding of life, all strength and all beauty.

We aspire to enhance and to elevate the divine illumination of all worlds, to strengthen and to uplift [them]. The divine ideas which have been narrowed because of the confinements of our limited existence we seek to liberate, and we extend to them aids of entry to a higher life in the realm of freedom, through the expansion of the flow of influences from our souls. They are fragmented in various directions, from the deep affirmations of faith to the shallow levels of action, from the zone of innocence and equity to the heights of criticism and scientific analysis, from the lust for life and existence to the charms of all beauty, all hope, and all freshness, from the darkest depths of a depressed spirit, of a grievous fall, to the head uplifted, soaring toward the heights. All is a robe for the eternal quest, for the farthest reaches of our eternal hills, of the Eternal One of Israel who will endure always.

Orot Hakodesh II, p. 591

Morality and the Law

In assessing the morals of character and the laws of behavior, we must say that the latter is needed for the good of society and the former for the good of the individual.

When one becomes so involved in the laws of behavior that one forgets their goal, there sometimes results a decline in the zeal for the morals of inner character. Those who are the champions of universal morality will then issue a protest that appears as a rebuke at the over-concern with the details of the law.

But the highest goal of morality is that society be well-integrated and in a state of vitality and, to assure this end, these laws are necessary and indispensable. Thus the law must always go beyond the moral norm, and the moral norm is to be its aid, to generate enthusiasm for the law with a flow of moral sensitivity.

Orot Hakodesh III, Introduction, p. 32

Morality Rooted in Faith in God

We are pervaded by a moral sensibility. We yearn to live a life of purity. Our imagination excites in our hearts a deep desire which conjures up images of the most exalted, the most beautiful, the noblest. Our inner desire is that our permanent interests be pure and holy, that our concerns be clearly focused on life's highest ideal.

All these aspirations can be realized only through our commitment in feeling and deed to the light of God, to the morality which emanates from our faith in God, which is made manifest in the Torah, in tradition, in reason, and in the intuitive sense of equity.

Morality that is rooted in a secular outlook does not run deep and does not penetrate the inwardness of the soul. Though a person is led by it to perform noble deeds, by recognizing the principles of equity as defined by logic, such pattern of behavior will be unable to withstand the stormy temptations which may assail him. Surely a morality so weakly based will be unable to offer guidance to society in all its depth and wide embrace, to penetrate the depth of the soul and to turn the heart of society and of the individual person from a heart of stone to a heart of flesh. There is no alternative to the guidance offered by a morality based on faith in God.

It is better that a person stumble on the path of his development, and seek to base his vision of the world and the moral principles of his life on the profound moral system rooted in faith in God, than minimize his stumblings and live a weak spiritual life through the shallow influence of a secular morality.

Orot Hakodesh III, pp. 1-2

The Morality of Existence

Morality is a component in the order of existence: it has its roots in the existential reality, to the extent that the universal rhythm of existence is dependent on it. This establishes a significant relationship between a person who has reached a high-level development in morals and the whole of existence. Society, which is a more significant manifestation of existence than the individual person, will reflect its own development by the state of its morality, and this will determine its relationship to the larger world.

The source of the moral dimension of existence is the divine order, which established existence and directs it toward its unfolding.

The souls endowed with a firmness of perception, penetrating to the light of morality and recognizing it as the soul of existence, which is resplendent and beloved even under the many veils of wars and horrors, when viewed superficially — these are the most precious in existence, and their significance is beyond assessment. These are the souls that enjoy the beneficence of nearness to God. Those persons endowed with them are endowed with divine strength to effect deliverance for many people. They illumine people with the light of divine justice and equity that shines with great profusion on them. They place on all society the mark of the quest for truth and the desire for life in all its purity and strength.

The moral purpose pervades the laws of the spiritual dimension of existence, in all their richness, with full force; but even in the laws of the material aspect of existence, its sparkling light is not extinguished. The bright light of the disposition which emanates from the principle of justice at the heart of all worlds is integrated with them, so that all are conditioned to release and to receive the influence which emanates from that pure morality that has its being in and has been cleansed by God.

The divine light which is robed in the great moral purpose of all existence penetrates to all forces of nature, which seemingly do their work as though without purpose, understanding and direction, and which appear to function for evil and destructive ends, as well as for everything that is moral and good. The sparks of divine light are, however, sovereign over everything and will carry what is darkness and evil to purification in the eternal purpose of the divine ideal, which abounds with justice and equity, and is the source of strength and vigor. It is this which endows life and existence with their vitality. Therefore "does His kingdom rule over all, and the design of the Lord will prevail" (Ps. 103:19, Prov. 19:21).

Orot Hakodesh III, pp. 4-5

The Unity of Morality and Wisdom

The scholastic philosophy tends to regard morality and reason as distinctive dimensions, separate from each other, which can be joined only in some technical way. It maintains that evil character traits impede clarity of perception, but that this is only a conditional impediment. At times a person engaged in the pursuit of wisdom may be able to overcome his evil disposition, though he may not be able to conquer it; his mind will still enable him to perceive lofty truths, except that he will do so with greater difficulty. As a result of this conception, which separates the basic dimensions of life, there developed subsequently a great breach between the substantive content of morality and of reasons, and of all the values of the different world outlooks.

But not so, states the Torah. The light of Israel emerges with divine and equitable force. It recognizes the all-encompassing unity. Reason and morality are not distinctive dimensions that can be joined only through outside aids. They represent one soul, one essence... "And you shall observe carefully and do them, for in this is your wisdom and your understanding" (Deut. 4:6).

And this unity of wisdom and morality indicates that every decline of morality is, in essence, also a decline of reason. Reason alone, no matter how far-reaching its development, cannot ever be self-sufficient. In the area where evil is rampant there is also folly. And the divine splendor will not reveal itself in any life that is spiritually defecting. "The divine presence does not abide in a defective place" (Zohar Bereshit 216b). Thus a penetential withdrawal from every sin is always a vital condition for the pursuit of wisdom in the conception of Judaism.

Orot Hakodesh III, pp. 19-20

The Universal Will

One cannot understand the wondrous will of man, in all the glory of its freedom, except as one spark from the immense flame of the great will which pervades all existence, a manifestation of the will of the Sovereign of all worlds, praised be He. When the [human] will is hallowed, the branch resembles its root. It draws from its source and is attached to it; it derives from its light the inspiration for its life; it is filled with it abiding and perfect abundance.

But when the private will is detached, when it is sunk in the triviality and particularity of its fragmented imprisonment, one severs himself from the source of his life, and he brings on himself futility, weakness, and darkness in the most inward dimension of his being, which is his will, his glory.

All have efforts of morality, all the spiritual manifestations in the world have as their highest objective the liberation of the will, returning it to the basic source of its life, to be planted in the house of the Lord, to bear branch and fruit, to bring forth buds and flowers and much produce, thus it will be joined in full and living unity with the universal will, which is the light of God and His glory, the soul of all existence.

Orot Hakodesh III, p. 39

The Ascent to Inner Greatness

There are great *zaddikim* [righteous persons] who are imbued with higher dispositions, who feel oppressed in their inner soul, because they do not penetrate into the inner greatness of their spirit. They do not believe with full faith in the holiness of their aspirations, and therefore they do not recognize sufficiently the enlightenment represented by the wide embrace of their thoughts. They go about bowed because of the secular burden of the world's folly, the anger of fools, which presses on them. For this reason they find themselves in a sea of spiritual afflictions. The narrow thoughts of the masses oppress their spirits, and they lack the strength to raise themselves to think their own thoughts, to affirm the firmness of their own will.

But they must finally awaken from their slumber. With all their attitude of peace and respect for the behavior of the masses, they will return to God, who always reveals Himself to them through their special windows and lattices.

If you aspire for the Torah, raise yourself and gird yourself to meet that higher sensibility which stirs inside your spirit. With all your movements, with all your talk, with all the burdens, physical and spiritual, that are placed on you, be brave and look straight toward the light that is revealed to you through the lattice.

Orot Hakodesh III, p. 122

Inner Greatness and Self-Assessment

How much good people throw away with their own hands because of low level thinking! The spirit of God is ready to seek admittance into their hearts, but they hold on to trivialities. They do not believe in the greatness of their own souls. It is neither the environment nor particular actions which form the basis for the inner treasure of the soul's happiness. It is rather the greatness of the self, the inner holiness and purity, the firmness of will and the potency of thought. The environment and the actions take a secondary place before the spiritual power when it rises to a high plane.

It is for this reason that the great *zaddikim* concern themselves primarily with inner growth. Obviously they are careful about their actions, they try to cleanse their environment. But all this is inspired by the inner thrust of the higher illumination, which streams in the soul with all its treasured splendor from the flow of the divine channel. But they will not lower themselves to be always involved with the smallness of endless particular concerns that fill the spirit when it is rising toward the heights.

In general, the real world with its exacting activities does not occupy the primary place in the eternal soul, which is manifest in its luminous grandeur in the higher souls. It is rather the august majesty of Him who is the life of the universe, in whom all is included, all the good of thought, the moral and the practical. The reach for perfection of all activities comes by itself when the great will for the divine good, in its immense purity, acts with its full strength.

But at times the *zaddikim*, in their immense greatness, will turn to confront the minutest details of their actions. After they have sated themselves with the higher delight, and their spirit, full of vitality, has been firmly established, and the yearning for the good and the pure abounding in the light of life has been vitalized in the heart, there comes a large and beautiful self-assessment concerning the most minute details of their actions. Then there also comes fright, and a spiritual and physical depression like an inundating flood and an awesome thunder; but also greatness, hope and confidence, and a desire to mend every defect, to embrace a higher penitence in which all mending is included.

When the righteous discover any defects in their actions, even when they realize that they cannot be mended, they do not on that account fall from their high station, for they realize that the reason for the inability to mend every defect is that the soul has not yet released its light. This is the true source of life's vitality in all its proliferating expressions.

They therefore seek to ascend to higher levels, in comprehension and clarity of spirit, so that the soul becomes more potent and reveals to them its manifestation. They are confident that, with the increase in the soul-force, all their strength will increase to a point where they will be able to mend all the defects, the spiritual and the practical, those immediate and those distant, whether in the relationship between man and God or those between man and man. For them there is no substantive difference between those two.

Orot Hakodesh III, pp. 123-124

The Mending and the Fall

The greatness of soul which aspires for the supreme holiness, and for great and noble vistas, must also concern itself with the perfection of one's own attributes of character and norms of behavior. At times one must descend to the depths of practical life, to probe its minutest particularities, to perfect them and direct them according to justice and law, on the basis of the Torah and the legal enactments, and to reach down to the most basic character traits, to remove from them every evil and every perversion.

If one should only focus on his [spiritual] ascent, and not on the purity and holiness of the mundane world, that higher light could be shattered and turned into a calamity. The greatness of soul could lead to a strange pride, the longing to probe the great mysteries could develop into an imagination that prides itself in the riches of its diverse pursuits. The vitality that raises the thrust of life could also stimulate fierce bodily passions: the greed for money, honor and the desire for sensual pleasures could break out of all bounds of propriety. From the highest reaches of angelic aspirations could come the most frightening fall . . .

Orot Hakodesh III, p. 125

A Higher Disposition

The righteous suffer spiritual weariness when they experience a decline of faith in themselves. They then think that they are like the masses of people. Even if they should seek to compare themselves to the most refined and learned among them, even then will they not be spared an inner decline.

They must know that the disposition of their soul is altogether different and of a higher nature, that the yearning for the light of holiness and for attachment to God is demanded of them at every moment, and that it is for them to influence all souls which are nourished from their great and all-embracing soul. Among such *zaddikim* are those for whom an inner yearning for the mystical dimension of the Torah and for contemplating holy wisdom has become a part of their nature.

And though at times they suffer a diminution of light, and though at times they fall into various lesser concerns — of them it is written, "the righteous will fall seven times and rise again" (Prov. 24:16). And after all that has happened to such a person, let him not lose faith in the essence of his holy soul. With a full mouth let him say, "Know that God has set apart the pious for Himself, the Lord will hear when I call to Him" (Ps. 4:4).

One who has been conditioned to the genuine fear of God, to piety [*hasidut*] and holiness, must know, that he cannot be at all like any other person, but he must strengthen himself to persevere in his distinctive attribute.

Orot Hakodesh III, p. 214

A Special Path

Each person must know that he is called on to serve on the basis of his own distinctive conception and feeling, according to the prompting of his own soul. In that world, which embraces endless other worlds, will he find the treasure of his life. Let him not be confused by suggestions streaming into him from alien worlds, which he does not properly comprehend, which he is not conditioned to introduce in his own pattern of life. Those worlds will find their perfection in their own place, among those especially suited to establish and perfect them. But he must concentrate on his own inner worlds which are for him full of everything and embrace everything. A person must say, "For my sake was the world created" [that is, the world to which he feels especially drawn] (Mishnah, Sanhedrin 4:5).

This humility will bring happiness to a person and will bring him to higher perfection, which stands and waits for him. By stepping in this sure way of life, in the path of the righteous especially meant for him, he will fill [himself] with the strength of life and spiritual joy. And the light of God will reveal itself on him. From the meaning in the Torah that speaks especially to him,[10] will go forth for him his strength and his light.

Orot Hakodesh III, p. 221

Engaging in the Holy Services

The *zaddik* always stands between God and the world. He links the speechless, dark world to the divine communication and light. All the impulses of a true *zaddik* are dedicated to linking all worlds with the divine. His passions, desires, inclinations, meditations, actions, conversations, customs, movements, griefs, joys, pains, delights, they are all, without exception, notes of the holy music. The divine life, when it acts within all the worlds, releases through them its voice, a mighty voice.

Numberless souls, endless treasure houses of life, which fill all existence in their endeavor to rise from the wasteland of their lowliness to the joyous heights of divine freedom, the source of delight and pleasure, they prod all the efforts of the *zaddik*, who is always engaged in the holy service. All his life is dedicated to God.

A great truth lives in his heart. A living and conquering strength is astir in his soul. He feels his greatness, and the great splendor of his desire, but to the measure of his greatness is his humility. He sees himself as less than a tiny spark of light against the vastness of all the worlds, against the grand splendor of the living God which is always striving in his spirit.

An endless love for God is his supreme joy. An inner love for all creation, a faithful friendship for all people, a dedicated love on all levels — to the family, to friends, to the nation, to the human being, to animal and plant, to everything that has being — is imprinted in the fullness of its equity in the wishes of his heart. Heavenly strength and immense respect fill all his thoughts. His speech is like a river of delight, full of life and creativity. He says and he does, he ordains and he fulfills. "You will decree a thing and it will be established, and light will shine upon your ways" (Job 22:28).

Orot Hakodesh III, pp. 229-230

The Higher Silence

Silence will be sought from the depths of a soul which is regularly devoted to higher contemplation that transcends man's capacity for verbal articulation. When a person with a silent soul pursues his exalted silence, many worlds are fashioned, noble songs rise with their holy tribute [to God], and a higher force with holy delight is raised over all spheres of the spiritual.

Silence, which abounds with life, gathers within itself the majesty of wisdom. The spiritual and practical worlds, with all their well-defined particularities, in their most precise formulations, reveal themselves with a mighty force to the wise person of higher stature whose vineyard is fenced in with a fence of silence, which is appropriate for the wise. This is the higher silence that rises above the wind, the tumult, the fire. "It is a still small voice" (I Kings 19:12), and "behold God is passing" (ibid., 19:11).

Orot Hakodesh III, p. 274

The Supreme *Zaddik*

The *zaddik* who has reached true holiness unites within himself all opposites and all the good which is diffused in the world. When these are viewed from a lowly perspective, each appears to negate the other. When he encounters them together, on one context, the zaddik unites them with his great and widely embracing power. For he always ascends in his thought and will to the higher realm of the spiritual where there is no confinement and everything can enter there. Automatically then all the good can be assembled together. He acts with his higher power so that the good which is diffused among all Jews individually, and in all the world, and in all worlds, shall be assembled together.

The *zaddik* of the highest stature embraces the most universal domain. There is no sternness in him, but he abounds with kindness and great mercy, and he is truly desirous of the good of all. He loves to see the side of innocence in all people, and he hates to see them in the wrong and to regard them as guilty.

But the world cannot tolerate such a degree of mercy and every higher *zaddik* must robe his higher righteousness in many robes. After these reduce the light, then it becomes possible for people to benefit from him.

The longing of the true *zaddik* is to be truly linked with God, which transcends all thought and all limited and confined aspiration. When he afflicts his soul by denying it this mighty longing through involvment in limited affairs which, from his perspective are prosaic, his affliction is felt in many worlds. Endless numbers of souls are pained by his inner pain.

Later, when the gates of light are opened, and he returns with penitence inspired by love, and the joyous light of the holy spirit sparkles and shines on him, then many souls are raised up with joyous acclaim, with eternal celebration, from their depths, and many worlds, with the heaven and the earth that exist in them, are filled with strength and gladness. "When the righteous are enhanced, the people rejoice" (Prov. 29:2).

Orot Hakodesh III, pp. 307-308

The Desire for the Good Deed and Its Value

When we rise above confined thinking, the significance of the good is enhanced to a point of stirring a desire like a mighty flame in the soul. The spiritual unity of existence, when it is perceived with a high-level inner sensibility, draws the self toward the good, toward good deeds and beautiful feelings, which in themselves spell delight in all worlds. The realization grows in the person so that by cultivating good deeds, good thoughts, and good speech, he thereby makes all existence more agreeable, he strengthens humankind and raises it toward the heavens.

The person knows that when the influence of the holy spirit acts on his soul, that whenever he raises himself through good deeds, through a higher stirring of desire for the divine, for wisdom, justice, beauty and equity, he thereby perfects the spiritual disposition of all existence.

All people become better in the privacy of their hearts through the improvement toward a higher way of life of one of them. The grief of many depressed people becomes mitigated, and is touched with some comfort, when one soul is stirred forcefully by divine comfort. Even wild beasts and all destructive creatures become more gentle.[11] Their poison is softened somewhat through the general swaying of a soul that rejoices in the Lord.

And good people grow in their goodness, and their rejoicing in the good and the equitable increases. All the higher worlds, the angels on high, are stirred to an agreeable, holy song, and they rise with beautiful and graceful singing, and the heavenly hosts are adorned with light.

After the tumult of all kinds of sophistication which have wrought the various forms of destructiveness, and after all the deepest probing in mystical teachings, we come to the conclusion that man's labors should be carefully directed to increase good in the world, between man and man, and among all beings on the face of the earth. And this thought should be pursued with many clarifying expositions, which endow those who engage in it a life of enlightenment. In the end, a good such as this gained by one individual is destined to touch the entire populace, to bestir each one toward merit, to the extent of his capacity. Then all existence will automatically become more exalted and enobled.

Igrot Hakodesh III, pp. 314-315

Good to All

When the desire to be good to all strengthens itself in a person, he should know that an illumination from a higher realm has come to him. Fortunate is he if he prepares an appropriate place in his heart, his mind, the work of his hands, and all his feelings, to welcome this exalted light, which is greater and higher than all the cherished things of the world.[12] Let him hold on to it and not let it go.

And all the impediments and obstructions, the physical and the spiritual, that might interfere with welcoming this holy thought into his inner being should not hold him back. He should wage war against all of them and hold fast to his resoluteness. Let him raise his vision toward the transcendent realm, to emulate the attributes of God who is "good to all, and whose mercy is over all His works" (Ps. 145:9).

Orot Hakodesh III, p. 316

Kindness and Inner Strength

It is necessary to refine the attribute of kindness so that it shall not remain merely a softness of heart, but that it be defined according to the attribute of reason.

In order to establish the enlightened dimension of the world, it is necessary that every spiritual person be strengthened in his position and not be swept along by the masses. Toward this end, there is need for sensitive knowledge on the part of the soul that thinks, that reflects, that envisions holy images, which is the goal of man's creation. One cannot elevate the world and bestow good on the mass of humanity without an awareness of the superiority of sensitive people, who have mastered wisdom and the knowledge of the Torah and morality. To be aware of this one must at times probe deeply into the evil traits of the multitude, their vulgarity. But this probing is not meant to cool the general love; it is rather meant to stimulate the spiritual potency, the force that works to elevate the world, which is the holy of holies, and its efforts are dedicated to inspire life and blessing and good in the whole world.

When one loves one's people in its total embrace, in all its forces, when one loves humanity in all its societal constituencies, when one loves all creatures, in their diverse forms of being, one must always be careful not to be caught up in the stream of low level [thinking] which is characteristic of the general populace. The whole objective of the higher forces, the stimulation of knowledge, morality, equity, and poetry is to elevate all, to define well the goal of life, its beauty and its holiness.

The source of kindness must therefore be established with inner firmness, and with an inner anger over the spiritual failure of the world. Obviously, this must also be directed at oneself. One must concentrate on the inner stirrings of the heart and act to improve one's disposition. Then will the words and expressions come forth, and paralleling them the actions and the relationships, and all the universal and personal values, in their fullness and goodness, in an appropriate manner.

In the end, the whole world is sustained through these heroes, who love the good and hate evil. They are the great critics and the mighty apologists who speak with an inner love. At times, from the lattice of their windows there breaks through a light of friendship for all, for all individuals, for all the masses, for the entire people, for all creation.

Orot Hakodesh III, pp. 334-335

NOTES
The Basis of All Thoughts

1. Rabbi Kook apparently alludes here to the Cabbalistic concept of the *sefirot* (divine emanations), that the *sefira* of *hokhman* (wisdom) is the primary emanation of divine potency which engenders the creative order.

2. The verse in Ecclesiastes is: "The excellence of knowledge is that wisdom preserves the life of the one who possesses it."

The Hidden Spring

3. The term used is *asameba* which is usually translated as "barns", but its original meaning is "store-houses", which were often underground.

Silence and Attention

4. The usual translation of this line is "day unto day utters speech", which seems justified by the context.

The Question About the Origin of Certainty

5. This is the mystery of the unfolding of ideas, when we are invited to see and to understand what was not communicated to us from the outside, but is generated in a spontaneous process of inner enlightenment.

The Unity of the Human Family

6. Rabbi Kook adds here the phrase *al afar ve-efer*, which may be rendered "considering that we are creatures of dust and ashes". The entire statement is a slight adaptation from Job 34:6.

The Basic Changes in the New Thought

7. The terms used by Rabbi Kook are *shekitah rekatnut* which mean literally "quiet and smallness".

8. The allusion here is to the Biblical account of creation.

General and Individual Providence

9. For a general discussion of the philosophic position on divine providence, see Isaac Husik, *A History of Medieval Jewish Philosophy* (New York: Macmillan, 1930), pp. 290ff; 375f, 393f; 421. For the specific views of Levi ben Gerson (Gersonides), see pp. 340ff.

A Special Path

10. Rabbi Kook uses the term *ot* which literally means "letter" or "sign". Mystics believed that the soul of every Jew has a special affinity with a particular letter in the Torah ("Bene Yehoshua", a commentary on the Talmud Kiddushin 30a). As Gerschom Sholem explained it, mystics believed that "the number of possible readings in the Torah was equal to the number of the 600,000 children of Israel who were present at Mt. Sinai — in other words, that each single Jew approached the Torah by a path that he alone could follow" (*Kabbalah*, New York, 1974, p. 172). The most general formulation of this concept appears in the Midrash Exodus Rabbah, ch. 5, that God's voice addressed itself to each person according to his reception capacities.

The Desire for the Good Deed and its Value

11. Joy Adamson has reported in her writings how a lion was tamed under the influence

of humane treatment in her home. Isaiah in ch. 11:6-10 describes the humanization of wild animals in the messianic age.

Good to All

12.   The term used is *nikhbade eretz,* which means literally "the honored ones of the earth", a phrase that appears in Isaiah 23:9.

V.

Aphorisms

Certainty of conviction alone, with all its seeming greatness, holiness and beauty, cannot be the basis of the spiritual life, unless the convictions believed in are of a significant nature. At times doubt may be far more important than certainty if based on a lower conceptual level.

Orot Hakodesh I, p. 219

It is necessary to seek spiritual harmony, which means that reason shall exert a direct influence on feeling, and feeling on the imagination, and the imagination on action. If there should be a contradiction between these elements, then destructive forces will have room to assert themselves.

Orot Hakodesh I, p. 249

A person cannot live by reason alone, nor by feeling alone. There must always be a synthesis of reason and feeling. If a person should immerse himself in feeling alone he will fall into the depths of folly, which bring about every weakness and sin. Only an equitable balance between the two will be his full deliverance.

Orot Hakodesh I, p. 257

When the higher holiness is activated in an individual or a society, it relates them to the higher will which is active in all existence. The private will is then no longer confined and confused, imprisoned in the narrow conceptions and aspirations based on the realities of limited existence.

Orot Hakodesh II, p. 298

As a fundamental principle we must declare that a life of idealism has its validity only if it is associated with a conception of the divine on its highest level.

The morality which is part of an atheistic outlook is devoid of significance, because atheism itself is based on a denial of the basic principles of justice and morality. In the case of atheists who are moral, their morality derives not from their atheism, but from the action of God which is hidden deep in their nature, of which they are unconscious.

Orot Hakodesh III, Introduction, p. 24

Holiness does not battle against self-love, which is deeply rooted in every loving being. But it places man on so high a level that the more he loves himself the more will the good within him reach out to embrace all, the whole environment, the whole world, all existence.

The substantive good in morality is already included in holiness in a more celebrated and edifying form.

Orot Hakodesh III, p. 13

The fear of God, the discipline of a higher religious faith, must be cleansed of all moral and scientific dross which man, and every narrow ideology, introduces into it.

The greatest cleansing is attained when a person realizes that there are no base elements; that everything is part of life and is good; that it is only necessary to assign to each its proper value. The functional element must be assessed in its proper measure in all areas, whether material or spiritual. It is the task of the scientific element to know how to assess everything. "Then there will be no adversary and no evil mishap" (I Kings 5:18).

Orot Hakodesh III, Introduction, p. 26

At times the will is weak because of a weakness of the body, and the spiritual dimension cannot be well-established because of a lack of a physical base. The physical neglect adds to this affliction, while a healthy body enables the spiritual light to come forth, and it strengthens it.

Orot Hakodesh III, p. 79

It is impossible to know the true nature of any person, not even of oneself, and certainly not of another, not of an individual and surely not of a people... We are engaged in conjectures, in approximations, judging on the basis of outer behavior which, for the most part, is concealed to us, especially the causes behind the acts... We must conclude that our knowledge in this area is feebly based, and "only God can judge" (Deut. 1:17).

Orot Hakodesh III, p. 119

We must always battle against darkness to liberate ourselves from domination by the power of lust, the blind power of evil that steps, skips, flies and hovers over the world. With all its power it spreads its domain of darkness over the person and all his faculties... It obstructs every enlightenment, from the higher illumination of holiness, impeding its spread and entry into the life of the person and the world.

Orot Hakodesh III, p. 132

When simple, common sense is at work in a person, it is incumbent on him to battle against the forces of dark chaotic lust which always seek to destroy the edifice of reason and equity, at the inception of their formation. Especially does it place its obstruction against the practical application of the rational concepts. There it deposits its poison, the germs of the snake.

Orot Hakodesh III, p. 133

Every philosophy which renounces the perfection of the physical world and the proper order of society, and floats in the spiritual realm alone, priding itself only in the perfection of souls and their success, is based on a falsehood that has no link with reality. And every philosophy which is unconcerned with the elevation toward eternal ideals, and places its attention only on the mending of material existence, even if it includes ethical programs and efforts toward justice and equity — will, in the end, be corrupted because of its smallness of vision and because of the filth with which material existence is afflicted by nature when it is detached from the basis of eternal life and the aspiration for it.

Orot Hakodesh III, p. 180

One who is prepared to experience the true fear of God, toward saintliness and holiness, must know that he cannot be like other people, but must strengthen himself to follow his distinctive path.

Orot Hakodesh III, p. 214

One who needs to draw nourishment from a higher source cannot draw it from a lower source. The simple morality will not be adequate for those who are prepared for higher contemplation. They must concern themselves with reflection and a style of life appropriate for their status. They must bring their nourishment from afar — the small place nearby will not afford them spiritual sustenance.

Orot Hakodesh III, p. 220

Though the Torah and the commandments refine one's character traits, we, nevertheless, cannot depend on this alone. It is essential to make special efforts to refine one's character traits and, particularly, to perfect one's moral state.

Zaddikum who never stop in their spiritual progress, but go from strength to greater strength, always pursue a discipline of penitence. One of its major aspects is the refinement or clarification of their moral traits.

Orot Hakodesh III, p. 233

The defects in a person's inner life, which manifest themselves in evil character traits — such as shrewdness, lower passions, anger and hostility — reflect the general defects of the world.

Orot Hakodesh III, p. 234

The righteous are always in a state of war against the elements of evil which are an admixture with the good that is in them.

Orot Hakodesh III, p. 241

When one experiences distress because of his wrong- doings, his evil character traits, his lack of attention to the study of Torah, and the alienation from God — this distress is the purging fire that comes to cleanse the soul, and through it one can anticipate deliverance.

Orot Hakodesh III, p. 249

When a person feels that he has suffered great spiritual decline, let him know that the time has come for him to build a new edifice, nobler and more exalted, more enduring and renowned than the previous one. Let him strengthen himself in perfecting his ways and his action in a proper order, with firmness of heart, with purity of desire, with strength and inner joy.

Orot Hakodesh III, p. 251

When a person feels his decline because of a weakening of spirit and moral lapses, let him resolve that in the lower state he can find previous jewels, and then he will return and rise again, and renew his spirit with strength and peace.

Orot Hakodesh III, p. 252

As a person's moral sensitivity is sharpened he sees his barrenness, and at times he becomes very bitter. However, every person of upright heart should be wise enough to accept with love this condition which serves to refine him and raise him to precious qualities and equitable inclinations.

Orot Hakodesh III, p. 254

When a great person becomes overly punctilious with details, whether in study or behavior, he is diminished and his status is lessened. It is for him to repent out of love, with greatness of soul, and to link the focus of his soul with great and exalted concerns. Obviously he must not disparage any detail, and should always strive to enhance his commitment to holiness in his practical affairs as well . . .

Unless he is enlightened to find delight and joy through contemplation of universal themes to eliminate the panic over particulars which are endless, he will be depressed by his anxiety and he will be impeded from the study of Torah, and prayer, and the contemplation of higher concepts, which is the most precious of all.

Orot Hakodesh III, p. 259

When one is always involved with the state of his own soul, without rising to the broad domain of free, universal, rational thinking, his perceptive powers will diminish, his character traits will decline, and his conceptions will be trivialized.

Orot Hakodesh III, p. 261

Silence is demanded by the deep recesses of the soul, where higher meditations, which transcend man's capacity of articulation, are a fixed pursuit of his inner being.

Orot Hakodesh III, p. 274

When one focuses truly on the good element in each person, people will come to love him with an inner love, and he will not need to stoop to any kind of flattery. His concern with the good, which he will always encounter, will conceal from him all evil. "A prudent man conceals shame" (Prov. 12:16).

Orot Hakodesh III, p. 324

If there should ever appear to us a contradiction between one truth and another, we must have a mediating principle, and that is to reach out for some new principle.

There is a limit to freedom of thought, but it is difficult to define the limitation, and it stands to reason that the limitation cannot be the same in all societies.

Igrot I, Letter 20

The outer expression of the love of the Lord God of Israel are less significant, less potent and luminous than the inner feeling, hidden within us.

Each person, of whatever people he may be, will embrace in himself the high as well as the low points of his people, for no person can liberate himself fully from the pattern of his people's way of life.

Our speculations, the pure philosophic inquiry, has only one objective — to safeguard our concepts from the ethical ideational dross that attach itself to them.

All the spiritually damaging ideologies that have come to the world have affected only the external forms in which the higher and absolute spiritual truth robes itself.

If a person should also wish to construct the general cosmological edifice, without the addition of a spiritual influence, and only on the basis of materialistic determinants, we shall be undisturbed and regard this childish construction as one which fashions the outer shell of life while not knowing how to build life itself.

The world will embrace the light of the God of Israel, not under the pressure of a dry logical necessity or as a strategy for coping with the violence of robbery and murder, but because the belief in God corresponds to the diverse realities embodied in the whole of existence.

We do not base our faith in God on an inference from the existence of the world, or the character of the world, but on inner sensibility, on our disposition for the divine.

We are not troubled if some tendency to social justice can be established without any reference to the divine, because we know that the aspiration for justice itself, in any form, represents the most enlightened form of a divine influence.

Man will not always remain in his low state. He will also discard the idols of love as he discarded the idols of fear, and he will recognize the general principle of the higher, all embracing love, which the people of Israel have proclaimed: the love of God.

Igrot I, Letter 44

We must never forget that in every conflict of opinions, after the furor passes, critics find that there are light and shadows on each side . . . Though we are resolute in fighting for the things that are close to our spirit, we must not be altogether committed to our feelings but realize that there is also ample room for the feelings that differ from ours. God of the spirits of all flesh made everything good in its time.

Igrot I, Letter 314

The sublime goal that divine justice shall prevail among us and in the world — this is our mighty over-all inner aspiration . . . All the religious acts, all the *mitzvot*, all the customs are only so many vessels, each of which bears some fragment of light from this mighty higher light. To the extent that the vessels are sturdy and pure and directed toward their objective . . . will the light be enhanced. And as knowledge, reason, and thought expand, the dew of life will fructify and vitalize every yearning heart and every thirsty soul.

Eder Hayakar, p. 124

Our whole way of life, proclaimed by the Torah of the living God, both its study and its observance... have but one objective, to reveal the enlightenment that comes from the aspiration after divine ideals.

Eder Hayakar, p. 137

In every subject of study there is a spark of the general light which is manifest in all existence. The significance of the spark is its relation to the whole, though it is in a state of great concealment, and only its particular dimension comes to expression. One who studies the Torah for its own sake focuses on the anticipation that he will glimpse the universal. The universal light will reveal itself to him and he will reach great heights in his understanding.

Orot Ha-Torah 3:7

As we are awed by the immensity of creation, by the vast realms of space where wondrous stars shine, by the mighty forces operative all through nature, so are we awed when we contemplate the wonder of creation in the realm of smallness, the tiny organs of the smallest of creatures, the delicate substances, and the precision of forces which act in the most distant places. Through knowing both dimensions, the vast and the tiny, will the perception of creation be properly registered in the human heart.

Orot Ha-Torah 3:8

At times a person cannot study because he is in a state where the general illumination which transcends verbalization shines on him, and he cannot confine himself to the study of a text. On embracing this illumination in holiness and humility, he will merit to study later with good joy and clear understanding.

Orot Ha-Torah 5:3

The world must recognize that it is not by one utterance, by the affirmation of one formula of faith that man can fly to paradise, while leaving untouched all the evil, the murder and the abomination imbedded in his spirit, in his flesh and blood, believing that he has no need of purification, of study, of concentration and progress . . .

The desire to establish one nation in the world to serve as a kingdom of priests and a holy nation was meant as a model of the way the divine light penetrates the life of nations. It is only when this people will exist strong and free, when it returns to its land and to its happiness, will it demonstrate to all that the ideal of holiness is not an extraneous ideal which can be grasped by soiled hands, but is a distinction which is achieved by fearsome exertion, with continued self-sacrifice.

Orot, pp. 32-33

When life is in bloom, when it manifests creativity and the knowledge of the sciences, opinions cannot then be established according to only one point of view.

Orot, p. 52

God was charitable toward His world by not endowing all talents in one place not with one, person, nor with one nation, nor with one country, nor with one generation, nor with one world. But the talents are diffused. The necessity of seeking perfection, which is the most important force that acts on us, causes us to seek an exalted unity that is bound to come for the world. In that day will the Lord be one, and His name one.

The disposition to universality always fills the hearts of the refined spirits of the human race. They therefore feel as though they are choking if they should be confined within the sphere of their own nation solely.,

Orot, p. 152

It would have been appropriate for humanity to be united into one family, and then there would have come an end to the controversies and other evil conditions which result from the division of nations within specified boundaries. But the world needs a program of refinement, through which humanity is perfected by the development of the riches in the distinctive characteristics of each nation.

Orot, p. 156

The most destructive thoughts are the unripe forms of the most exalted thoughts, but they reach us without their full development, that is, they do not come with an indication of their significance or of the circumstances for their application.

Maamore Ha-Rayah, p. 40

In general the spiritual life does not assert its authority except through the challenge of heresy to all its restraints, inspired by inner conviction and feeling, free of all timidity and weakness. Out of this challenge is engendered the light of pure faith that is the mightiest force in the world.

The need to speculate about God marks a great decline, and it is needed by man as a therapy. Atheism is a negative setting for the higher ascent, when there will be no need to speculate about the divine for life itself will be a manifestation of the light of God.

Who can know the deep anguish of a heart of wide aspiration, of a soul that aspires for the widest horizons, when it is imprisoned in a narrow confinement? It is like an eagle enclosed in a chicken coop.

The light of God does not reveal itself except when thought is free. Only lusts for the vulgar which produce timidity in those that become addicted to them will rob the human heart of freedom of thought.

The slogan "freedom of thought" is distorted when it is invoked by those who are enslaved to some ideology n their battle against those enslaved to other ideologies.

When mankind is in a condition of spiritual weakness then its rationale for freedom of thought is that all ideologies are in a state of doubt. But mankind will soon recognize that doubt is only a weakness, that it erodes all the firmness and zeal necessary for creativity and constructive work, and it will begin to have freedom of thought on the firmness of a principle.

When the agitation of heresy focuses on some moral goal t is veritably a divine mandate. Morality and its expansion, the enhancement of life, its delights, its aspirations — God summons us to pursue these more so than other goals which remain in the heart but offer nothing for the practical improvement in the ways of life.

But people are unfortunate as long as they do not realize that every effort for moral enhancement, and the quest for the good, constitutes what God demands of us. And they are due for a great enlightenment when this secret is revealed to them.

Maamore Ha-Rayah, pp. 40-41

At times we see that people of deep spirituality, the *zaddikim* of the generation, are inclined to asceticism and to solitude, and that they show disdain for material existence. But this is an indication that the world has become corrupt, and in order to heal themselves of this corruption they are using radical medication. The healthy person has no need of these at all.

Maamore Ha-Rayah, p. 235

The nationalist goal of the people of Israel is distinctive in its hope... which is focused not on itself but on the general good... This cannot be attained except through the perfection of the world under the kingdom of the Almighty.

All nations have a mission which becomes a specialized pursuit necessary for the perfection of the world. This is the unique role of each nation, according to its disposition, its background, its philosophy and its historic potentialities, and it bequeathes to mankind all its particular achievements...

There are many particular paths in different specializations of endeavor which all nations must pursue together in the service of humanity, each according to the bent of its own nature. But what is distinctive in the wisdom of Israel, the wisdom of the Torah, is the clarification how all the labors of all the nations in the field of culture [wisdom] join toward one objective: to know God, and to develop paths toward universal justice, which will help to bring peace to the world.

Olat Rayah I, pp. 386-387

Literature, painting and sculpture are due to express all the spiritual concepts which are imbedded in the human psyche, and as long as any phase hidden in the psyche has not been expressed, there is an obligation for the work of art to express it.

Olat Rayah II, p. 3

There is no falsehood which does not contain some truth. If we do not clarify that truth, and declare it openly, and establish it in proper form, the power of falsehood will spread over everything.

Hazon Ha-Geulah, p. 108

The wise person yearns for the inner essence of the good. He recognizes it and knows that it alone is truly good. But the fool seeks the outer form of the good, according to his shallow judgment. He does not recognize the greater good which is in the inner dimension, and for this reason he is short of the perception to recognize the defect that marks the outer form of the good.

A person should always strive to know the truth about himself, and he should always focus his concern on what he lacks toward his perfection. He will never think that he has what he does not have. His awareness of what he lacks toward his perfection should not inhibit him from rejoicing in whatever little he does have.

Musaz Avikha, pp. 67-72

There are many causes for melancholy. One of them is the inclination to pursue vulgar pleasures which drag the soul to a domain of darkness. It is in order to turn this immense grief to joy. For as the soul rises from the bonds of its exile which held sway over it, a great current of joy rises from the lower to the higher domain, and a richer treasure of spirituality emerges.

Arpele Tohar, p. 2

The more the world becomes perfected, the more its constituent elements are seen as embraced in a comprehensive unity, and its nature as one organism becomes more clearly discernible. The higher unity is the correlation of human reason and will with the whole cosmos, in its wholeness and in its particularities.

Arpele Tohar, p. 10

A person in whom the light of religious faith is manifest in its purity loves all people without any exception, and all his efforts are directed at elevating and perfecting them. The ways of their perfection are pervaded with the values of morality and equity, commensurate with the state of religious faith embraced in his heart.

Arpele Tohar 13

Life surrounds us on all sides. When we rise, everything rises with us; when we decline, everything declines with us. When our own essence is elevated, then all our life's expressions, wherever they be, are elevated. And the more original our elevation is, the more it is broadened to affect our most distant relationships. The ascent toward godliness, to the extent that it becomes manifest, raises with it whatever is related to us, no matter how distant the relationship.

Arpele Tohar, pp. 21-22

Without the service of God one cannot exist. The human spirit which aspires for greatness, for the embrace of the universal, will be depressed when it is imprisoned in smallness, in spiritual confinement. The entire rhythm of existence will suffer from the shrinking of this mighty, universal spirit of any person. There is no other road toward the light, except through the service of God, the eternal God, the God of life, holy and blessed is His name.

Arpele Tohar, p. 24

The knowledge of God must necessarily take flight from the life that is defective, fragmented, and deficient, toward a life expressive of and abounding in perfection — even in this world. One spark of the divine light that shines in any one heart can overcome endless centers of darkness.

Fools who are without understanding say that the knowledge of God diminishes the quality of life. They stand outside. A people is yet to arise in this world imbued with the knowledge that life finds its perfection in the light of God.

Arpele Tohar, p. 25

The feeling of love must develop in all its dimensions, to embrace life's treasures, the intellectual, the emotional and the imaginative. Then will this love rise to its spiritual plane, which bears God's name. Similarly the aesthetic sense must develop well so that the soul will be able to envision the spiritual dimension of beauty which will invest it with its highest significance. The literary creations of our generation, and their expanded interest in the beautiful, though they are oriented toward the secular, at times even descending toward the profane — they are all preparatory stages for the higher purification in the majesty of the spiritual that will yet emerge in the world.

Arpele Tohar, p. 30

The basic cause for spiritual weariness and the lack of inner contentment which develops in a person is his dissociation from the concerns to which he is suited by the nature of his inner disposition.

Arpele Tohar, p. 32

From the perspective of the higher divine truth there is no difference whatever between conventional religion and atheism. Neither of them offers the truth. From our point of view religion seems closer to the truth and atheism to falsehood, and automatically we see good and evil as deriving from these two opposites . . . The truth emanates from religion and it thus appears as the source of the good, and falsehood from atheism and it appears as the source of evil. But before the light of the *En Sof* [the Infinite] they are all alike. In atheism, too, is manifest a life-force in which is robed a higher illumination. It is for this reason that heroes of the spirit draw from it many good elements [sparks], and they transform its bitterness to sweetness.

Arpele Tohar, p. 32

A great soul aspires to embrace all the gradations of existence, to reach out to the very last stratum of being, in order to bring vitality to all, to draw all near to itself, to elevate all. To the extent of its outreach, it raises its own stature, and is enhanced. It reaches higher levels. Great and mighty concepts of compassion appear before it. It sets straight all paths. But then little people come and hinder its outreach and automatically shrink its stature, and it is aggrieved, cramped, and depressed. At times it conforms to the will of those who impede it. It is bowed down in a narrow sphere, but its eyes are raised with the desire to bring light to all, even to those who hinder it, to all manifestation of life, those above and those below it. It is filled with hope for the wide horizons of the world, for an inheritance without confinement, the inheritance of Jacob, the high places of the earth.

Arpele Tohar, p. 33

We experience spiritual speechlessness. Alas, how much there is for us to say! How deeply we feel the stirrings of righteousness and wisdom within our souls! But how shall we reveal it, how shall we explain it, how shall we bring it to utterance? How shall we formulate even some small dimension of this majestic splendor? The channels of communication are closed to us. We begin with prayer; we petition, we raise our voices in song and praise, and we attempt to formulate analogies and concepts. We stand watch at the doors. Perhaps a tiny crack will open up and we shall be filled with speech and torrents of light with precious delicacies of thought will stream forth.

Arpele Tohar, p. 40

Those who contemplate higher themes experience true freedom, and they cannot bear any kind of servitude. Every form of servitude is a subjugation to a creature of flesh and blood. Even the submission to the disciplines of religion, as prevalent among people, is a servitude to mortals, because the sovereignty of God itself descended from its grandeur and was narrowed as mortals dimmed its light.

The aspiration for absolute freedom is an expression of high-level penitence, and from its supernal height it sets in order and builds all the lower worlds, turning them toward higher glory. It reinvests them with all the attributes and dispositions toward perfection and equity, of Torah and the commandments, which develop progressively. They rise as an expression of higher freedom, which is adorned with discernment that emanates from God.

Arpele Tohar, p. 40

The truly great people feel an inner resistance to scholarship, for thought is all astir in them and radiates from their spirit. They must always reach down deeply into their own inner being. Study is for them only an aid, a peripheral pursuit. What is primary for their perfection is their own Torah, and in their own Torah they meditate day and night.[1] At times a person does not appreciate his own worth, and he turns his back on his own Torah and he seeks to become a scholar. He is moved by habit or by some teaching such as the adage: study, and you will be rewarded. Then there begins his decline, darkening the world of these great weaklings.

Arpele Tohar, p. 43

When religion is on a low level, it is thought that whatever people do to establish their position — battling against the evils of the world to acquire knowledge, strength, beauty, order, rationality — that these are outside the divine concerns. For this reason many people are disdainful of all worldly progress. They hate culture, the sciences, the political activities of the Jewish people, and the nations. But this is all erroneous, and a deficiency in religion. The refined position discerns the divine presence in everything that perfects life, that of the individual or of society, the spiritual or the physical.

Arpele Tohar, p. 47

There is no reason to be confused when confronting great contradictions, as they are commonly defined. What many envision as conceptual separateness and contradiction is only the result of their narrow mentalities and outlooks. They see no more than a tiny aspect of the higher perfection, and even this only in a distorted form. The masters of clear thinking reach out with their thought into various realms and broad horizons, and they embrace the treasures of the good in all places and unite all in the togetherness of a comprehensive whole.

Arpele Tohar, p. 66

NOTES

1. Rabbi Kook makes the latter statement by quoting Ps. 1:2, "and in his Torah he meditates day and night", but here *his* refers to God.

General Index

Cited Passages

Tantakh

Genesis
1:27 32
5:1,2 48
15:6 65
49:26 31
Exodus
4:22 50
31:14 123
33:16 70
Leviticus
10:1,2 146
11-13 53
18:5 123
19:18 48
Numbers
23:23 72
Deuteronomy
1:17 195
4:4 177
4:6,8 50
4:6 181
27:9 28
28:18 151
29:28 129
32:3 50
Samuel
I 2:6-7 166
I 12:22 56
II 1:18 125
II 23:4 89
Kings
I 5:18 194
I 19:11 187
I 19:12 187
Isaiah
2:3 56
2:7 27
2:17 34
6:3 29
9:5 149
11:6-10 192
23:9 192
26:2 26
27:12 69
29:18 137

33:6 107
40:8 35
42:21 56
49:3 49
49:6 32
52:15 158
60:1 56
60:19 72
60:21 72
Jeremiah
13:17 46
30:17 113
31:7 133
31:15,16 133
Hosea
4:1 34
9:10 50
14:10 7, 63
Malachi
1:15 134
Chronicles
I 16:22 120
I 16:27 98
Psalms
1:2 210
4:4 185
9:11 56
16:5 133
19:3 152
25:8 174
29:4 39
50:20 94
66:7 46
89:9 169
93:5 165
96:3 122
103:19 180
103:20 163
104:31 160
117 70, 137
118:5 24
119:74 8, 143
119:76 23, 24
119:174 63
139:12 89
139:15 166
141:5 92

145:9 189
Job
2:4 88
5:16 34
14:19 56
21:15 94
22:28 186
28:12,23 159
34:6 191
Proverbs
8:34-35 36
12:16 199
16:4 97
19:21 180
20:12 154
24:16 185
25:25 149
29:2 188
29:3 28
Song of Songs
2:16 155
Ecclesiastes
7:12 150
8:5 34
Lamentations
3:24 176
Daniel
12:7 72

Mishnah

Avot
1:6 130
2:12 68
2:15 130
4:1 150
6:1 56, 105
Sanhedrin
4:5 185

Talmud Yerushalmi

Sanhedrin
7:12 108
Shabbat
1:3 51

Talmud Bavli

Berachot
40a 60, 125
63b 28
Eruvin
13b 46
64a 28
Yoma
69b 71
85b 123
86a 49
Rosh Hashanah
30a 113
Hagigah
3b 46
5b 46
9b 60
12b 33
Gittin
43a 105
Kiddushin
30a 191
57a 67
Baba Kamma
38a 70
Baba Metzia
84b 68
Sanhedrin
21b 125
45a 72
92b 56
Nidda
30b 38
61b 146

Midrash

Genesis Rabbah
44:1 48
Exodus Rabbah
ch. 5 191
ch. 41 65
Leviticus Rabbah
10:1,2 146
Midrash Tanhuma
Pekude 7 94
Tanna Debe Eliahu
ch. 25 72

Other Works

Guide to the Perplexed
II:45 52

Hovot Halevavot
intro. 56

Zohar
I 216b 181
I 13a 72
I 37a 89
II 22a 31
II 109b 31

Tikkune Zohar
30 126
70 59

Netivot Olam
Netiv Ha-Torah, ch. 14 62

Cited passages from Rav Kook's writings

About the Editor and Translator

Ben Zion Bokser was born in Lubomb, Poland in 1907, and raised in the United States. He first encountered Rabbi Abraham Isaac Kook as a high school student when he was deeply moved by Rav Kook's address to Yeshivat Rabbeinu Yitzchak Elchanan.

Throughout a career that included a half century as spiritual leader of the Forest Hills Jewish Center, Rabbi Bokser turned again and again to Rav Kook, as a beacon for his own spiritual path and writings, and in his role as a translator and popularizer of the work of the rabbi he considered his inspiration.

Rabbi Bokser's articles in *Tradition* and *Judaism* helped introduce Rav Kook to an American audience in the 1960's. These were followed by Rabbi Bokser's translations of *The Lights of Penitence, The Moral Principles, Lights of Holiness, Essays, Letters, and Poems* as part of the Paulist Press "Classics of Western Spirituality" series.

This, his second selection of Rav Kook's writings, was published posthumously.

Other books by Rabbi Bokser include a biography of Rabbi Eliezer ben Hyrcanus entitled, *Pharisaic Judaism in Transition* (1935), a study of the Maharal of Prague (Rabbi Loew ben Bezalel) entitled, *From the World of the Cabbalah* (1954), *Judaism and Modern Man* (1957), *Judaism: Profile of a Faith* (1963), and *Judaism and the Christian Predicament* (1967).

Rabbi Bokser translated and edited a prayer book for weekday, Sabbath and festival use, and one for the High Holidays.

Don't be without the "Essential" Rav Kook. Order your own copy today!

Check your favorite bookseller,
or order here:

[ ] **YES,** I want ____ copies of *The Essential Writings of Abraham Isaac Kook* at $19.95 each, plus $3 shipping per book (New Jersey residents please add $1.20 sales tax per book). Canadian orders must be accompanied by a postal money order in U.S. funds.

My check or money order for $_____ is enclosed.
Please charge my [ ] Visa [ ] MasterCard

Name _____

Organization _____

Address _____

City/State/Zip_____

Phone _____ Email _____

Card # _____Exp. Date _____

Signature _____

Please return to: **Ben Yehuda Press**
430 Kensington Rd.   Teaneck, NJ 07666
email: sales@BenYehudaPress.com
buy online at http://www.BenYehudaPress.com

Books make great gifts! We'll happily enclose a card, inscribe the book to the recipient, and wrap it. Just let us know the details!